Using Technology to Support Learning and Teaching

The climate of higher education (HE) ... are more likely to see themselves as cor... high expectations regarding teaching and ... in part, being used to meet this need wh... ...access to teaching materials outside the classroom or the use of interactivity in lectures. Although there is no illusion among HE institutions that technology is a panacea, it is clear that technology is a vital tool in meeting expectations, and one that will be used more and more.

Using Technology to Support Learning and Teaching fills a gap in the market by providing a jargon-free (but pedagogically-informed) set of guidance for teaching practitioners who wish to consider the variety of ways in which technology can enrich their practice and the learning of their students. It integrates a wide range of example cases from different kinds of HE institutions and different academic disciplines, illustrating pedagogies that are easily practicable. Full of advice, hints and tips for practitioners who want to use technology to support a style of teaching and learning that is built on sound pedagogical principles, it provides a quick user-friendly reference on how to incorporate technology into HE in a way that adheres to their learning principles and values.

This book is an essential tool for HE teaching practitioners and students studying HE. It will also be of value to newer teachers (perhaps taking teacher training programmes) who wish to see where recommended approaches link to pedagogy.

Andy Fisher is Associate Professor at the University of Nottingham, UK.

Kate Exley is Senior Staff Development Officer at the University of Leeds, UK, and a consultant in HE.

Dragoş Ciobanu is Lecturer in Translation Studies at the University of Leeds, UK.

Key Guides for Effective Teaching in Higher Education Series
Edited by Kate Exley

This indispensable series is aimed at new lecturers, postgraduate students who have teaching time, Graduate Teaching Assistants, part-time tutors and demonstrators, as well as experienced teaching staff who may feel it's time to review their skills in teaching and learning.

Titles in this series will provide the teacher in higher education with practical, realistic guidance on the various different aspects of their teaching role, which is underpinned not only by current research in the field, but also by the extensive experience of individual authors, and with a keen eye kept on the limitations and opportunities therein. By bridging a gap between academic theory and practice, all titles will provide generic guidance on teaching, learning and assessment issues, which is then brought to life through the use of short, illustrative examples drawn from a range of disciplines. All titles in the series will:

- represent up-to-date thinking and incorporate the use of computing and information technology (C&IT) where appropriate
- consider methods and approaches for teaching and learning when there is an increasing diversity in learning and a growth in student numbers
- encourage reflexive practice and self-evaluation, and a means of developing the skills of teaching, learning and assessment
- provide links and references to other work on the topic and research evidence where appropriate.

Titles in the series will prove invaluable whether they are used for self-study or as part of a formal induction programme on teaching in higher education (HE), and will also be of relevance to teaching staff working in further education (FE) settings.

Other titles in this series:

Using Technology to Support Learning and Teaching

Andy Fisher, Kate Exley
and
Dragoş Ciobanu

Routledge
Taylor & Francis Group
LONDON AND NEW YORK

First published 2014
by Routledge
2 Park Square, Milton Park, Abingdon, Oxon OX14 4RN

and by Routledge
711 Third Avenue, New York, NY 10017

Routledge is an imprint of the Taylor & Francis Group, an informa business

© 2014 A. Fisher, K. Exley and D. Ciobanu

The right of A. Fisher, K. Exley and D. Ciobanu to be identified as authors of this work has been asserted by them in accordance with sections 77 and 78 of the Copyright, Designs and Patents Act 1988.

British Library Cataloguing in Publication Data
A catalogue record for this book is available from the British Library

Library of Congress Cataloging in Publication Data
Fisher, Andy, 1976–
Using technology to support learning and teaching / Andy Fisher, Kate Exley, Dragos Ciobanu.
pages cm. — (Key guides for effective teaching in higher education)
1. Information technology—Study and teaching (Higher) I. Exley, Kate, 1964–
II. Ciobanu, Dragos. III. Title.
LB2395.7.F57 2013
371.33—dc23   2013024603

ISBN: 978–0–415–63049–8 (hbk)
ISBN: 978–0–415–63050–4 (pbk)
ISBN: 978–0–203–07449–7 (ebk)

Typeset in Perpetua
by RefineCatch Limited, Bungay, Suffolk

Printed and bound in the United States of America by
Edwards Brothers Malloy

Contents

Series preface

THE SERIES

The *Key Guides for Effective Teaching in Higher Education* were initially discussed as an idea in 2002, and the first group of four titles were published in 2004. New titles have continued to be added and the Series now boasts twelve books (with more in the pipeline).

THE SERIES INCLUDES

Giving a Lecture: From Presenting to Teaching, Exley and Dennick (2004), 2nd ed. (2009).

Small Group Teaching: Seminars, Tutorials and Beyond, Exley and Dennick (2004).

Assessing Students' Written Work: Marking Essays and Reports, Haines (2004).

Using C&IT to Support Teaching, Chin (2004).

Designing Learning: From Module Outline to Effective Teaching, Butcher, Davies and Highton (2006).

Assessing Skills and Practice, Brown and Pickford (2006).

Developing Your Teaching: Ideas, Insight and Action, Kahn and Walsh (2006).

Enhancing Learning Through Formative Assessment and Feedback, Irons (2007).

Working One-to-One With Students: Supervising, Coaching, Mentoring and Personal Tutoring, Wisker, Exley, Antoniou and Ridley (2008).

Inclusion and Diversity, Grace and Gravestock (2009).

It has always been intended that the books would be primarily of use to new teachers in universities and colleges. It has been exciting to see them being used to support postgraduate certificate programmes in teaching and learning for new academic staff and clinical teachers, and also the skills training programmes for post-graduate students and graduate teaching assistants (GTAs) who are beginning to teach. A less anticipated, but very valued, readership has been the experienced teachers who have dipped into the books when reviewing their teaching, and have given the authors feedback and made further suggestions on teaching approaches and examples of practice.

THIS BOOK

This book, on the use of technology to support learning and teaching and assessment, has proved to be a real challenge to produce. The field is so broad and fast moving that the authors have had to make choices and set priorities that perhaps some readers will not always agree with. However, the aim has been to provide an overview of the key ways in which teachers and course designers are embracing technology, and where the scope of the book has limited the depth of coverage we have tried to give further reading and website suggestions to compliment what is discussed.

The book has also been a joy to create, as it has prompted each of the authors to explore the work of colleagues, talk to e-learning specialists and the learners using technology to gain a better insight into the potential (and the pitfalls) of integrating technology in teaching – and we thank all case scenario contributors wholeheartedly.

KEY THEMES OF THE SERIES

The books are all attempting to combine two things: to be very practical and provide lots of examples of methods and techniques, and also to link to educational theory and the underpinning research. Articles are referenced, further readings are suggested and researchers in the field are quoted.

There is also much enthusiasm here to link to the wide range of teaching development activities thriving in the disciplines, supported by the small grant schemes and conferences provided by the Higher Education Academy. The need to tailor teaching approaches to meet the demands of different subject areas and to provide new teachers with examples of practice that are easily recognisable in their fields of study is seen as being very important by all the authors. To this end the books include many examples drawn from a wide range of academic subjects and different kinds of Higher Education institutions.

This theme of diversity is also embraced when considering the heterogeneous groups of students we now teach. Student cohorts include people of different age, experience, ability, culture, language, etc., and all the books include discussion of the issues and demands this places on teachers in today's universities. Inclusive teaching and learning practices are explicitly discussed in Chapter 2 – however, the ways in which technology can be used to support all learners is a theme that reappears throughout the book.

In the series as a whole there is also more than half an eye trying to peer into the future – what will teaching and learning look like in 10 or 20 years' time? How will student expectations, government policy, funding streams, and new technological advances and legislation affect what happens in our learning spaces of the future? You will see, therefore, that many of the books do include chapters that aim to look ahead and tap into the thinking of our most innovative and creative teachers in an attempt to crystal-ball gaze – here this is the topic for the final chapter.

So these were the original ideas underpinning the series, and my co-authors and I have tried hard to keep them in mind as we researched our topics and typed away. We really hope that you find the books to be useful and interesting, whether you are a new teacher just starting out in your teaching career, or you are an experienced teacher reflecting on your practice and reviewing what you do.

Kate Exley
Series Editor

Note on reading this book

This book isn't meant to be read from cover to cover. We expect and would encourage you to dip in and out of it. To pick it up when you are considering various developments in your, or your colleagues', teaching. Technology changes very fast, and although we have tried to future-proof this book as much as possible, no doubt some things will date quickly. Our hope though is that the technology presented here is not simply an end point, but a springboard for further thinking and discussion about technology and how it relates to teaching and learning in HE. Unless otherwise stated, all URLs are correct as of July 2013.

Chapter 1

Learning theory and the use of technology in HE

INTRODUCTION

When someone learns something, what is happening? In broad terms learning theory tries to answer this question. How this question is answered will lead to the learning theorist making recommendations about how teaching *ought* to take place. At its heart, learning theory is both descriptive and prescriptive. It attempts to describe how informa tion and concepts are communicated, absorbed, translated, interpreted, integrated and retained during learning. But it also helps individuals make informed choices about the educational strategies to use in designing teaching and learning with and without the aid of technology.

Given that learning theory is about how *people* learn, it is no surprise that the ideas and disciplines that it draws on are wide and diverse. People are minded, they use language, they interact socially, they have certain physiological responses to environments, they are emotional, etc. The learning theorist might draw on developments in philosophy, psychology, sociology, neuroscience, anthropology, etc. It will not surprise the reader then that this is a complex, subtle and multi-dimensional area of study.

To make things even tougher, a little reflection will show that these topics are in no way self-contained. For example making a discovery about certain neurological-pathways might give us insights into the way the mind works that in turn gives insights about how relationships are formed, about how values are embedded in those relationships, about the roles in the classroom, etc.

There is of course another question that the reader might have asked: why bother about 'theories' of learning? Many practitioners might balk at this chapter and will cry 'just tell us about the technology!' However, we believe there is great benefit in giving learning theories consideration. And this is especially true when dealing with technology.

We believe that readers will get more out of this book if they are sensitive to some of the key learning theories we present. For example, if you believe that the way people learn is primarily through *activity*, then this will help guide you with regard to which technologies you might find useful, and how they might best be implemented.

In the rest of this chapter we will outline some well-established learning theories. These theories are not presented in chronological order or order of importance. They were selected because they are arguably the most useful when considering the use of technology, but we fully appreciate that this chapter is only able to provide an introduction to the topic. Our goal is to give the reader a 'way-in' to thinking about the bigger issues that the rest of the book brings to the fore, and a theoretical framework to help situate some of the developments in using technology to enhance learning and teaching. We have provided some further reading that will give you a wider and richer set of information on which to draw with regards to learning theory.

Behaviourism

Perhaps unsurprisingly, when thinking about learning the behaviourist is interested in how we *behave*. What is surprising though is that for the behaviourist this is all they are interested in. That is, the idea of the 'internal' mental states that accompanies our behaviour is at best of secondary value and at worst irrelevant. For the behaviourist, learning happens when a learner obtains new or changed *behaviour* as a result of a stimulus.

When it comes to teaching and about the role of teachers, behaviourists talk in terms of *conditioning*, and by conditioning they really do mean this as distinct from the more cognitively engaged 'training'. The best way to get to grips with this distinction is to recognise that for the behaviourist there is a close analogy with the conditioning of animals.

Imagine a dog that is given the task of returning a ball to her owner. After many attempts the owner – through offering treats and witholding treats – can modify the dog's behaviour so as to condition the dog to return the ball on command. In a similar way, from the behaviourist point of view, the teacher can either create or reinforce conditioning in their students' behaviour using repetition, rewards and punishments.

The assumption is that through more and more testing and controlling conditions regarding stimulus and environment, we can scientifically study behaviour and hence learning and teaching. The student is seen as a passive receiver of stimuli, and the student is, as it were, programmed. This lends itself to the codification of behaviours and an accompanying predictability. That is, if we know that certain conditions can be met, then we can predict that certain behaviours are likely to occur; the behaviourist maintains that this predictability can help improve teaching.

Success in teaching therefore amounts to how quickly and successfully behaviour can be modified to align with the determined aim or required competency. Behaviourism is by definition a reductive and scientific approach to teaching and learning; a scientific approach where drilling, repetition, class testing and learning objectives are the norm.

 PAUSE FOR THOUGHT

Do you find behaviourism a plausible position? What aspect of technology in teaching might fit particularly well with the behaviourist model?

Cognitivism

Cognitivism is often talked of as the 'opposite' of behaviourism. It is a theory of mind which focuses on the 'internal'. If behaviourism is thought of as objective in its focus on behaviour, cognitivism can be thought of as subjective, with its focus on the individual. In particular, the cognitivist thinks learning is about internal cognitive processes; roughly speaking, the handling of symbols in the mind. Understanding such manipulations and how certain internal frameworks arise and operate promises – the cognitivist argues – to help us understand learning and give insights into teaching.

If learning is about symbols, structures, formation and reformation, storage, etc. in the mind, then it is the teacher's job to create environments to encourage this symbol manipulation, construction and reconstruction. The teacher ought to strive to grab the students' attention, to help them organise and make connections between ideas and concepts. A cognitivist model might thus lead to a focus on problem solving and the processing and reflection of information. Arguably, the

3

teacher will do this most effectively if they can help the learner be immersed in a rich and engaging environment.

Given the generality of cognitivism – it is about the 'internal' in individuals – it acts as a *starting point* for other influential theories. Put simply, if you think that mental activity is the focus of learning then this leaves open the stories people might tell about how that mental activity should be understood. One such highly influential cognitivist theory is *constructivism*.

 PAUSE FOR THOUGHT

Do you find behaviourism or cognitivism more plausible? What aspect of technology in teaching might fit particularly well with the cognitivist model?

Constructivism

Constructivism is about construction – to construct is to be *active*, hence constructivism is about *actively involving and engaging learners*. It focuses on individuals and the mental structures they possess, and how those structures and past experiences/knowledge speak to and influence the construction of various things. What these 'things' are will vary depending on what type of constructivist theory is being defended. Constructivism can be about 'knowledge', 'reality', 'meaning' and 'truth'.

For the constructivist, the teacher is not someone who imparts knowledge as pre-packaged discrete parcels; rather, the teacher is best thought of as a *guide* or *facilitator* who helps students actively construct knowledge. Consequently, if the teacher is a facilitator, then the role of teacher has to be rethought.

Peers can act as teachers – which is particularly interesting given that technology allows millions to be involved in the development and sharing of ideas. New ideas and learning can develop through collaborating with others rather than having knowledge didactically conveyed. This means that constructivism leads naturally to thinking of each learning experience as unique for each student, as each student brings with them their own experiences and knowledge that form the basis of the construction.

Because the constructivist puts the learner at the heart of learning, there are various approaches to teaching which are particularly well suited

4

to this theory – namely, student-centred and active learning, which we discuss below.

Furthermore, in the constructivist classroom there is a realignment of 'power' and 'trust'. Specifically, the centrality of the student means that teachers must trust them and be ready to allow them to fail. For constructivist approaches to 'work' there needs to be collaboration and the creation of a 'safe' and 'judgement-free' environment. Again, you might think that the anonymity and multiple-connectivity that technology affords is particularly well suited here.

The need for construction and engagement means that the best types of learning will be those that involve choices that the student can make, and learning where there are meaningful contexts where the student is engaged. Assessment is not seen as discrete and standalone, but as part of an ongoing process. Constructivism is particularly suited to formative assessment not summative assessment, and this approach to assessment is well supported by developments in technology (e.g. ePortfolios, blogs, wikis, etc. See Chapter 5 for a detailed discussion of assessment).

 PAUSE FOR THOUGHT

In your view, what are the pros and cons of the constructivist model?

Humanistic theories

The basic idea of humanistic theories is that students learn best when their natural desires and inclinations – to be creative, to grow, to learn etc. – are *harnessed* rather than changed or suppressed. If learning is aligned with these inclinations and desires, then – according to the humanistic theory – students will feel less alienated and disengaged from the learning task. Moreover, they will be motivated to go 'deeper' into the subject area.

Consequently, unlike in the case of behaviourism, there is no need, or at least less need, for punishments and rewards. Moreover, because learning is about harnessing the student's own desires and inclinations then, in as much as the student retains these desires and inclinations, the learning will be seen as relevant; hence teaching practice inspired by humanistic theories will lead naturally to the development of lifelong learning.

The humanistic approach highlights the importance of developing the *person*, so that they can achieve all they can achieve and become all they can become. This is *holistic* in that humanistic theory isn't directly interested in the student getting a certain degree, or a certain job, etc. To focus on these goals is too narrow and will typically frustrate a learner's natural inclinations. Rather, learning and teaching ought to be about self-actualisation (e.g. see Maslow, 1943). Notice the idea isn't that there is *no* talk of achievement and advancement, but that these are attained incidentally in virtue of aiming for the goal of self-actualisation.

Key to developing an individual's desires, motivations, inclinations and their overall self, is for the individual to *know* which desires and inclinations they have. So such a theory requires reflection and ongoing challenges to make these features transparent to the student. The teacher needs to provide opportunities for reflection, and offer a wide range of options for students to recognise and realise their passions.

 PAUSE FOR THOUGHT

How might technology help students: (a) identify their own desires/ inclinations better; (b) have the chance to reflect more; and (c) have greater choice?

Connectivism

On balance, we might think that constructivism, behaviourism and cognitivism are going to be less relevant theories, given that they were developed at a time when technology was in its infancy. This contrasts with the theory of connectivism, which is a fairly recent learning theory and arguably particularly suited to understanding and prescribing within the digital/technological age. It is therefore particularly important in this book.

For the connectivist, education is about preparing people to be social: to be resilient and flexible in an ever-changing world. This is done through helping students create an optimal capacity for connections among information. Education is not about specific, discrete bits of knowledge, and it isn't about a set of pre-determined goals for learning. The value of learning is about social identity, and groups communicating and connections forming naturally.

We can then see why connectivism is so well placed in the ever-developing world of technology. The Internet connects people, and starts to create and recreate social learning groups by allowing a multitude of connections. Further developments (e.g. Facebook and Twitter, see Chapter 3) enable us to generate connections.

Connectivism starts by thinking we are beings who make connections – conceptual, social, spiritual, etc. – and that consequently teaching ought to build on this; it should be about working out connections. For the connectivist, in order to understand and respond better to the student's needs, we should boil their educational experiences down to connections.

One reason that connectivism is particularly important in relation to this book is that it makes explicit one particular problem which is perhaps at the heart of the use of technology in higher education. Technology brings about the democratisation and fragmentation of information. This brings many benefits that we will discuss later, such as individuality, creativity and the centrality of students. However, the aim of education might also be about students making sense of lots of things, and being able to tell a coherent and meaningful story regarding the information they have. Moreover, to this end we need students to be discerning and able to evaluate the information they have.

These different aims appear to conflict with each other. We are encouraging students to use technology that leads to a decentralisation and fragmentation of information, in order to form a coherent narrative and connected end point.[1]

In fact, connectivism is well suited to dealing with this issue. If learning is about connection, then teachers ought not to simply assume that *technology* can do the connecting. This needs to be something that is explicitly developed by the teacher. In fact, this need – in one form or another – is at the forefront of the development of new technologies. In particular, more recent developments in technology are around reviewing, archiving and curatorship (see Chapter 10).

One important difference between connectivism and the previous theories is that while the other theories situate learning *within* the individual, connectivism situates it *outside* the learner. For the connectivist, learning can take place within communities of learners and social networks. So the connectivist theorist is most interested in learning how to locate and connect knowledge, as opposed to internalising it. We summarise some of the main points raised in regards to each learning theory below (see Table 1.1)

TABLE 1.1 Summary of some key learning theories

Theories	View of the learning process	Approach	Major contributors to the field
Behaviourist	Seeking to change learners' behaviours	Providing stimuli to reinforce or challenge behaviours (rewards and punishments)	Pavlov Watson Skinner
Cognitivist	Opening the black box of the mind. Individual learners construct their own internal mental processes and knowledge through the development of schema and mental frameworks	Building internal mental processes and frameworks through active experimentation. Learners develop theories through experiences and using what they already know, which they test out with others	Piaget Ausubel Bruner Vygotsky
Constructivists	Individuals (through active and dialogical activities) construct their own meaning from knowledge and experience	The process of constructing knowledge and understanding when new information and experiences are integrated with existing knowledge. It is closely linked with cognitive theory and emphasises active learning and the personal motivation and responsibility	Davey Piaget Vygotsky Kolb
Humanistic	An individual acts to fulfil their potential and self-actualise. Concerned with the development of the person	Driven by a desire to be the best you can be, and a desire to learn and improve with experience	Maslow Rogers Kolb
Connectivism	Education is about helping students create an optimal capacity for connections. Learning can take place outside the individual within a network, or connected community	The teacher should encourage the student to discover their own connections between seemingly discrete information, using different means (e.g. Twitter, wikis, blogs, open educational resources)	Siemens Downes

Given the different learning theories, there are a number of different *approaches* to education which have developed and which fit, to various extents, with each theory. These are useful to keep in mind when considering the uses of technology to support teaching and learning in HE.

ACTIVE AND STUDENT-CENTRED LEARNING

What is urgently needed is an educational program in which students become interested in actively knowing, rather than passively believing.

(Volpe, 1984)

Active learning is a process in which the learner engages with the topics and concepts to be understood actively – perhaps by selecting information, solving a set problem or engaging in a planning task. This forces learners to reflect upon learning tasks and take stock of their own ideas about them. It also prompts learners to self assess their own level of understanding, and to take responsibility for checking and filling gaps in their knowledge. Therefore, at the heart of active learning is the process of learners being cognitively, and perhaps even physically, engaged and active.

Coupling the notion of active learning with a student-centred approach is a very natural next step for educators to take. Being student-centred means providing learners with more control and choice in their learning, so that they can influence what is studied, and to some extent when and how it is learned. This may involve people learning independently or with others, as well as learning directly with and under the direction of a teacher.

 PAUSE FOR THOUGHT

What problems might there be when using a student-centred approach to learning? Do you think using technology would increase these problems, or help solve them?

SITUATED LEARNING

A challenge for educators is the extent to which learning is context dependent or 'situated' (Halpern and Hakel, 2002). In medicine and health training, for example, much store is placed on the need to provide real or simulated learning situations that expose the learner to the environments in which they will be required to function (Jenkins and Brotherton, 1995).

'Transfer' is a key notion in situational learning, and can be considered in two different ways. To what extent can learners transfer what they have learned in one context to another, and to what extent can they transfer their factual understanding and knowledge into real action in their own situations (sometimes also thought of as a transfer between having 'declarative' knowledge to developing 'procedural' knowledge – the move from 'knowing what' to 'knowing how', first identified by Ryle in 1949).

One aspect worthy of consideration is the cultural context experienced by the learners, in terms of both thinking and communication styles. These are seen to be culturally based and culturally sensitive, and yet many of the models that are used to explore education have been derived within a Western context and using a Western set of assumptions. You might think that technology, with its talk of immersion and virtual learning situations, is particularly well suited to this approach to learning. That is to say, the situations are far more accessible to all students as technology advances (in particular, see Chapter 2).

COLLABORATIVE SOCIAL LEARNING AND COMMUNITIES OF PRACTICE

What often comes to the fore in reviews of education and references to learning theory is the power of collaborative learning, and the simple truth that most people learn far more when they learn with others than when they try and learn alone. In science and health disciplines there is a wealth of studies that have long shown this to be the case (e.g., Dougherty et al., 1995; Johnson and Johnson, 1986).

A key feature of collaborative learning, in all its forms, is that co-learners speak to each other. Formulating questions and responses, sharing experiences, using each other as sounding boards for new ideas, etc. This learning conversation is increasingly thought to be central to the importance of collaborative learning (Michael, 2006).

Jean Lave and Etienne Wenger's views on 'communities of practice' builds upon this social view of learning, and states that learning involves a deepening involvement with a group of people with a shared set of interests or a common goal (Wenger et al., 2002).

> In a nutshell: Communities of practice are groups of people who share a concern or a passion for something they do and learn how to do it better as they interact regularly.
>
> (Wenger, 2006)

The community, in this case, is more than a network of people, but a group who share a commitment to a topic or domain and who are prepared to help and support each other which, over time, enables members to learn from each other. Communities of practice have been considered as a mechanism to support professional development and the promotion of communication between novices and those who have more experience and expertise within a field of interest (Li et al., 2009).

 PAUSE FOR THOUGHT

What are the pros and cons of using technology to promote collaborative learning?

CONCLUSION

We have outlined a few influential and important learning theories, and related approaches to learning and teaching. We have hinted at how these theories might help answer the question at the forefront of this book: how might technology be used in HE?

We have identified five themes that you might want to keep at the forefront of you mind when reading this book. In particular, the reader might consider these in relation to learning theories and the approaches to teaching we discuss.

1　Technology gives students a voice. It moves learners from being the consumers of information to being producers of it.
2　Technology helps create a richer experience through generating different situations and contexts – ones which are not limited in traditional ways (e.g. through geography).
3　Technology helps collaboration despite physical separation.
4　Technology helps with accessibility, meaning that the teacher can better meet the needs of students with disabilities and

learners drawn from a broader range of social and economic backgrounds.

5 Technology is immersive and can bring an element of fun to HE.

NOTE

1 For an excellent discussion of connectivism, and especially this point, see: http://www.elearnspace.org/Articles/connectivism.htm

USEFUL RESOURCES

Beetham, H., & Rhona, S. (2007). *Rethinking Pedagogy for a Digital Age: Designing and Delivering E-learning*. Oxford: Routledge.

For a good overview of learning theories, try: http://www.learning-theories.com/

For a good overview of connectivism, and how it relates to behaviourism, constructivism and cognitivism, see: http://www.elearnspace.org/Articles/connectivism.htm

A short and accessible piece: http://onlinelibrary.wiley.com/doi/10.1111/j.1365–2729.2011.00437.x/abstract

Chapter 2

Inclusive practice

Disability and diversity

INTRODUCTION

An inclusive approach to teaching and learning centres on the teacher's ability to anticipate challenges that learners might have in accessing course resources and activities, as well as assessment methods, and therefore design these components from the outset to be accessible to all students.

Technology can provide a wider range of options *for teachers*, in the ways that they can deliver the syllabus. Content can be provided in different formats, at different times and in different learning environments. Technology can play a significant role in a way a course is structured; for example, by blending face-to-face and distance learning.

Teachers can also make full use of technology in the ways that they monitor, evaluate and ensure the quality of their programmes (e.g. real-time electronic signup, electronic prompts to update learning objectives, etc.) The ability to oversee the take-up and engagement of different groups of students can help course leaders ensure that what they offer is fit for purpose and meets the students' needs.

Technology can also provide greater choice to *learners*, offering them alternatives for engaging with the curriculum, as well as organising their own learning materials and personal study. For example, students can choose digital learning resources (e.g. online portfolios instead of physical folders, or interactive quizzes as opposed to printed workbooks), and different hardware and software to support and enhance their learning experiences (e.g. smartphones and various social media platforms).

As with later chapters, the scope of this chapter is potentially very broad. As such, we have narrowed its focus to individual classroom teachers – concentrating our discussion on the ways they can, through their face-to-face and online presence, adopt an inclusive approach and, with the help of technology, embrace 'variety' in their teaching.

To this end, the chapter is divided into three main sections: first we consider how the use of technology can support inclusivity in the classroom; second we consider how technology can be used to support distance learning through online provision; third, we consider the ways in which technology can provide specific assistance for students with a disability.

INCLUSIVITY IN FACE-TO-FACE TEACHING AND LEARNING

There are three key ways in which technology can be used to enhance the experience in face-to-face learning:

1   To provide a richer and wider range of learning resources.
2   To provide ways in which participation, collaboration and exchange can be facilitated within and beyond the classroom.
3   To provide ways in which teaching and learning experiences and outputs can be captured.

We will expand on each of these in turn, and provide some specific guidance and examples of practice.

Providing a richer and wider range of learning resources

As with most guidance concerning the use of presentational media – such as 'Keynote', 'Prezi', or 'PowerPoint' (e.g. Exley and Dennick, 2009) – the tips are often devised with particular needs in mind (e.g. dyslexia, cognitive impairments, etc.), but are nearly always universally beneficial.

Neurological studies point to the fact that human brains treat each word as an image, which needs to be decoded before being processed for meaning (Medina, 2008: 205). This process is complex and time-consuming when large bodies of text need to be read. Contrary to public perception, human brains cannot actually pay attention to several concurrent and different stimuli – such as visual and auditory.

So using text sparingly and replacing it with images means that *everybody* in the audience will spend less time working out the meaning of the slide and more time concentrating on what the presenter has to say.

These points and others are reflected in the 'good practice' guidance given below.

Basic good practice for accessibility within PowerPoint[1]

General slide content

Presentation slides are meant to be visual aids rather than a transcript. Many teachers do not have extensive contact time with their students, so it is important to make those moments count by challenging students to engage with a topic rather than reading from a slide.

Ideally, teachers should use engaging and relevant visual content; for instance, by illustrating several points of view on the same topic with images and video. This in turn can lead to engaging in-class debates.

If text is needed, then keywords are the best approach. If keywords are not enough, short, concise bullet points will ensure your audience's attention is directed at you. A very effective recipe for cognitive overload is a student having to keep up with lots of text on a slide as the teacher is talking generally – but not exclusively – about the same ideas, while perhaps also demonstrating the practical use of a device. Remember, when it comes to actually paying attention, humans cannot multitask

Aim for one idea per slide, even though this may mean that the presentation has many slides. Don't be afraid of blank space on slides, as this can direct the student's attention to the slide content (Figure 2.1 is an example of this mix of keywords and images).

Slides can also include hyperlinks allowing the presenter to skip between different sections of the presentation. This is a useful inclusion, as it allows the same set of slides to be delivered in a bespoke way depending on the student's interests and progress – more on this technique in Chapter 4.

Ideally you ought to use a sans serif font of at least 24 points in size, and limit the number of lines to about eight. If your presentations cannot be redesigned to move away from text to relevant and engaging visual content, you will at least need to give your students significant time to read and take in the content.

Slide layout design

There are a number of slide layout designs built into the software, and when utilised appropriately, these will enable a presentation to be

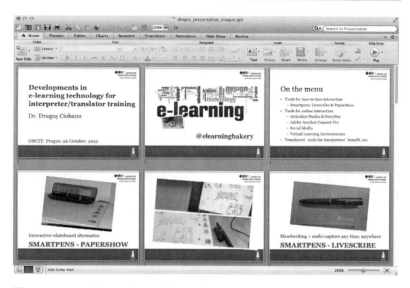

FIGURE 2.1 Image-based PowerPoint presentation with keywords on slides

exported to a number of different formats (e.g. as a Word document), while retaining all the textual information. This is particularly important for those students who need alternative access to the presentation.

Having said that, not all designs are equally suitable. Do not feel you need to fill every corner of a slide: recall that blank space can itself be a useful aspect of the slide design. Busy slides are challenging for anyone who sees them for the first time, and the more 'stuff' there is on a slide, the harder the student will have to work to discern what is important and what is not.

Consistency of formatting is beneficial (e.g. that headings, bullets and themes are consistent, using the same fonts, colours, and sizes, etc.). Becoming accustomed with using slide and handout masters helps, and this will also increase speed and productivity. The incorporation of relevant images can also help ensure that slides do not look identical, better enabling students to navigate the presentation at a later date.

Appropriate text and background colours

It is important to consider the environment in which a presentation will be delivered, as this will determine the appropriate background and text colour. For example, design agencies generally advise the use of a dark background with light text in large open spaces, and light background and dark text in smaller presentation rooms (Duarte, 2008). In general, it is best to avoid the use of patterned backgrounds as they make text less readable.

In addition to the issues of readability, it is important to remember that colour can convey meaning. For instance, while Western cultures are likely to view content written in red as being important, in other cultures red will signify that one should avoid doing what is written. Or, for example, one should be aware that in Chinese and Japanese cultures only the names of the dead are written in red. So, writing a researcher's name in red to attract attention to his/her importance will in fact signify to your East Asian students that the researcher has passed away, or that something bad is about to happen to them.

Use of the 'Notes' field

The 'Notes' field can offer a way to provide additional detail, further clarification and links to further reading suggestions. The Notes field can help avoid the problem of producing overfilled slides, and make the resource more useful when viewed at a later date.[2]
Additionally, the Notes field in PowerPoint can include contextualisation and explanations of any visual content in the slides (e.g. keywords, graphs or photographs: see Figure 2.2). This will ensure that those using screen readers – software that attempts to identify and interpret what is being displayed on the screen – are not disadvantaged by the use of images.

If the presenter needs access to these notes, they can be printed out, or they can be accessed electronically during the presentation, depending on the presentation application used and also the hardware setup.

Figure 2.3, for instance, shows how a presentation is displayed on a computer with two screens: while on the presentation screen (the one on the left) slides are displayed in slideshow mode, the screen on the right allows the presenter to access content in the Notes area, as well as see which slides follow.

17

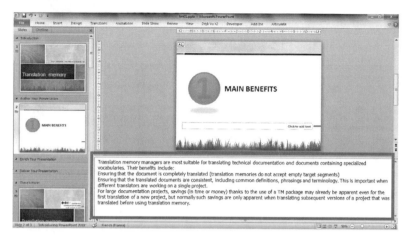

▓ **FIGURE 2.2** The use of the Notes area in PowerPoint keeps slides uncluttered

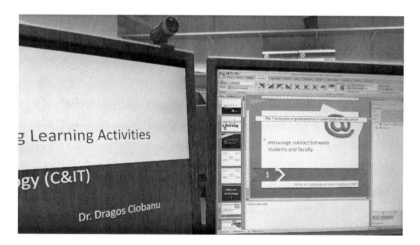

▓ **FIGURE 2.3** A PowerPoint presentation on a computer with two screens

Animating PowerPoint slides

When explaining the complexity of a concept or the stages in a process, it can be very helpful to be able to present information sequentially in an animation. There are three ways in which this can be done in PowerPoint.

▓ **18**

Sequential text display

Parts of the text on the slide are programmed to appear with the click of a mouse by using the Animations tab and the Custom Animations icon. This is a good approach because it ensures students do not have to grapple with all the bullet points on the slide at once. Having said that, having different ideas on different slides is an even more effective approach, which can be implemented using the following technique.

Graphical animation via a sequence of slides

A picture can be built by adding additional parts of the picture through a sequence of individual slides that provide an animated effect. Because the individual parts of the animation are easily isolated, this approach can provide a helpful resource when printed out as a handout.

Moreover, bullet points can be sequenced on different slides too. This will allow teachers to make better use of the Notes field to insert additional information, and will result in handouts which are easier to follow and understand. Also, this will result in more effective session recordings, as many of the current lecture capture tools create automatic bookmarks when slides change, which makes it significantly easier for viewers to identify points of interest in long lecture recordings.

Animation on a single slide

A less effective – but currently more popular – way to structure information is to have as much text as possible on a single slide, and then use Custom Animation to configure its appearance. Such an approach may sometimes be appropriate – for example, it may make it easier to update information.

 PAUSE FOR THOUGHT

Each one of the three methods outlined above has pros and cons, and thinking about how you and your students will be using the slides – maybe at different times, and on different platforms, such as their computers, tablets, smartphones, or as a printout – will help you decide the best approach. Consider some of these issues. For example, do you expect your students to use the slides as a pre- or a post-lecture study/ revision aid? Do you want them to see how an answer to each part of an equation fits together? Do you want them to access the presentation on their smartphones?

Presenting pointers

When presenting using any technology, a handful of common-sense measures can ensure that you communicate effectively with most of your students, most of the time.

One key principle is to do one thing at a time. Face the front when speaking, so that your students can see your face and expressions – this will not only ensure those using lip reading techniques have access to your words, but it will also benefit non-native English speakers who use body language and expressions to gain a fuller meaning (Khuwaileh, A. A., 1999). Above all, it will ensure that you make eye contact with your audience in order to engage them better and estimate when you need to make adjustments to the presentation.

It is also important that you pay attention to the pace of delivery, particularly for your hearing-impaired students who might have note-takers with them. Note-takers are rarely subject experts and are trying to summarise the key points of a lecture on an unfamiliar topic. Delivering the session at a slower pace, stopping regularly to recap and summarise, and giving time for any interactions (such as question and answer sessions) will benefit *all* your students.

Try and verbalise all the points you make on each slide without resorting to simply 'reading out' the text line by line. Visually impaired students will need you to explain pictures, graphs and other images. This is easier said than done, and you might want to include prompts to do this in your own lecture notes and materials. In later chapters – namely 5, 8 and 9 – we talk about how technology might allow fuller explanations and understanding of pictures and graphs.

Facilitating participation within and beyond the classroom

The inclusive use of student response systems (SRSs)

Student response systems – also known as clickers, crickets or voting pads – can be used to encourage greater engagement and facilitate student interaction in teaching sessions. They make it significantly easier for teachers to find out whether their students are following the lecture. The students' replies can be anonymous or tracked, depending on the purpose of the activity. Evaluations show that most students find their use to be engaging and useful (Schell et al., 2013); however, care needs to be taken to ensure *all* students can gain from their use. To this end:

- Select a system which is suitable for all your students – be aware that some systems, in an effort to make the clickers as small as possible, have reduced the size of the buttons (and occasionally increased the pressure with which they need to be pressed), which makes them challenging for students with motor impairments, or conditions such as arthritis.
- If you choose a web-based or a smartphone-based system instead of purchasing physical clickers, think of how you will address aspects such as data protection when students register their devices and start submitting data with them, as well as how you will ensure that all students have a suitable device in the first place.
- Ensure that module information provided to students tells them that SRSs will be used – we appreciate this may be too much for occasional trials using this technology, but as a minimum, you need to ensure that all students know why this technology is being used, and that their personal data is safe.
- Confirm confidentiality of responses and/or explain how any captured data is to be used (e.g to track class responses or individual progress).

Ask the students if they have used the handsets before – and if not:

- Provide an explanatory diagram or a labelled photograph of the handset.
- Demonstrate the use of the equipment.
- Insert a 'test' question so that the students can have a practice run.
- Display the questions *and* read them out loud. Some students may also prefer to read them from a hard copy in a handout provided in advance.
- Ensure students are given enough reading and thinking time to be able to respond effectively.
- Be flexible – allow students to work alone or in groups.
- Consider including an option on the slides marked 'I don't know' and/or 'Abstain', giving students the possibility to opt out. Alternatively, you could include an additional question element that allows students to indicate their confidence level while voting.
- Consider the readability of the slides (as for PowerPoint slides) and, if possible, upload question slides onto the Virtual Learning Environment (see Chapter 7) before or during the class, so that students can download them onto their laptop and tailor them to

suit their accessibility needs (e.g. increase the font size or change the background colours).

■ Display the class voting results and comment on the results. You can also choose to have a discussion before displaying the results. (The use of Student Response Systems (SRS) is discussed in more detail in Chapter 4.)

Facilitating learner collaboration and exchange within and beyond the classroom

Facilitating student interaction

Many small-group teaching sessions (e.g. seminars and tutorials) are built around the need for discussion and interaction. Real-time, verbal communication can be both stimulating and challenging, and for some particularly difficult. This may be because they are non-native English speakers with a different set of cultural expectations, or they may have a disability that makes listening/speaking more difficult (e.g. Cohan and Smith, 2007; Fuller et al., 2004).

Technology provides different ways in which students can contribute – for example, through the use of interactive whiteboards, tablets and mobile phones (for more examples, see Chapter 4).

The use of mind-mapping software can also support productive discussion and allow students to construct and visually represent knowledge and concepts. Mind-mapping was first described by Tony Buzan as a method of note-taking that adopts a more open, nonlinear approach that better mimics the natural thinking process (Buzan, 1976; Buzan, 1993). Concept-maps are a form of mind-map (Novak, 1990) that can be used to represent the connectivity and interrelationships within and between ideas and subjects.

Bringing the visual and the discursive approaches together can be very beneficial for dyslexic learners, who sometimes struggle to find the structure and form to present their ideas and understanding coherently (Chanock, 2007). Dual coding theory (Clark and Paivio, 1991) suggests that students code information both in verbal and non-verbal formats, and as such the use of graphic organisers and mind-mapping is particularly helpful. This approach is also supported by a constructivist learning theory, in which the student develops internal mental frameworks and schemata that allow them to organise and retain knowledge (for a discussion of constructivism, see Chapter 1).

22

CASE EXAMPLE

Podcasts and interactive mind-maps to increase participation

Richard Field, School of Geography, University of Nottingham

In 2006, I moved about 60% of my regular lectures in a second-year biogeography module to 'podcasts' (not true podcasts, though the audio and visual content went online rather than using an RSS – please see Chapter 5 for further information). Using a high-quality MP3 recorder, I recorded the audio as a series of short MP3s, mostly in my dining room, but some in a tropical rainforest in Honduras, livening up the content with background birdsong!

Each short MP3 was paired with 1–5 PowerPoint slides, and these were organised using interactive 'mind-maps' (diagrams visually grouping and linking topics) online – see Figure 2.4 for a mind-map example. Students click on the topics to access the MP3, PowerPoint and a transcript; there is also an option to download all in one go, in a pre-specified order (more like a lecture). This system is still in operation in 2012; the class size is usually approximately 100.

Of the various reasons for the move, the main one was to diversify the teaching from traditional lectures to a mix of lectures, student-centred learning (via podcasts) and in-class discussions. Students work through the podcasts in their own time, freeing up classes for two main things.

Firstly, updates: with the basic, core material covered in podcasts, I now use some class time to tell the students about some of the more interesting latest developments.

Secondly, discussions: 3–4 times in the semester the students read specified recent journal papers before the class and (with a colleague) I ask difficult questions with multiple-choice answers (typically no one correct answer) that students vote for using a student response system, having discussed the question in small groups for a few minutes. My colleague and I then delve into the issues raised, highlighting anything from subject-specific knowledge to the nature of research and contested knowledge.

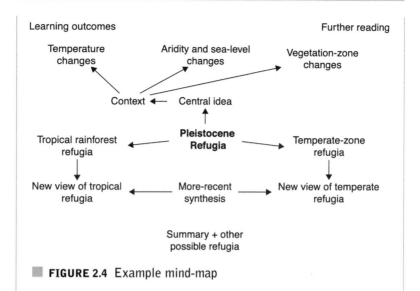

FIGURE 2.4 Example mind-map

In Figure 2.4 the week's topic is Pleistocene refugia, which are places where local conditions allowed the persistence of species during the great environmental changes of the ice ages in the last two million years. In the interactive version of this mind-map, each term can be clicked as a link to specific audio and visual content.

The benefits include more interesting, topical and varied teaching. An unanticipated benefit (though expected in hindsight) was the improved performance of dyslexic students. In my experience, traditional lectures, assessed by examination, are very challenging for dyslexic students, with performance often hindered. The podcasts allow the students to go through the core material both at their own pace and ahead of time. The increased focus on discussion and evaluation seems also to benefit a wider range of learners than only using traditional lectures.

Capturing 'live' teaching and learning experiences and outputs

Lecture capture

Lecture capture can take a variety of forms. Probably the most common method is for lecture rooms to be equipped with hardware that records the teacher's voice and the images he or she displays through the projector.

These will include images from the computer, PowerPoint presentations and displays of other sources, such as from the web, as well as projections through a visualiser (for more details on this, see Chapter 6). Many institutions have taken the decision not to seek to capture the video images of the teachers – assuming that many would feel more inhibited and self-conscious if they felt they were being 'filmed'.

Once captured, the material is usually sent to the teacher, often in the form of a web link, which he or she can then make available to their learners. This approach is ideal, as it gives the teacher control of the captured lecture, and they can then decide how best to use it. Key questions the teacher must answer when considering lecture capture are:

- Is all the audio-visual content included on the slides appropriately referenced?
- Is the content in the presentation allowed to be republished through a lecture recording?
- Should the whole lecture or an edit be provided to the student?
- Should the recording be made available immediately or should it be delayed?
- Should the lecture be available for download?

PAUSE FOR THOUGHT

Given your own lecturing context, what are the relative pros and cons of the different lecture capture options available to you? How might these impact on the types you use when teaching?

CASE EXAMPLE

Lecture capture system

Carol Summerside, Development Officer in the Educational Development and e-Learning Team, Newcastle University

As part of its strategic plan to enhance the student experience, Newcastle University decided to pilot a lecture capture system called ReCap[3] in six venues. The intention was to provide a scalable solution that would allow lecture capture to be made available in multiple locations and be as automated as possible. Following the success of the pilot, the service has grown and is currently available in 62 venues across the University's main campus and three at the Medical campus in Malaysia. Staff can also record additional material on their own desktop computers using a version of the same system.

ReCap records the teacher's voice and any projected audio-visual material they choose to show, including slides and visualised documents, and it makes the recording available for online publication, via the university's Virtual Learning Environment (VLE). It does not record any video of the teacher.

The anticipated benefits for students were that they would be able to review lectures and additional material, helping them better understand complex topics, assisting their revision for exams, and allowing them to catch up on lectures missed for valid reasons. It was also felt that there would be significant benefits for students with dyslexia and other disabilities, for non-native English speakers, and those whose circumstances make regular travel into the University a problem. Feedback from students has begun to bear this out:

I think the system is really good and it is a special help, or I must say a gift, for international students like me. I would like to thank my teacher for trying this type of technology as I believe because of the ReCap sessions I was able to achieve 83.33 per cent in my exam, otherwise it would have been impossible.

I learn much better interactively and through listening than by reading, so for revision ReCap is the most helpful tool ever; please encourage more lecturers to use it.

I have dyslexia and find it very difficult to take notes, listen and understand in lectures. The ReCap system allowed me to listen to complicated lectures for a second time with the ability to pause so I can take notes and digest the information. I found I did better in the modules where I used the system to take additional notes for revision, combined with background reading from textbooks.

Success of the project can be attributed to the support provided by the university's senior management team, who fully backed ReCap implementation after seeing the results obtained during the initial pilot study. Two project teams were tasked with taking forward the strategic goals: an Implementation Group which was tasked with delivering the technical and ICT solutions required, and an Educational Steering Group which was tasked with ensuring that an appropriate pedagogical approach was taken.

The main challenges faced by the project have been associated with staff concerns and misconceptions about the system, particularly about student attendance and the security of recordings. In order to address these concerns, a ReCap usage policy has been introduced and a staff training programme has been delivered extensively across the University.

Evidence obtained via surveys indicates that student reaction to ReCap is very positive, with 90% of users surveyed rating it as 'useful' or 'very useful' and ~80% of students stating that they accessed recordings to make additional notes, to revisit difficult concepts, or for general revision purposes. Usage statistics confirm that peak student usage is prior to exams, and that an average student watches 2.5 hours of recordings. Since its introduction in 2007/2008, over 24,000 recordings have been made using the ReCap service, and these have received over 900,000 viewings (as of January 2013).

For more information on ReCap, please visit the project website: http://teaching.ncl.ac.uk/recap/furtherinfo.php

Using technology to capture *student-generated* content

In more discursive or practically oriented classes it may be extremely valuable for the students to be able 'capture' their contributions or the work outputs that they have generated in class. For example, the students may wish to share class experimental data after a laboratory class, or to summarise the views generated in the seminar debate.

Note-taking in an active, discursive class is not easy, even for a non-dyslexic, native English speaker; therefore, using technology to both capture and then make available notes or materials can be especially helpful for all learners. This might simply involve using a smartphone to photograph the whiteboard or flipchart and posting it online after the class, or may involve the use of more advanced technology – such as electronic flipcharts or whiteboards that can automatically save and digitise such images for you (also see Chapters 4 and 10).

CASE EXAMPLE

Combining technologies to provide access for deaf and hard-of-hearing students

Alina Secară, Teaching Fellow in Translation Studies, University of Leeds.

The aim of my project was to combine innovative technologies to provide live access to lectures to deaf and hard-of-hearing students, and to assess the extent to which same language subtitling (SLS) can enhance the access of international students to lectures. This was based on established research, which demonstrates the benefits that SLS has on word acquisition, comprehension, literacy skills and academic skills for foreign-language learners (Danan, 2004; Garza, 1991; Vanderplank, 1988, 1993).

The approach we suggested for providing and enhancing access to lectures was the result of consultation with the Equality Service at the University of Leeds, staff and note-takers, professional captioners, and our student who had the hearing impairment. The solution consisted of combining a range of technologies and skills which included Adobe Acrobat Connect Pro for lecture capture, Dragon Naturally Speaking for live SLS, and live note-taking using trained note-takers. The integration of all the lecture sources of information – the PowerPoint Presentation, the lecturer video feed, the live subtitles and the live note-taking – into one screen within the Adobe Connect platform area allowed uninterrupted live access to the lecture for the hard-of-hearing student.

The student, present in the lecture theatre, used a laptop, but smaller portable devices such as tablets and smartphones were also tested. This approach offered significant advantages over the previous model, where the student's concentration was interrupted by the need to direct her visual and cognitive focus to different points of interest – the projected slides, the lecturer's face and gestures, and the notes taken by the note-takers on a laptop or on paper.

The Adobe Connect session recordings were then made available online to the rest of the students via the VLE. Statistics regarding access to these resources clearly indicate all our students' interest in them. The results of the evaluation questionnaire distributed at the end of the module highlight the importance that international students attach to these recordings for revision purposes, but more specifically the perceived advantages of SLS in their learning. These echoed existing research in that SLS resources were perceived as serving different learning styles (visual versus auditory), they were used as a priming device, they drew attention to concepts not known (Vanderplank, 2012), and they were also seen as leading to enhancement of comprehension through double exposure (Kruger, 2012).

For more information on the use of Adobe Connect for a variety of learning and teaching purposes among others, please watch Ciobanu, Secară and Morris (2011): http://goo.gl/pW3MB

Using technology to support integration

An increasing number of universities are opening campuses in other countries and aim to offer to their new local students the same experience that all their other university students have. Even without these remote campuses, it is becoming increasingly common to teach the same course to groups of learners based in several locations MBA programmes have led the way regarding this approach. Challenges that often arise with this setup relate to difficulties in maintaining student engagement and succeeding in making the remote students feel part of the wider university student community.

A particular challenge facing some teachers is brought about by particular course designs and structures. For example, a new programme in pharmacy has adopted a two-plus-two course structure, in which students spend the first two years studying at an overseas-based campus, and the second two years at the UK campus. The overseas group of students join an existing UK cohort and need to integrate with the UK-based students, as well as adapt to a new learning environment.

This situation raises two challenges in which technology could be of assistance:

- Making a transition in learning environments.
- Integrating different groups of learners and engaging them with their subject matter.

Technology can be used to meet these challenges through the provision of a common online learning environment that can be accessed by all

29

students concurrently and throughout their studies. Students can be put in contact with teachers and peers before they move to the new campus, and video tours and immersive environments (see Chapter 9) can introduce new surroundings and learning spaces.

CASE EXAMPLE

Using tailored mailing lists to support integration

Yuka Oeda, Japanese, University of Leeds

In order to support exchange students from Japan, I create a tailored mailing list to communicate with them. Through this mailing list, I invite Japanese students to attend my Japanese language classes. I find this helps them to make friends with students who are studying Japanese here, and helps them to feel less isolated and lonely when studying away from home. At the same time, it is also beneficial for my own students who are learning Japanese to have native Japanese speakers in class with whom they can have discussions and exchange opinions. I also use the mailing list to link with the Japanese Student Society and East Asian Research Society.

Whenever they want to advertise their events, I can post their emails through the mailing list to let the visiting Japanese students know about interesting things happening on campus.

INCLUSIVITY IN ONLINE TEACHING AND LEARNING

The majority of university programmes now include online learning – and for some learners these are particularly valuable and supportive components which aid inclusivity in a number of ways:

- VLEs and e-learning in general consist of useful tools for making materials, information and learning resources readily accessible. This is particularly helpful for disabled students.
- It is also possible to provide opportunities to communicate, discuss and collaborate with colleagues via discussion boards, blogging and social networking (see Chapters 3 and 7).

- Technology can provide 'simulated' learning experiences, for example in recreating fieldwork or laboratory-based work for students who might find it very difficult to experience these forms of study; either because they are studying at a distance, or have a disability (see Chapter 9).

However, simply providing online learning does not ensure inclusivity, and teachers and designers need to take time to consider the needs of online learners.

Making online content accessible

The IMS Global Learning Consortium[4] Accessibility Guidelines for Developing Accessible Learning Applications give an overview of the factors that need to be considered in order to give maximum accessibility to e learning content. The guidelines cover a range of topics, such as text, audio, visual, multimedia, real-time and posted communications, tests and assessments.

The W3C[5] (World Wide Web Consortium) WAI[6] (Web Accessibility Initiative) has produced a set of WCAGs (Web Content Accessibility Guidelines) which are widely used to check the usability of websites. TechDis, the UK tertiary education's accessibility advisory service also provides excellent advice and guidance.

An important general principle in these guidelines is that of providing alternative auditory and visual formats for online content. Some users will not be able to make use of the visual or the auditory elements of a webpage (e.g. diagrams, statistical charts, video clips, etc.), but well-designed online resources should provide the same information in a text format.

Providing all the information in a text format gives flexibility, enabling content to be delivered in a variety of ways. For example, the text can be presented in a larger font or be converted into speech using a speech synthesizer — often provided as part of the computer operating system — or changed into Braille.

However, diversity of medium is the key as some learners may instead have difficulty reading text, so it can also be beneficial to provide non-text equivalents of the text (e.g., pictures, videos and audio).

Sharing control with learners

In terms of their disability, nobody knows what a student needs more than the student, and so mechanisms that give them the ability to control and manipulate the technology and online environment are clearly advantageous; in fact, as technology advances, it is this ability to control and manipulate which is becoming increasingly popular (see Chapter 10). Of course, giving the learners the control has an obvious problem. Learners often start as novices, and simply may not know what they need in order to become experts. With that in mind, providing mechanisms that allow the *sharing* of control allows experts to provide a learning route, which can then be tailored by individuals to their personal needs.

However, there are ways in which resource designers can unintentionally raise barriers, by incorporating features that dictate the ways in which a learner 'should' or 'has to' engage with the material.

For example, when a website has automatic scrolling or where the text or images on the page are automatically updated, students with cognitive or visual impairments encounter difficulties becase they are often unable to read moving text quickly enough or even at all. The moving text (or images) can also distract, so that the rest of the page becomes unreadable. Automatic scrolling or updating text and images may also prevent *screen readers* from being able to read the text. Furthermore, students with physical disabilities might not be able to move quickly or accurately enough to interact with moving objects. Therefore, incorporating the ability to switch off or pause any automated features in the resource design is very desirable.

Readability

Reading text on a screen can be tiring and very challenging for some students. A number of those with specific learning disabilities such as dyslexia suffer from a visual-perceptual disturbance, also known as Meares–Irlen syndrome,[7] which affects the way black text on white paper or on a white screen is seen.

We can predict some of the features that will make text easier to read:

- *Font style and colour* – using a sans serif font (such as Arial or Tahoma) is widely acknowledged as being more readable. Moreover, ensuring there is good contrast between the text and the background colour is also effective. Some find that dark blue is clearer than black font (Pearson and Koppi, 2006).
- *Background* – having uncluttered backgrounds that give good contrast is key. Some students find it helpful to be able to manipulate the background colour, preferring to avoid a bright white one.

■ *Layout and line spacing* – for some students, text can appear more squashed or even distorted, so having well-spaced text and leaving plenty of white space between sections is beneficial. It is better to link a series of pages than have very long and dense sections of text. This will require very clear and consistent use of navigation prompts, such as hyperlinked text menu items or hyperlinked icons whose meaning is known to the students.

Using technology to teach students at a distance – some issues for inclusivity

As universities open overseas campuses, recruit international distance learning students, and establish international educational collaborations, it is clear that technology will be central to the success of many of these initiatives. 'Transnational education' is the term coined to describe education in which the learners are located in a different country from the awarding institution (UNESCO and Council of Europe, 2000). Learners in this situation are most prone to experiencing possible clashes between cultural norms, as they remain situated in their 'home' culture while being expected to learn in a different one (Volet and Jones, 2012).

For some students, adopting a self directed and autonomous way of working with online distance learning materials will be effective, while for others, perhaps used to more teacher-centred and tightly structured learning modes, it may be less so (Ziguras, 2001). It is, therefore, important to check assumptions, understand how things are done within the residential culture, and take these findings into account – particularly at the beginning, during induction and in deciding the level of guidance that needs to be provided for new learners (Smith and Smith, 1999).

Online collaboration: synchronous and asynchronous communication

Synchronous communication – 'virtual chat'

Technology can provide several ways to communicate in 'real-time'. Using the VLE to do this is becoming increasingly common – especially when supervising students undertaking projects or doing fieldwork at a distance (e.g. Martin, 2012).

The 'chat' area in the VLE may include a set of tools, such as whiteboard space for collaborating on diagrams, or notes and quick links to key course documentations that might be needed during the conversation (e.g. previously agreed work plans). Sessions can also be archived for the purposes of revision, reflection and monitoring progress.

CASE EXAMPLE

Video conferenced workshops with colleagues overseas

Nuala Byrne, Course Director, Postgraduate Certificate of Higher Education, University of Nottingham

At the University of Nottingham, video conference workshops are being used to enhance flexibility and expand choice for new academics at the China and Malaysia campuses that are enrolled on the Postgraduate Certificate in HE course.

Traditionally, all workshops were delivered face-to-face during an annual visit of the UK-based PGCHE course team, which meant that the range of workshops was limited and, if participants missed part or all of the week, they would have to wait for the next visit to attend the missed sessions. The video conference sessions are facilitated from the UK, need to be shorter than the standard length (1.5 hours compared to 3), are scheduled to account for the time difference (7–8 hours), and facilitated and managed differently from face-to-face workshops. A few things to consider are:

- Taking more time to brief the group before starting (e.g. what to do if the connection is lost).
- Establishing how they will indicate to you that they have finished a task.
- Communicating clearly what you expect from them in terms of participation.
- Numbering or naming working groups clearly to ease communication and feedback.
- Allowing some time for the group to see you and get used to you before you start showing slides.
- Thinking about how you will find out what they have been discussing, as you cannot circulate around the groups and hear their discussions or see their notes.

34

- Planning how you will collate their contributions (flipcharts are difficult to read).
- Extensive signposting – using video conferences means that workshops are available throughout the year and on more than one occasion.

The result is that we have been able to offer China and Malaysia participants a learning experience that is closer to that of the UK participants.

For some students with disabilities, especially with physical impairments, studying can be an isolating experience. This is also true for many distance learning and part-time students too. Online learning and discussion can generate an autonomous learning community manifested through formal and informal exchanges among students and between tutor and students.

Online tutoring, mentoring and peer-to-peer exchanges can provide a mechanism for supporting such learners and giving the important sense of being part of a learning community. Holography – the use of holograms – is perhaps a next step this area, as it can incorporate many valuable face-to-face features that mere video chat cannot (e.g. body language). We discuss this further in Chapter 10.

Asynchronous communication – 'intermittent conversations'

Asynchronous communication tools, such as discussion boards, enable students to post questions, replies or feedback online in their own time. Within the online forum, conversations are grouped as threads that contain the initial posting and all the associated responses.

Discussion boards are often set up to run for set periods of time to support particular parts of a module or course, but within that students can post their comments at any time and from any place that is convenient for them.

For many students, not just students with disabilities, online discussions provide a forum in which they feel comfortable to exchange information and ideas. Students can feel freer to participate and have the time to construct their postings and put their thoughts into words at their own pace.

> The removal of social cues and social distinctions like disability, race, and facial expression through text-only communication can make even shy people feel more confident about communicating with others
>
> (Burgstahler, 1997)

The fact that these online discussions are also captured and stored means that unlike a face-to-face conversation, they can be reconsidered at a later date. This has its own rewards, for both learners and teachers. For example, conversations can be revisited, perhaps for revision purposes or assessment, and archives of conversations can be kept over a longer time period and effectively form banks of frequently asked questions together with their replies. Making this wider set of student-generated learning resources available also gives a greater sense of equality and inclusion. However, encouraging all students to participate in online discussions is not without its problems (see Chapter 6).

Just as in synchronous communication, being very clear and explicit about what is expected in online communication, and providing a schedule of tasks and contributions in advance, is important and will enable students to organise their workloads and manage their time; again, this is an aspect of study that is particularly challenging for some disabled students.

Simulating 'real-life' learning experiences

Simulations are instructional scenarios where the learner is placed in a 'world' defined by the teacher. They represent a reality within which students interact. The teacher controls the parameters of this 'world' and uses it to achieve the desired instructional results. Simulations are, in a way, a lab experiment where the students themselves are the test subjects (see: http://olc.spsd.sk.ca/DE/PD/instr/strats/simul/index.html).

Being able to immerse students in virtual worlds means that a student who has difficulties travelling to or engaging with study in more 'challenging' real-world situations can access the experience through a different means – see Chapter 9 for an in-depth discussion of immersive environments. For example, such an approach has been particularly valuable for students with a physical disability who wish to study geography or geology in the field. Virtual reality simulations also enable learners to work in a risk-free environment in which they can practice and experiment, and be exposed to situations and circumstances that in the real world would be difficult and problematic to provide – for example, a nursing student learning how to carry out an invasive clinical procedure (Jenson and Forsyth, 2012).

ASSISTIVE TECHNOLOGY

Technology has also provided a range of tools, devices and software that have greatly improved the support available to many students with learning or physical disabilities, so that they can access their programmes of study and learning environments effectively.

Having said this, some of the technologies may also be useful for non-native English speakers, or those who have any difficulties in reading and writing (at speed).

 CASE EXAMPLE

Assistive technology to aid inclusion

Kerry Pace, Specialist Teacher, University of Hull

Assistive technology (AT), such as mind-mapping (as well as text-to-speech and other software), is often seen as a specialist 'add-on' provision for students with disabilities, or a tool limited to visual representations of theories and models, and not generally accepted as an academic form, like traditional essay plans or 'finished' work.

However, mind-mapping software is versatile and powerful, and should be seen as part of an inclusive, supportive approach for *all* students. This approach formed the basis of a project I was part of, involving two university departments, sports rehabilitation and nursing, with the aim of enhancing lifelong learning and professional development, through promoting analytical and evaluative skills, and in applying theory to practice (Wray, Aspland, Taghzouit and Pace, 2012).

Students' learning styles were assessed through tools such as questionnaires, which raised awareness that learning is not a set, one-size-fits-all function, but rather a varied, individual one, and students were encouraged to engage and interact with materials in a way that best

---

37

suited them, with timetabled sessions dedicated to exploring how AT could facilitate this.

Students quickly grasped how mind-mapping software is able not only to visually represent thoughts, ideas, concepts and so on, but also to easily convert mapping into bullet-point lists, PowerPoint slides, topic/subtopic forms, Word documents, as well as capturing web pages, university learning platforms, files, emails, etc., so that the map becomes a central source for learning, aiding organisation and time-management.

Mind-mapping software features a wide variety of interactive 'templates' and multisensory mapping, and encourages the most novice users to add to an existing map form, rather than start one from scratch.

The project further promoted inclusion through YouTube video podcasts demonstrating software, site licenses enabling access to software, drop-in skills sessions for staff and students, and through the use of mind-maps in teaching sessions and materials, thereby normalising and mainstreaming AT.

To find out more, see http://www.Diverse-Learners.co.uk

The following is a list of some of the assistive technologies that are now commonly used in universities and colleges:

- *Screen readers and text-to-speech software* allow text on a computer screen to be read out loud by a computer-generated voice. Software such as *Jaws* is designed for people who cannot navigate around a screen using sight, and instead use a set of keyboard shortcuts to have the screen text read out to them by the software. In addition to the proprietary Jaws software, the major operating systems now come with built-in text-to-speech capabilities. Moreover, the *Write Out Loud* software similarly enables students to hear the text that they type on screen and so review, correct and edit it.
- *Magnifiers* such as *ZoomText* and *SuperNova* are readers and magnification tools which display a magnified text on screen, as well as read it aloud.
- *Voice recognition software*, such as Dragon Naturally Speaking, allows you to speak navigation commands to the computer, as well as dictate content, thanks to its conversion of the spoken word into digital text. Such spoken voice recognition needs to be

trained to recognise individual voices, and to develop specialised vocabularies. Just as in the case of text-to-speech software, the major operating systems also have built-in voice recognition capabilities, and their quality is approaching that of commercial systems such as Dragon Naturally Speaking.

- *Optical Character Recognition (OCR)* uses relevant software that can also be linked to a scanner to recognise printed text and convert it to digital text. This allows it to be accessed and edited by other assistive technologies such as Screen readers.

- *Literacy support tools* such as TextHELP Read and Write Gold are study skills support software that assists students with reading and writing. The package includes text-to-speech features, phonetic spell-checkers and predictive text functionalities with a speaking dictionary to check pronunciation.

- *Spell-checkers and related word finders* check the spelling of particular words, or look for synonyms/antonyms and alternative meanings. There is also a speaking dictionary and thesaurus called the Language Master.

- *Predictive text* works in conjunction with a word processor. The first letter of a word is typed and the programme then offers a list of possible words beginning with that letter. If the desired word appears, it can be selected and the word is inserted into the sentence. If not, additional letters can be typed and the computer continues to offer alternative suggestions until the right word is found.

- *Maths technologies*, such as Talking Calculator; *Metroplex* produces a range of voice-operated mathematics programmes.

However, there are still issues for users of such assistive technologies. Some e-learning applications do not dovetail well with them and particularly in the case of science-based resources, there can be difficulties in scanning and translating these for screen readers and text-to-speech applications. In addition, the time and commitment students need to devote in order to become proficient users of the technology is significant when these students may already be under very real time pressures in their studies (Draffan, 2011).

Accessibility

A key concern when using any technology to support teaching and learning is its ease of use for all students – its accessibility. Microsoft,

Apple, as well as the free and open source software community behind the numerous flavours of the Linux operating system, have developed a range of accessibility features that give computer users increasing control to tailor their operating systems and user-interfaces to best suit their needs and preferences.

Please see the Accessibility Guide produced by the LExDis – *Technology Strategies for Studying*[8] – project for detailed accessibility guidance and a set of 'considerations' to take on board when designing and using e-learning that is inclusive.

CONCLUDING REMARKS

In this chapter we have explored several ways in which technology can support teaching and learning that have the happy side effect of making it easier for students who have a disability, students who are non-native speakers of the course language, and students who are working at a distance, to participate fully in the course activities. Inclusive approaches, in reality, often improve the experience of all learners, but the benefits are most keenly felt and most appreciated by those who have different abilities and requirements.

In addition, we have also considered the special role that technology can play in providing assistance for those who have particular learning needs, and the ways in which technology can level the playing field of HE.

It is, however, also important to remember that the use of technology may bring its own barriers. Gaining confidence and skill in the use of different hardware and software tools takes time and may also require additional training and support. It is also worth remembering to keep the needs of all students in mind when developing resources and tools, and to ensure that students are pre-warned of the need to use different technologies in the module outline and pre-course information that is provided (Grace and Gravestock, 2009).

Although this whole chapter has focused on the topic of inclusivity in teaching, many of the later chapters will revisit this theme and give specific examples from practice.

NOTES

1   Based to some extent upon JISC TechDis: *Accessibility Essentials, Implementing Inclusive Practice.*

2   PowerPoint slides can also be turned into a standalone e-learning resource which can be accessed after the presentation. By using rapid development tools such as Articulate Studio, Articulate Storyline or Adobe Presenter, the main ideas of the slides, or even the accompanying narration and the resulting transcript, can be integrated with the slides automatically – a feature that is particularly beneficial for learners who have a hearing impairment, for learners whose first language is not the one the lecture takes place in, or to mitigate the situation in which the lecturer is not easy to understand because the language of the lecture is not his/her first language.

3   There are several other lecture capture tools available, as well as online conferencing tools which have also been used for lecture capture purposes: Adobe Acrobat Connect Pro, Big Blue Button, Blackboard Collaborate, Echo360, Panopto, Mediasite, and many more.

4   Instructional Management Systems: http://www.imsglobal.org/index.html

5   http://www.w3.org

6   http://www.w3.org/WAI/

7   For further information, see: http://www.irlen.org.uk

8   http://www.lexdis.org.uk/guides/accessibility/

USEFUL RESOURCES

Academic Development to Enhance Professional Teaching (ADEPT) aims to support the continuing professional development of academic and support staff involved in learning, teaching and assessment. The site's pages on inclusivity provide a good set of links to online materials on inclusive practice:

Inclusivity Online Resources. http://goo.gl/YIxAmm

The Worldwide Web Consortium (W3C) has developed a programme called the Web Accessibility Initiative (WAI): see http://www.w3.org. It aims to promote accessibility through the development and implementation of open technology standards.

W3C has set out guidelines for authors of web-based content to follow in order to achieve certain levels of accessibility. These guidelines explain how to make Web content accessible to people with disabilities. The guidelines are intended for all Web content developers (page authors and site designers):

W3C (1999). *WCAGs W3C Recommendation.*
http://www.w3.org/TR/WAI-WEBCONTENT

A suite of learning resources and advice on the use of technology in teaching in five areas: Preparing Your Learning; Delivering Learning (Lecture/Classroom); Delivering Learning (Practical/Fieldwork/Placement); Delivering Learning (Online); Assessing Learning:

41

Teaching Inclusively Using Technology – JISC TechDis – Inclusion Technology Advice. http://goo.gl/t1gfeB

Useful Contacts in Disability – the HE Funding Council for England (HEFCE) has compiled a helpful list of organisations involved in improving the provision for disabled students in tertiary education at: http://goo.gl/XUPqdw

Chapter 3

Collaboration and networking

The use of social media

INTRODUCTION

The rise in popularity of social media and networking tools such as Facebook (FB), Twitter and LinkedIn has been startling. Many young people use their FB accounts and Twitter feeds as their primary means of communicating with their friends and family. Even back in 2010, Roblyer et al. commented that 'the data indicate that students communicate as much with Facebook as they do with technologies traditionally used in colleges (e.g., email)'. News, information and celebrity gossip can be passed through a community of users so rapidly that the analogy with infection and 'going viral' seems very apt.

Although many will point out that the web is inherently 'social' and Internet applications have existed for the last 30–40 years, it is the scale of use that is now so different. Selwyn (2011: 2) observes:

> social media of the 2010s now boast a sufficient critical mass of users and applications to be of genuine collective benefit and social significance.

So what is the significance of such a pervasive technology for HE? There is no doubt that many students entering university education today are already skilled in the manipulation of their online environments, and in exerting choice in the ways they interact with web content and with their wider networks of contacts. Not content to consume prepackaged and one-size-fits-all web material, today's students are already very used to authoring, producing and customising – in short, controlling – the content for themselves (Tapscott and Williams, 2007).

> Social media encourages contributions and feedback from everyone who is interested. It blurs the line between media and audience . . . [it] is better seen as a two-way conversation.
>
> (Mayfield, 2008: 5)

Many students entering HE in 2013 have never known life without the web, and its use is completely integrated with how they communicate, learn and live. This is who they are. Arguably then, the educational experiences that we design and plan for them have to recognise this and seek to maximise the potential of social media, or what has come to be known as Web 2.0 tools.

Some argue that the use of social media tools will have a profound effect on how students will approach university life (Ulbrich et al., 2010). For these students, networking and collaboration, the perception of effective multitasking, and the reliance on the web to find information and opinions, are approaches which they are increasingly likely to bring to university. Moreover, prospective students are likely to be very used to publishing their views and contributions on the web, as well as seeking the opinions and advice of their peers and fellow contributors in this way.

While it can be anticipated that students are more likely to view learning as a 'participatory, social process' (McLoughlin and Lee, 2010) and expect to have some role in actively shaping and contributing to knowledge themselves, one can also easily see a role for educators in facilitating a better understanding of social media etiquette, use of appropriate register, and web-based content-creation advantages and pitfalls – with special emphasis on the long-term implications of one's personal digital footprint.

However, integrating the use of social media into formal HE is not without its difficulties and obstacles. It can be difficult to engage learners and encourage regular interaction in an educational context.

One possible explanation is that the preference for different social media platforms is itself dynamic and changeable and, as such, it is very easy to look outmoded and old fashioned.

It may also be that there is some resentment when social spaces are used for the purposes of providing structured education processes and experiences. After all, they are *social* spaces, and it seems reasonable to think that in some ways providing formal education via social media tools reduces the very essence of what makes their use desirable in the first place (see, for example, Andrews and Drennan, 2009).

Another inhibitor may be that much of the informal learning that goes on, while using social media tools, is not recognised and appreciated officially. Jay Cross (2006) and others have emphasised the value and importance of informal learning, but how best to integrate it within the formal course (and particularly assessment) structures still remains a considerable challenge and an inherent paradox.

In many of the existing social media environments, contributions are appreciated and validated by the community of users with simple endorsements, such as a 'thumbs up' or a 'like' posting. Usefulness or 'value' is recognised by the number of retweets or shares for a particular piece of information, or through the award of star-ratings for contributors (e.g. 'Was this review useful to you?').

This way people see that their voluntary efforts are rewarded in their social or professional circles. In some ways it is easier to see the progress from 'newbie' to 'expert' in a community of practice (Wenger, 1998) in social media and online communities through such recognition endorsements and signifiers of value, but these do not fit with traditional assessment and feedback strategies readily.

In this chapter, we will consider the pedagogic use of social networking, particularly the use of blogs and wikis, and discuss four different social media tools in a little more detail: Facebook, Twitter, Skype and LinkedIn.

VIEWS ON USING SOCIAL MEDIA IN TEACHING AND LEARNING

Possible benefits

Social media use is so widespread that knowledge about it and experience of using it should be part of a general education in its own right.

This argument focuses on the need for graduates to be aware of the various ways in which social networking is used in research, in business, and more generally in society as a whole – in particular, the way that potential employers are increasingly likely to use social media to recruit candidates, and the fact that many will research an applicant's online profile as part of their selection process. Students, therefore, need to understand the concept of the 'personal digital footprint', and recognise the potential of social media in job hunting, as well as the dangers of 'saying' something in the heat of the moment that cannot then be retracted or controlled once published. A lesson in this respect was a recent legal case involving a second-year biology student who received a 54-day jail sentence for his racially offensive Twitter postings (BBC News Wales, 2012).

Apart from employability, another benefit is that the appropriate use of social media tools can lead to higher levels of student engagement and participation. For example, students can showcase their knowledge and skills through their use of blogging and contributing to wikis. They can expose their ideas and thoughts to a wide and varied community of followers, and learn how to debate and defend their particular viewpoints. They can also discover and engage with the global research and user community in their field of study through Twitter.

Social networking tools can enhance the levels of a variety of types of communication between students and teachers. Examples include making course announcements, giving feedback, setting preparatory tasks for class, and sharing interests and enthusiasms perhaps in relation to research interests (this ability to share interests is an area discussed in the 'many-to-many technology' section in Chapter 10).

Moreover, although making educational decisions based on trends is a very dangerous activity, you may want to consider the reality that numerous schools and colleges use this technology already, and thus universities run the risk of appearing outdated and old fashioned if they do not keep up with the latest developments in social media.

 CASE EXAMPLE

Supporting early student engagement

Russell Gurbutt, School of Healthcare, University of Leeds

The experience of new students during the early period of their studies via a blended learning approach is highly important to their continuing progression. Typically there are factors on both sides (educators and students) that can either enable or inhibit engagement.

On the student side, there are particular issues surrounding making sense of the technology being used (such as Moodle, WebCT or Blackboard VLEs), and problem-solving when it is not immediately obvious where resources and information are located. Furthermore, the fact that the education experience could initially appear to be a collection of assorted texts, pamphlets, guidebooks and online resources, means that there is a strong likelihood of feeling detached and isolated from the student community. Additionally, there may be some inhibition about contacting academic staff.

From the academic side of the equation, there is the danger of familiarity with the process and content, to the extent that any initial anxieties that a student may have about understanding the process sufficiently, such that they become absorbed in the content, are overlooked. Like students, academic staff may also have some reservations about the accessibility and reliability of the technology, and the additional work that it involves compared to pure classroom-based lectures.

One intervention package that addresses this situation, drawing on experience at three universities, has been to develop online communities of students using social networking tools (such as blogs), thus providing initial plain-language, friendly communication via letter or email (or both), introducing oneself and outlining online the communication arrangements.

An ongoing group blog with regular contributions from the staff can work well to offer a focus for informal discussion, as can student-led blogs or discussion boards to facilitate sharing personal experiences of learning, although some will prefer other social network sites outside of a VLE. Included in this will be initial online ice-breakers, as well as classroom-based shared activities, so that students develop friendships that transcend the subject matter so as to develop a sense of belonging.

Robust guidance on problem-solving selected technology issues and routes of referral to technical support are also necessary to facilitate workload regulation, while plain-language guides to how the study process is designed do help. Continuous feedback is essential, and can be gained via online survey points at set junctures during the first few weeks so that group-wide responses can be made.

Overall, the sequencing of regular online discussions, and the provision of clear information and support, help orientate students to the process of study. Activities designed to develop interaction, and gather feedback using technology as a conduit and not a barrier, further contribute to promoting engagement and confidence during the initial phase of their studies.

Potential difficulties

Like many of the technologies in this book, social media was not designed with formal education in mind, and one of its key features – its accessibility and openness – presents many with their biggest concern. Practitioners use the metaphor of the 'walled garden' to describe the safe and enclosed space they try to create for their learners, be that in the classroom or online (Dron, 2006). The need to feel safe to take intellectual risks while learning is important, and hosting learning events in a 'public' space seems to fly in the face of this need (see also Chapter 6 on open immersive environments).

More practically, social media could potentially be distracting rather than an enhancer of learning.

 PAUSE FOR THOUGHT

Divided attention and face-to-face communication

- Is encouraging students to log onto their FB accounts really a good idea when their undivided attention and concentration are needed for specific course tasks?
- Could the greater use of social media actually inhibit the development of face-to-face communication skills?

If students felt that their computer screens and smartphones could replace the need to interact and speak with teachers and their peers, this would clearly hinder their abilities to develop presentation and dialogue skills. This concern is even more serious given that employers still seem to rate the 'ability to verbally communicate with persons inside and outside the organization'[1] as the most important quality they look for in their new recruits.

Furthermore, online behaviour can become less respectful, and in extreme cases be considered bullying or harassment. Cases of cyberbullying and trolling have recently hit the headlines, and social media sites have been closed because of poor conduct. This brings with it two clear considerations: first, the actual bullying and harm done, but also the second issue of increased workload, for it seems to follow that if universities want to use social media, the interactions which take place within it would need to be monitored and moderated.

Another often-voiced concern is that social media encourages free riding and passivity – precisely the two characteristics which universities try very hard to 'teach-out' of students. In fact, it is the case that most social media sites have far more observing 'lerkers' than active contributors. Even very well-used sites, such as Wikipedia (see below) rely on the activity of a few thousand people[2] who add and edit entries, while most of us simply treat it as an information source. In the words of Selwyn (2012), most social media activity is 'appropriated for the one-way passive consumption of content'.

A final concern focuses more on the role and skills of the teacher, and the requirements and workload involved in acquiring a new skill set. Social media has a language and a modus operandi of its own – and nothing is more embarrassing than 'older generations' trying to adopt a 'youth culture' style. Of course, embarrassment itself need not be a problem; the problem comes because this gap might lead to the communication feeling 'inauthentic' and 'manipulated', which most likely would be a huge demotivator for students.

 PAUSE FOR THOUGHT

Where do you stand in this debate?

Take a moment to consider your own position. What do you see as being the most persuasive arguments for and against the use of social networking tools in your teaching?

Security and privacy considerations

One of the most important considerations when using social media in teaching is that of privacy and security. Some teachers seek to compartmentalise the different aspects of their lives online by registering at least two different accounts, and using one for work and the other(s) for their own social and personal interactions. Relatedly, some thought ought to be given to which privacy settings should be selected, so that contributions are only seen by those for whom they are intended.

Using blogs and wikis in teaching and learning

A blog or a 'web log' is an online set of 'journal entries' – termed 'posts' – which are shared with an open or closed web-based community.

There are currently free options for hosting a blog (e.g. WordPress, Blogger, Posterous, etc.), which offer a range of free functionalities, as well as an additional, extended range at a price.

Blogs may be the work of just one 'blogger', or they can be co-authored by a group. Sometimes blogs are very personal and maintained as a kind of open diary, while others are written on particular topics or themes, or to accompany particular ventures or projects. For example, a colleague working abroad for six months recently maintained a 'travel blog' to keep in touch with friends and family. Also, students studying abroad (for example, as part of a language degree) or undertaking longer-term research projects, are sometimes required to do the same thing.

Blogs are authored by the blogging individual or team, and the posts cannot be created or modified by externals without first being given editing rights. Interactivity is usually limited to the opportunity for visitors to post comments, questions and messages to the author and other readers at the end of the blog.

The recent rise in micro-blogging (blogging with an imposed word limit) via tools such as Twitter, has led to significantly more interactivity, with posts triggering more responses. Provided that all contributions have a common tag, they can take the form of an asynchronous, online conversation with the most recent posts appearing at the top of the page.

Many teachers have found that blogs provide an excellent vehicle for formative and summative assessment, because they allow them to understand their students' expectations better and to provide feedback more promptly (e.g. by asking students to post a brief comment very early in the course). Moreover, blog posts can also be used to gain evaluative feedback from learners, both during and after the module (for a further discussion of the use of technology in assessment, see Chapter 5).

 CASE EXAMPLE

Using social media to teach undergraduate theory

Carole McGranahan, Lecturer, Cultural Anthropology, University of Colarado

Students taking an introductory-level anthropology course were asked to write two 500-word essays, in which they applied two different anthropological theories that had been studied in class. The essays related to two different themes – food or love – and submission deadlines were staggered so that some students wrote about food first and while others wrote about love.

Teaching assistants marked the essays and, together with Carole McGranahan, selected a sample of them to post on the blog – using gender-neutral pseudonyms. All students were then asked to make six 'substantive comments' on the posted essays – three on love essays and three on food. Their essays and postings contributed 40 per cent of the course grade. The outcomes were considered to be a great success, with students making insightful and constructive comments, practising applying the theory they had recently learned about. These students were also able to remember and use the theory when taking more advanced anthropology courses later in their degrees.

For further information, see Carole McGranahan's full blog at: http://goo.gl/WFzfni

A *wiki* is a particular kind of web page that can be created by a group of designated users, all having the power to add to or edit existing content on the wiki pages. It is this extra collaborative editing, as well as the fact that the result of the collaboration is a coherent webpage rather than a long list of comments, which distinguishes wikis from blogs. Wikis were first developed by an American computer programmer – Ward Cunningham – in 1995. As an aside, he is also known as the author of Cunningham's Law:

The best way to get the right answer on the Internet is not to ask a question; it's to post the wrong answer.

The most famous of all wikis is probably Wikipedia, which was launched in 2001 and is a freely available and collaboratively edited encyclopaedia. Because any authenticated user can create and edit existing pages, this has led to the common criticism that some information is unverified and inaccurate – in fact, even its creator has suggested that academics do not use it (Young, 2006). However, and following Cunningham's law, these inaccuracies are often challenged and corrected by other readers and users of the site. In fact, a 2005 experimental study by *Nature* indicated that Wikipedia came close in terms of the accuracy of a range of scientific entries to the *Encyclopaedia Britannica*. The latter has disputed the result of this study, the title of the article, the methodology and several other aspects, yet *Nature* rebutted the complaints in 2006.[3]

Wikis are therefore shared online spaces in which collaboration and joint working and learning can be facilitated. They can be made completely open access (like Wikipedia), or they can be restricted to an 'invited' membership (by setting appropriate permissions). It is in this latter form that they have been most widely used in HE. The wiki saves all previous versions of its pages so that there is a log of all the changes that have been made, and who has made them.

For example, a wiki can be set up for the PhD student and his/her supervisory team, so that progress can be reported by the student and commented on by all members of the supervisory team in an open manner, with all feedback visible to everyone involved. This transparency can help reduce the difficulties arising from a student receiving conflicting advice. Research papers can be collaboratively developed using a wiki, with all authors accessing and editing a developing manuscript at the same time. In the same way, students undertaking a group project can use a wiki to write their joint report or dissertation. Blogs and wikis are widely used in university teaching in a wide range of disciplines and with a varied set of foci (see the Case Examples box).

 CASE EXAMPLES

Using a wiki to generate a reading list

Alec Couros uses an open-access wiki on his educational technology and media course at the University of Regina, and invites his students (and past students) to help him create the reading list for the course and discuss assignments. He has chosen to allow new students to access the wiki history for his course, as he feels it helps them learn from their peers: past and present.

Using a wiki to generate lecture notes

Richard Buckland at the University of New South Wales has used wikis for many years, and uses them to write his own lecture/teaching notes, and to share them with his students so that they also become the class notes for the students.

He has experimented with a number of ways of doing this: he finds his students want to see his bullet-point notes for the lecture (and know that these are 'official'); he then asks a study group of students each week to make some very quick 'raw' notes and post these later the same day (each study group does this once in a 12-week semester and get a very small percentage of marks and a public grade for doing this). Then he has what he calls the 'nice notes', which are developed and added to by the students and become the best set of notes that the students later revise from.

Richard also talks about the importance of 'wiki-nature', and how this drives his students to want to develop a really good set of notes that they can be proud of and contribute in a way that is driven by wanting to do a good job; he has found that the minute he starts trying to drive student contributions by grading and assessing this, the quality of the notes goes down.

See him talk further about these experiments at:
http://www.youtube.com/watch?v=m1-800rBi0o

SOME SPECIFIC SOCIAL NETWORKING TOOLS

Facebook

Facebook (FB) is currently the most popular social network in the world, with hundreds of millions of users drawn from all ages and walks of life. Users need to register and set up an FB account, and then they can personalise their own FB page to include the information they wish to make available both to the users they have selected to be their 'friends', and other users, by modifying their FB privacy settings.

It is this ability to customise information distribution channels that is often cited as the main reason why FB became such a market leader. Users can share information, photos, video footage, their likes and dislikes, and they can join FB groups that share similar interests. They can comment on postings made by their 'friends' and participate in public and private chat. This platform therefore provides many of the tools necessary for people to be able to communicate, collaborate, develop and share ideas in an online environment. It also has the advantage that the vast majority of students will already be familiar with how FB works and already be engaged users.

Grosseck et al. (2011) reviewed the recent literature on using FB in teaching, and identified a wide range of potential benefits for both students and teachers. For learners using FB, it can be motivating and can help foster positive relationships with peers and teachers. The range of skills used and developed is also highlighted, with special emphasis on those of communication, evaluation and critical thought, in addition to the enhancement of personal traits such as self-confidence, autonomy, tolerance and respect for diversity.

For the teacher, FB provides a vehicle to involve students more actively in shaping their own learning, and in interacting with them and fellow teachers outside the classroom. In a survey of staff attitudes and experiences of using FB, Bosch (2009) noted that teachers felt that their students could ask questions online that they might not feel comfortable asking in class.

In addition, some teachers indicated that using FB meant that class time could be spent more effectively, because student queries had already been dealt with. Moreover, students could also indicate which areas of the material they would like extra help with, and the teacher was then able to come to class prepared for these discussions.

However, FB raises a number of issues. For example, should teachers be 'friends' with students? Some will argue that it is important to maintain boundaries between the teacher and his/her students, and being FB friends blurs this professional relationship. Meanwhile, others feel that becoming friends with current and past students helps a teacher really get to know their students, which in turn means they can tailor their support and teaching. There are colleagues who have more than one FB account, allowing them to keep their personal and teaching life separate, and enabling them to communicate with their learners freely.

> Having two Facebook profiles does mean I have to log in twice when I want to use Facebook, but it also means that I am only ever one click away from contact with a colleague or former student. It's an invaluable resource for maintaining an alumni network and securing guest speakers to come to my classes, and sometimes I even get requests for career advice from former students, giving me the opportunity to mentor them in their careers, one of the great joys of teaching.
>
> (Michel, 2009)

Alternatively, it is possible to use the 'list' feature on FB to set up distinct areas for teaching and personal conversations – currently this is done by 'Creating [a] List' using the 'Friends' tab and adding students by clicking on their profile pictures, typing in their names in the 'Add friends to this list' field, or by accepting FB's own suggestions if appropriate.

After creating the list, you will need to go to your account menu and select 'Privacy Settings' in the top right corner, then click on 'Edit' next to the appropriate features which you only want to make available to the list. Another area you may want to look at is 'Blocking', where you can use the 'Lists' function to exclude some of your contacts from seeing your information and posts unless you make them 'Public'. After making appropriate selections, you can then choose to keep your posts, contact information, location, photos, etc. private if you wish. In a similar way, you can set up groups and restrict access through privacy settings, too.

In addition to the 'Lists' function, FB also enables users to create groups with various levels of privacy – from 'Public' to 'Secret'. This can be useful to create safe environments for collaboration and idea sharing.

 CASE EXAMPLE

Facebook groups for educational purposes

Erik Mobrand, Political Science, National University of Singapore

I regularly teach a fourth-year seminar of 25–30 students at the National University of Singapore (NUS). I use a Facebook (FB) 'group' as a supplementary learning medium. FB's settings controls allow me to make the group closed to our class. My students join and we don't have to be 'friends'! With FB groups, instructors can create autonomous educational spaces that do not require sharing personal information with students.

Our FB group serves two related functions. Firstly, for each seminar I require 2–3 students to post a link to a relevant article, video, or other resource to our group. The content becomes mandatory reading for their classmates. This exercise allows students to play a role in creating the course syllabus. Secondly, students engage in online discussion of course materials through the FB group. Online exchanges before class prepare students for seminar discussions, and the debate often continues online after class.

FB groups hold one fundamental advantage over other online discussion formats: educators can bring the learning environment into the students' social space. Accessing university-hosted discussion boards requires students to make a conscious decision to cross into an academic space and engage in schoolwork. An FB group does not.

Most students at NUS spend time on FB for personal purposes already; once on FB, interaction with our class is just one click away. When they stumble across web content related to the class, sharing and commenting is easy. In addition, since many students access FB on their mobile phones, they can easily engage with the course on the go. In these ways, FB groups allow educators to adapt to the shifting social and technological habits of students and tap into those habits to facilitate learning.

Adapted from Mobrand (2011).

Twitter

The basics

Twitter (established in 2006) is a free micro-blogging environment that limits the size of the messages posted (called 'tweets') to just 140 characters. Tweets can also include links to images, websites, other blogs, etc. In addition to posting, users also choose whom they wish to 'follow', and so quickly build up a personalised Twitter feed that combines their varied interests. The tweets can be posted and read from any computer, smartphone or tablet, making them instantly accessible and mobile.

SETTING UP A TWITTER ACCOUNT

1 Go to http://www.twitter.com/signup
2 Enter your name, email address and a memorable password. Choose a username that makes it easy to identify you.
3 Click 'Create my account', and your account is live.
4 Then compose a brief profile that describes you and your interests – you have 160 characters to do this. You can link to other sites and

blogs if you wish. Include a photograph, and provide any relevant professional or personal details you wish. All of this information can be changed whenever you wish.

Following others

You can use the 'Search' box function of Twitter to look for friends and colleagues. Once you have found someone whom you would like to follow, you can check to see whom they are 'following' in their turn, and thus you are likely to find other individuals with similar interests to you. Twitter is easy to use and very intuitive. You can also use keyword searches to look for people tweeting in your discipline, in your research area, or from your own institution. There is no limit to the number of people you can follow.

You can un-follow people just as easily by putting your cursor over the green 'following' button and clicking when it turns red to un-follow. Similarly, you can block people whom you do not want to be followed by, by clicking on their head and shoulders icon and clicking on the 'Block (their name)' option when it appears.

Tweeting and retweeting

The thing that makes Twitter different is the limit of characters allowed – which means postings are short, punchy and to the point. Saying something interesting, witty, or meaningful so succinctly is a real skill, and the medium has generated its own stars who have thousands of followers.

It is easy to retweet somebody else's tweet and include it in your own Twitter feed (so all your followers get to see it too). When a tweet is retweeted it shows with a small arrow icon, so that readers can see that it has been reposted and was written by somebody else.

From a teaching and learning perspective, Twitter can also be seen as a human-filtered search and referencing engine, allowing individuals to engage with the global community, as well as develop a relevant and supportive group of followers by posting relevant updates, retweeting items of interest and being consistent. This feature can be useful both to a teacher preparing teaching materials and to a student exploring a topic, perhaps in order to write a dissertation or undertake a project.

Not using your professional Twitter account to post updates regarding your personal life can have a significant positive influence on your professional profile. In terms of topics worth tweeting about, the relative – and often overestimated – anonymity of the medium, as well as the disconnection manifested with all forms of social media, can often lead to individuals sharing information that you will very likely find inappropriate or irrelevant in an HE context.

However, building a relevant network will protect you from most of the irrelevant content. Regarding your own contributions, updates on projects and developments can help maintain your network's interest; many academic meetings and conferences now use a common Twitter hashtag to communicate about the event. It is common for following to become reciprocal, with the people you follow returning the compliment.

Backchanneling and hashtags (#)

Backchanneling is the term used to describe an online conversation about a particular theme or topic. This may be conducted alongside a live conversation or presentation – for example, students tweeting questions or comments during a lecture (Atkinson, 2009), academics posting tweets while papers are presented at conferences, or journalists and pundits posting tweets about a political speech as it is being broadcast.

There are several ways that Twitter can be used to backchannel tweets for a specified or intended group of users, but the use of the hashtag is probably the most common. Here a topic, event, acronym, or keyword, is preceded by the hash symbol (#); search engines or Twitter clients can then easily identify the hashtagged items and group them together. It is increasingly the case that professional meetings and academic conferences will pre-announce a hashtag so that both those attending and those wishing to follow events can stay in touch easily.

Some teachers are also beginning to use the same approach for their modules or classes – announcing a course hashtag which students are encouraged to follow. The teacher can then make course announcements, tweet articles or questions, links or news items; students can be encouraged to join in and add tweets of their own for the class, too (Rinaldo et al., 2011).

Taking care on Twitter

The main attraction of Twitter is that it is open, and anyone – with or without an account – can look at and read any unblocked tweets:

everything is in the public domain. Thinking carefully about what you write is therefore extremely important, particularly because, although you can delete a tweet you have posted, you cannot control what others may have done with your original tweet; for example, perhaps others had retweeted your message before you deleted it.

In addition, there are numerous automatic tweet harvesters on the web, which capture all tweets in order to mine the information you share for clues regarding your mood, favourite products, pastimes and purchases you are likely to make. This is valuable information that a growing number of companies are willing to pay for in order to try and sell you whatever they happen to be selling at the time.

On a similar note, it is also worth bearing in mind that not everybody is who they claim to be on Twitter – it is very easy to set up 'fake' name accounts, and so you may not be following whom you think you are. Especially if you need to follow economists/politicians/public figures for your studies, make sure you research their profiles thoroughly to ensure you are following the right person.

All in all, however, Twitter represents a valuable learning and communication tool, despite the need to still alert students to their online profile and how they present themselves in the virtual world.

Using Twitter

In this section we have been focusing on the use of Twitter in teaching and learning, but many also use this media to promote their professional and research activities. This could be on an individual basis or as part of a research group. When appropriate, remember to include your Twitter account in your email signature, your letterhead and business cards, as well as in relevant information that you provide when you present at conferences or teach.

Using Twitter in your teaching

A common use of Twitter is to set up a separate Twitter account for each of the modules or courses that are taught, using the name and course code of the class in the username. Teachers cannot sign students up to Twitter, and therefore ensuring that they follow the course tweets can be a challenge. However, it is possible to arrange for the course tweets to be relayed via an RSS feed to other online environments, such as the VLE

(Blackboard, Moodle, etc.); for more information on RSS feeds and VLEs, see Chapter 7.

If a teacher uses Twitter, two features worth highlighting are:

1   How to stop Twitter pushing notifications to their phones; and

2   How to 'track' their own username so that they will get an alert on their phone if anyone responds to their tweets (by sending a tweet from their phone, 'track @insert the particular account name here').[4]

Reasons to tweet include the following:

- To give quick feedback to the class
- To encourage in-class participation
- To provide encouragement and further guidance
- To suggest further readings or study topics
- To make 'course' announcements
- To follow up on in-class discussions
- To answer student questions and queries
- To share successes and research findings
- To prompt preparatory thoughts before seminars
- To remind students of deadlines or assessment requirements
- To offer ongoing support for homework or self-study assignments

Twitter can provide a very helpful way of keeping in touch with students who are working at a distance. This might be while they undertake field-work, when doing their year abroad on language programmes, or if they are part-time or distance learners.

Like the other social media mentioned, using Twitter to communicate and keep a record of developments on a dissertation or research project can also be very helpful. As a research supervisor, Twitter provides a mechanism to maintain contact – albeit completely in the public eye – with a student while they are conducting their own studies.

Some teachers and individuals are beginning to experiment with more creative ways of using Twitter by, for example, setting up fictional twitter accounts for literary or historical characters and using the medium in a form of role-play[5]; this approach may help students and other members of the community to better understand different ways of thinking about a situation, a problem, or to identify and contextualise the people and events being studied.

Tweeting in class

Research has revealed that with micro-blogging, students are able to participate in classroom discussion at a level that they would not normally do. Junco et al. (2011) report that the use of Twitter encouraged online participation from some students who otherwise might not be active participants in class. Similarly, Rankin (2009) noted that the integration of Twitter as a communication tool allowed more students to participate in classroom discussion than before.

For example, a professor at the University of Texas, Dallas – Monica Rankin – had her class tweet messages and questions *during* the lecture. These messages were then displayed on a large screen for all the students to see (Miners, 2010). She reports an increase in involvement and participation from her students, and also states that it is clear to see how getting those questions and comments would also provide her with very valuable 'live' feedback on the learning of her students.

In order to do this, ask students to bring their laptops or smartphones to the lecture; issue a class hashtag and invite the students to post questions, comments, suggestions etc., *during* the lecture or class, in order to extend the possibilities for interaction and debate beyond the traditional question and answer session.

Display the tweet postings, in the class, on a large screen, and give the teacher and the learners the chance to reply, either verbally or also via Twitter, then and there or later after the class. Plan your session to enable your students to concentrate on each task in turn – remember that multitasking is not possible in terms of paying attention to concurrent stimuli.

Dunlap and Lowenthal (2009) also found that *students* perceived Twitter as a tool that could facilitate their informal and independent learning, by helping them locate appropriate information sources and gain help by asking peers about coursework assignments and course elements that confused them. They also found that online learning communities established via micro-blogging often remain active long after the particular module or course has finished.

Students can also be set learning tasks that use Twitter; for example, they could be asked to host a twitter chat on an assigned topic, or track a current event or news story by analysing relevant trending topics.

61

CASE EXAMPLE

Using Twitter

Gill Swan, Lecturer in Architecture, University of Central Lancashire

Gill Swan recently reported her experiences of using Twitter to help her architectural studies students 'tap into a wealthy resource of professionals online, without demanding too much of their valuable time' at the University of Central Lancashire. Her students were encouraged to engage with prospective employers by tweeting examples of their work over a three- or four-day period. They received feedback and suggestions from the professionals and gained very useful experience and confidence in talking to this group of experienced and knowledgeable individuals.

PAUSE FOR THOUGHT

What are your views on in-class tweeting?

This seems to be a bold approach that very much changes the dynamics of a traditional 'teacher-centred' lecture. What do you think are the main pros and cons of micro-blogging in a lecture in your discipline? Is it something you have tried or would consider?

How about taking a few moments to see what the latest discussions are in the area of teaching and learning technologies by following these Twitter hashtags: #edtech and #elearning.

Using the 'idea' of tweeting in face-to-face teaching

The teacher need not actually tweet, as the very idea – or principle – of tweeting can be used to enrich face-to-face teaching. For example, one could ask students to write, with pen and paper, a 'tweet' on a topic on a sheet of A4 paper, and then exchange their papers and add a reply or comment to the first tweet – perhaps passing this around a group of three or four people to collect thoughts, views and reactions to their original tweet.

CASE EXAMPLE

Tabletop paper 'tweet' activity

Clare Kell, Postgraduate Certificate in University Teaching and Learning, University of Cardiff

With contact time on our PgC so precious, each activity we introduce is designed to offer multiple learning experiences and reflection potential. The first ten-credit module challenges participants to think about the context of UKHE and their role within it, and illustrate how their thinking translates into the development of one teaching session.

With the inclusive curriculum and technology-enhanced education agenda, key discourses at Cardiff, and central features of formatively assessed elements of the module, there is a lot to help participants see the HE world they work in, and themselves as learners and teachers, with new insight and with a fresh perspective.

Just before lunch on Day 1, participants' brains reel from discussions about the UKHE agenda, and earlier activities will have enabled them to meet just a few of their peers. How could we create a learning trigger for other elements of the day and give each participant a voice, with some degree of safety, to anchor and write down some of the possible confusion going around in their head? We assumed that participants would be familiar with writing short snippets of text to voice opinions on social media-based forums. We thought a social media-aligned activity could act as a bridge between our module's contact and VLE-based non-contact time learning activities.

Already seated at tables of four or five, participants were asked to each take a sheet of paper and, using not more than 140 characters (or about 20–25 words), write down a comment, statement or question that was running through their mind. When done, participants passed on their sheets and neighbours responded to the 'tweet' they received and passed it on again. When the paper returned to its originator, the group discussed both the activity and the issues arising in the 'tweets'.

While all papers were collected and used to post onto the module VLE, issues that remained unanswered/unclarified after the period of discussion were put on flipcharts. All participants, armed with Post-it notes, walked around the various posters adding personal thoughts about each, posing more questions, etc.

63

The session drew to a close with a discussion about the relevance of the activity to the e-based formative elements of the module, digital etiquette, etc.

How did it go?

While many participants relished the immediacy of the 'tweet' writing, some were caught in the headlights initially and needed to verbalise their thought to a PCUTL team member before they could write it. Once started, though, all flowed and the activity generated three or four distinct 'threads' from each table. This was a powerful learning trigger for many newer staff who had not appreciated how individuals could look at the same issues so differently. The walking plenary worked well and helped the whole group to both gel and recognise the wealth of experiences and perspectives within the room that could be harnessed by teachers to facilitate rather than control learning.

Reflections and suggestions for next time

Participant reflections suggested that using ideas from social media interactions to support learning was not something they had thought about before, but many have now repeated this and similar activities in their own teaching to benchmark learner groups, while others have set up class-time Twitter accounts for immediate learner–teacher in-class interaction. Even the participants who 'froze' used the experience to reflect on their personal learning styles, ways to manage in-class learning 'wobbles', etc., and concluded that uncertainty gives us room to grow.

Next time we are going to repeat the activity in exactly the same way. While on the day we discussed knee-jerk adjustments, reading participants' reflections suggests that we leave things alone and enable participants to learn from the activity what is relevant to them.

Skype: free (PC–PC) calls

Skype provides a cost-effective and easy way of communicating between PCs, laptops, tablets and Internet-connected smartphones.[6]

Originally launched in 2003, Skype is the most well-known Voice over Internet Protocol (VoIP) application, and allows users to make free PC–PC calls all over the world. If users have webcams, Skype also allows them to see and be seen by the person or people they are talking to.

However, Skype effectively connects computer-to-computer(s), thus allowing large-screen projection and a teacher/student to speak to and present to a distant group of people.

For teaching, it is key to know that Skype may be used to connect individuals, one individual to a group, or one group to another group.

(Eaton, 2010)

Consequently, course leaders, teachers, assessors, supervisors and learners in HE can use Skype in many ways, for example:

- To aid student recruitment and selection – course convenors are beginning to offer potential applicants the opportunity to Skype chat about the course and their applications.
- Guest lecturers – without the cost, time and inconvenience of travel, guests can be invited to give presentations to students.
- Interviews – external experts can be interviewed about their specialisms in a class by both students and the teacher.
- Feedback – students can seek feedback from a range of tutors and experts by talking through their work in progress; this can be very helpful when shaping a research or dissertation project proposal.
- Supervision and one-to-one support on assignments, research degrees or research publications – supervisors and authors can liaise with students and peers at a distance.
- Fieldwork – to keep in touch with students who are out doing fieldwork or to bring the field into the classroom for students who are unable to travel to distant sites.
- Language practice and cultural appreciation – talking to non-native speakers and/or those from other countries and cultures.
- Students based at different sites or campuses can join in online lectures or seminars.
- To support student interactions, and preparation for tasks such as in-class debates or collaborative group work and projects.
- To support distance learners (DL) at home and overseas. Having the chance to actually talk to a teacher and to fellow learners is often very much appreciated by DL students who can get isolated and become demotivated on their own.

65

TABLE 3.1 Other features of Internet chat software

Feature	Function
Text chat/instant messaging	Users can use the text chat function alongside or in addition to a real-time audio/video call, and so type a message to let a caller know if there is a problem with their connection or briefly explain or comment on a situation
Conference calling	Depending on the solution used, more than two participants may be on the line at the same time and take part in audio conversations together
File sharing	This feature allows a user to send a file to another user in real time – for example, a student could send a Word document to get feedback, or a teacher could send an additional learning resource to discuss
Screen sharing	Users can share part of or their entire computer screen with a caller – for example, to show a PowerPoint presentation, label diagrams, work out maths problems, or show a video clip provided they have the necessary rights to re-broadcast it

Teaching with Skype

 CASE EXAMPLE

Making full use of Skype to support learning

Kerry Pace, Specialist Teacher, University of Hull

Social media is often seen as a domain for the young and less so a valid tool of delivering information. You do not have to be a technical wizard to use packages such as Skype, as it is simply using the Internet to make telephone calls with video. I am not technically gifted (nor young), but in using Skype for the last six years, I firmly believe that whatever can be done in a traditional learning environment can be done via Skype.

Its ease of use and inbuilt tools mean it is a flexible teaching and learning, as well as assessment, tool. As only a computer and webcam are required, the student and member of staff can be located anywhere in the world, making working from home, supporting placements, flexi-working and evening sessions viable options. The lack of travel has a positive impact on carbon footprints and, in addition to reduced demands on teaching space, increases sustainability.

Higher education is changing and so are the needs of students. In reality there is no longer a 'traditional student'. Students often have difficulties accessing support from staff for a number of reasons: placement, caring responsibilities, multi-campus sites, disability-related issues, travelling time or distance. Skype is one way of addressing such barriers, ensuring opportunities to access and engage with staff/support.

In its simplest form, it can be used to replace sessions that would usually take place face-to-face – for example, for direct feedback, discussion, mentoring, or reviews. However, the options are endless and Skype has been used to deliver dissertations via viva voce, presentations, peer observations, dissertation meetings, as well as to conduct and attend interviews.

Skype is widely available, as well as free on a number of devices including games consoles and TVs. I have delivered sessions on a laptop via hotel WiFi while the student(s) have been in placement in a hospital on a mobile device (tablet, iPad, or smartphone) using MiFi (personal WiFi).

The most popular function with the students I support is 'screen share', which allows the viewer to watch a skill being demonstrated on the other's computer screen. This is not an interactive tool, so there is no security risk. A tablet and stylus can be attached so that written text, equations or drawings on the tablet can also be seen.

Screen share can be used to demonstrate many skills – for example, performing a literature search or using comment boxes to critique a piece of writing. I use it to demonstrate technologies such as mind-mapping. The student then shares their screen, enabling the teacher to assess that skill or offer guidance in the form of scaffolding. Demonstrating and assessing can also be done by simply placing a flip-chart or whiteboard behind the presenter and focusing the webcam on it.

Other tools in Skype mean files can be sent in real time, so assignments and documents can be speedily sent back and forth during the session. The text (IM) box is used to send links and make notes, and free software enables users to record the audio and/or visual streams.

I used Skype as a specific learning difficulties tutor supporting students with dyslexia and other disabilities at Hull University. It proved so popular that it was adopted as a means of supporting students and increasing access to staff for a cohort of more than 250 nursing students. This transition is documented in a Skype blog, and evolved into Diverse-Learners that provides support exclusively via Skype.

For further information and recordings of students using Skype and the Skype blog, see: http://www.Diverse-Learners.co.uk

LinkedIn and employability

LinkedIn is reportedly the world's largest professional social networking website, with 80 million members at the time of writing. It has been developed primarily with business communities in mind, and the reason for including it is to focus on another dimension of university-level education. This is a dimension which – given the changing face of HE – is becoming of paramount importance in teaching, learning and recruitment: *the employability agenda*.

The employability aspect in HE education is emphasised by most national governments, and increasingly universities and colleges are actively seeking to prepare their students for lifelong learning and being able to contribute effectively in society. LinkedIn is a social media tool that is used to connect professionals who have similar interests, work in similar fields, and therefore may have the potential to conduct business with each other. Human Resources departments use such tools to advertise work opportunities, and to seek individuals who have the skill set and experience that they are looking for. Recruiters may also research a job applicant's online profile, and search for information about them as part of a formal recruitment process.

An obvious consequence is the need for social media education to be part of a graduate experience, namely to ensure that students are aware of the opportunities that can be harnessed through such sites when it comes to promoting themselves, conveying their skill sets and securing future employment.

At the same time, it is very important that they are aware of the possible dangers of sharing personal information on the web, and they may require help to navigate the potential pitfalls of using social media. For example, many students and graduates using social media without appropriate security and privacy settings in place may have the messages and files intended for friends and family seen by a future employer.

An additional feature of LinkedIn that can be useful for students and teachers is the ability to ask specific questions of their networks, and connect with experts and professionals working in their area of interest. The feature is called 'Answers' and, at the time of writing, can be found under the 'More' tab in the banner at the top of the page. Questions can be asked, and answers can be given either publicly or privately. Some students have used this network feature to survey or poll their colleagues on LinkedIn for research projects or work assignments. If students are conducting a group project and all members are LinkedIn users, then they can also use it to share files, discuss ideas and make group announcements online securely – in as far as their data and conversations are actually stored on the LinkedIn servers, and their existence therefore depends on LinkedIn functioning.

> Used properly, LinkedIn can be a very effective way of raising our profile and marketing ourselves. It's less about a list of what we have done in the past and more focused on letting people know what we can do and how we can help.
>
> Being on LinkedIn means you can use this as part of your job search strategy, seeking out job posts, doing your research, identifying people for fact-finding interviews and so on.
>
> (Taylor, 2012)

A number of universities and colleges have established their own LinkedIn profiles and alumni groups, which not only promote the institutions, but also put alumni in touch with each other to enhance career progression and business opportunities. MIT and Caltech, for instance, have alumni groups which they allow their students to join before they graduate, so that they can begin to connect with alumni in their search for future work opportunities.

 CASE EXAMPLE

Using LinkedIn in MA education

Dragoş Ciobanu, Lecturer in Translation Studies, University of Leeds

MA students on the University of Leeds MA in Applied Translation Studies have a variety of linguistic and professional backgrounds.

Traditionally, those who enrol on the MA immediately after an under-graduate language degree have a long and challenging road ahead of them to achieve a specialism in a domain they will be translating in – such as law, medicine or economics.

It was for that reason that we have been using LinkedIn to put current students in touch with alumni who are now professional transla-tors. Questions and answers have ranged from effective methods to fast-track achieving such subject matter expertise in various domains, pros and cons of joining specific professional associations and online subscription services, and evaluations of recent specialised software.

These LinkedIn discussions complement effectively the in-class hands-on practice element, the comprehensive use of the VLE for asyn-chronous study and reflection, the international team projects, and the regular events with an employability focus that we organise for our students. They also help build effective professional relationships between current students and alumni, which are further strengthened by the access our students have to professional face-to-face events that members of the alumni network are involved in.

Teachers, too, can use LinkedIn in a number of ways. They can find contacts online who share similar interests, both in terms of their research and their teaching responsibilities, can ask for advice, can find experts on topics they are less familiar with, and perhaps invite visiting speakers who can provide inputs on their areas of expertise or professional experience.

CONCLUDING REMARKS

The experience of our learners is to a large extent shaped and influenced by the way in which they use and engage with social media in their everyday lives. It is also clear that the use of social media tools has a growing importance in their experiences of learning and study, creating a very particular set of expectations as they enter HE.

An increasing number of teachers will seek to incorporate learning activities and assignments using social media, and in this chapter we have seen a range of ways in which this can be achieved. However, even for more traditional teachers, the impact of social media is already firmly here.

The ways in which human beings communicate with each other, find others with similar interests, look for solutions to problems, and seek answers to the questions they have, has been dramatically affected by the developments in social media, and we are only just beginning to see the range of impacts and effects it will have on HE.

NOTES

1 http://goo.gl/yyAcgi
2 In 2005, Wikipedia was reported to have only 13,000 active contributors compared to the millions of users:
http://news.bbc.co.uk/1/hi/technology/4530930.stm
3 http://www.nature.com/nature/britannica/eb_advert_response_final.pdf
4 As Twitter clients become more and more sophisticated, such functionalities are increasingly being built into the client application for the user's convenience.
5 http://www.huffingtonpost.co.uk/2012/02/17/twitter-fakes-literary-characters_n_1284211.html
6 There are, of course, a number of similar free 'video conferencing' software available; for example, Oovoo.com which, at the time of writing, would connect up to 12 friends in HD free of charge. The points made here can be generalised to any similar software.

USEFUL RESOURCES

The *Guardian* Teacher Network. Social media for schools: A guide to Twitter, Facebook and Pinterest. http://www.guardian.co.uk/teacher-network/2012/jul/26/social-media-teacher-guide

Chapter 4

Technology for interaction

INTRODUCTION

Online courses are hugely popular, and are becoming more so. Arguably this is due to their capacity to bring knowledge to the masses for no – or very little – cost. As a result, institutions have been forced to reflect on the role of the university, and in particular the place of face-to-face teaching.

In the context of such raised expectations, technology is likely to be looked on increasingly as the key to providing a more engaging and comprehensive live interaction between all. This may cause anxiety for educators who on the one hand feel passionate about their subjects, but on the other feel less at ease with technology. In this chapter we explain a variety of suggestions that would suit a wide range of teaching settings, and would enable and stimulate a fruitful conversation between educators and students.

 PAUSE FOR THOUGHT

We claim that in HE there is an 'increasing pressure to provide more engaging and comprehensive live interaction between all'. Do you recognise this in your institution? If so, what form does this pressure take, and where is it found?

A key idea which we will illustrate with case studies is that, despite technological advances, course and activity design is still of great importance, and that simply adding a layer of technology on top of existing provision without changing anything or reflecting on the pedagogy will not magically increase student engagement.

We have structured this chapter to consider face-to-face interaction between teachers and students in a number of different teaching and learning settings: the traditional classroom, labs, fieldwork and tutorials. All of these settings have distinctive features which make certain technologies more appropriate and effective than others.

TECHNOLOGY FOR FACE-TO-FACE INTERACTION IN THE TRADITIONAL CLASSROOM

The lecture format continues to be a popular way of delivering information to big audiences, despite the several voices questioning the validity and effectiveness of such a format (e.g. Bligh, 2004). One of the biggest challenges teachers face is whether their students are engaged with the subject matter throughout the face-to-face sessions, and whether there are any easy ways of checking regularly how much of what is being presented is actually retained. This challenge becomes greater as the number of students in lectures increases.

From a design point of view, such a challenge could be addressed using a few very effective presentation techniques: engaging the audience's emotional intelligence rather than their analytical one; building visual presentations which stimulate rather than tire the brain (see Chapter 2); building time for reflection into the presentation in order to foster information retention; and introducing activities/elements of surprise every 10–15 minutes (Duarte, 2010; Heath and Heath, 2008; Medina, 2008).

If the size of the group allows, audience intervention can be sought, although that in itself involves mastery of group management techniques such as agreeing with the audience the start and stop signals which will be used to mark audience contributions and other similar interactive activities. For further guidance on engaging the audience without a particular focus on technology, we recommend the following:

- For examples of telling stories that people remember – Heath and Heath (2008).
- For building striking and effective visual presentations that tell meaningful stories – Duarte (2008).

- For gaining a much better understanding of how the brain works, and how educators can and should keep their students engaged – Medina (2008).

In using technology, teachers have several options that would allow them to conduct more interactive sessions.

'WORKING' THE ROOM

Traditionally, presenters tend to stand next to the presentation computer to deliver the sessions. While this approach is helpful to lip-readers, and is effective in certain cultures such as Japan where a presenter with true authority will stand still and not gesticulate while talking, there are several additional aspects worth considering. What if, for example, the layout of the room (pillars, unhelpful seating arrangements, etc.) does not allow your entire audience to see you? Is there any technology that would allow you to address such challenges?

WIRELESS PRESENTATION CLICKERS

The wireless presentation clicker is an inexpensive device. One component plugs into your computer's USB port, and the device allows you control the presentation from anywhere in the classroom. In their most basic format, these presentation clickers will have one button to go forward and backwards in your presentation, as well as a laser pointer. Most basic presentation clickers also have buttons to black out the presentation screen so that you can have a conversation with your audience without any visual interference from your slides.

More expensive are presentation clickers that control the position of the mouse on your slide (be it through a physical ball built into the unit, by using a built-in trackpad, or even by using your own hand gestures). You can use such devices to click on links, open up new windows, and essentially drive a more dynamic presentation from anywhere in the lecture room.

Spend a bit more yet and your presentation clicker could have a built-in timer which vibrates to let you know when you are close to running out of time or when your time is up.

Mastering the advanced functionalities of presentation clickers will require a small investment of time, but will result in a more accessible, engaging and professional-looking presentation on your part.

TABLET AND SMARTPHONE APPS TO CONTROL PRESENTATIONS

As smartphones are becoming increasingly 'smarter', the need for additional devices reduces – in fact, one of the recurrent themes of this book is the anticipation that even more learning and teaching technologies will eventually be combined into smartphone functionalities.

One can easily locate wireless presentation clicker apps which could be installed on the teacher's own smartphone or tablet, allowing control of the presentation computer. Figure 4.1 is an example of such an app

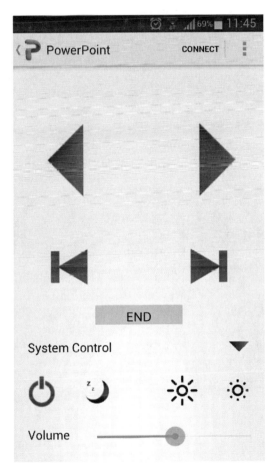

FIGURE 4.1 MacRemote app on an Android device

(MacRemote) available for Android smartphones, which allows users to control various functions of their laptops – including running PowerPoint presentations – remotely.[1]

CONTROLLING PRESENTATIONS USING NATURAL GESTURES

When it was launched in November 2010, few people outside of the Microsoft development team expected the Microsoft Kinect device to enter the *Guinness Book of World Records* for the fastest-selling consumer electronics product.

However, the Kinect is a truly impressive piece of hardware which can be used to track human motion, as well as the human voice. Gestures and voice commands can be interpreted by computer software, thus removing the need for using a computer mouse or keyboard.

Such software is still being developed – see Chapter 10 for a fuller discussion of its future use in education – but consider a few examples: shortly after being released, the Kinect was used in medical settings to analyse patient scans in real time during operations without the need to touch any equipment, thus removing any danger of contamination from external objects. It also found uses in engineering, design and the arts, for controlling presentations, zooming into maps, and rotating 3D objects.

MAKING THE MOST OF INTERACTION FUNCTIONALITIES OF EXISTING PRESENTATION SOFTWARE

A lot of teachers make extensive use of presentation software in their sessions. Locally installed software such as Microsoft PowerPoint, Apple Keynote, or Open Office Impress, as well as online presentation editing environments such as Prezi, are very popular options for combining static and multimedia materials. Thus presentations can be delivered to an audience which will have an increasing expectation of clarity and dynamism from the face-to-face sessions they attend.

Blacking out the screen

However, not all presenters make the most of the basic built-in functionalities of their chosen presentation software. One of the most straightforward options available is blacking out the screen during the live session in order to connect more effectively with your audience at a certain stage – perhaps to tell a meaningful and relevant story, to ask a question and listen to the answers, monitor a task, etc.

We have already seen how to achieve this effect by using a wireless presentation clicker, but in its absence it will be useful to know that pressing the B key on the presentation keyboard has the effect of pausing the slideshow and displaying a black screen, while pressing the W key will pause the screen and display a white screen; to resume the presentation, one only has to press the initial B or W key again. It is also worth bearing in mind that deaf or hard-of-hearing students may, in the absence of note-takers, rely on text displayed on the screen to understand what is happening in the session – see Chapter 2.

 PAUSE FOR THOUGHT

For your next presentation, think about how you might incorporate blank and/or white screen(s).

Live annotation and highlighting

In addition, presentation software also has built-in functionalities for live annotation and highlighting of the content on the slides. Figure 4.2

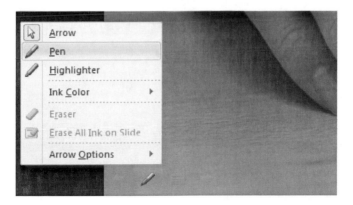

▨ **FIGURE 4.2** 'Pen' and 'highlighter' annotation functionality in Microsoft PowerPoint slideshow

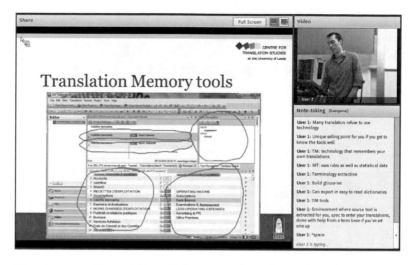

FIGURE 4.3 Manual PowerPoint annotation using built-in functionalities

shows a screenshot of such options available to the presenter during a Microsoft PowerPoint slideshow. The 'pen' tool can be used to annotate points of interest on the slide, or if the computer is a tablet PC by using a custom pen which comes with the device. Figure 4.3 shows this functionality in an actual lecture – despite the annotation lines being less than perfect, the teacher was successful in drawing the students' attention to various components of a specialised software interface he was talking about. As the lecture was recorded, this simple technique ensured that students watching the recording subsequently would have less trouble identifying individual elements the teacher was commenting on at any given time.

Using hyperlinked objects to create interactive, nonlinear presentations

In addition to annotating a presentation in a face-to-face session, speakers can also design their slides to be more interactive, thus breaking the general trend of creating linear presentations. Everyone will be familiar with the concept of hyperlinks from their experience with web browsing. Hyperlinks can also be used *within* presentations: either to link to slides, or link slides to external resources such as webpages, other presentations, or individual files.

78

Hyperlinks can be created from text, as well as images, and they can be placed anywhere on the slide. They can be invisible to the audience by using transparent hyperlinked shapes.

Designed in this way, presentations can become thought-provoking mazes for students and teachers to navigate through, debate and discover together. For example, the first slide can contain a situation and several choices, and each of these choices can hyperlink to separate subsequent slides detailing the implications and consequences of those individual choices, perhaps offering further better or worse options and teaching the negative consequences of wrong choices. This technique can be combined very effectively with e-voting software – see Chapter 5 – in order to run such an activity successfully with very large groups in real time.

Such interactive presentations can be subsequently published using software such as Articulate Studio or Articulate Storyline, and the interactive experience can be taken even further online. Figure 4.4 shows an example of an interactive PowerPoint presentation in which, with the exception of the main video displaying on the slide, everything else is a hyperlink to separate sections of the overall presentation:

- The 'home' icon links to the resource menu.
- 'The interpretations' image links to the section in which two interpreters work on the same speech from their different individual notes, which are annotated in sync with their interpretation.
- 'The original speech (full)' image links to the complete speech on which this section of the interactive resource was built.
- The NNI logo links to the full website of the National Network for Interpreting project, which contains numerous interactive multimedia resources of this kind.[2]

Figure 4.4. is not a screenshot of a PowerPoint presentation viewed in PowerPoint. However, having built the interactive multimedia elements in PowerPoint – hyperlinks, images, audio and videos – it was then very easy to publish the full presentation as an online resource using Articulate Studio. Articulate have recently released the Articulate Storyline rapid development tool, a powerful alternative to Articulate Studio – full details and examples are available on the Articulate website.[3]

FIGURE 4.4 PowerPoint presentation with hyperlinks published as an interactive online resource with Articulate Studio

ALTERNATIVES TO PRESENTATION SOFTWARE FOR LIVE ANNOTATION PURPOSES

However interactive one may succeed in making a presentation by using mouse drawing, highlighting or hyperlinking, sometimes it is necessary to annotate slides with more precision. For those situations where natural handwriting or drawing movements are required, presenters have again several choices: touch screens, visualisers, smart pens and tablets.

Touch screens and their predecessors: interactive whiteboards and graphics tablets

Following the success of graphics tablets, which allowed users to employ freehand movements in order to write or draw in various computer programmes, and thus create digital graphical objects, touch screens have gained popularity by being integrated straight into portable tablet PCs.

They are pressure-sensitive screens that allow users to use special pens to draw directly on them without the need for additional graphics tablets – they are essentially a cross between a laptop and a graphics tablet. These drawings can be slide annotations, but they can also be annotations of screenshots of webpages, diagrams drawn from scratch, etc.

80

Figure 4.5 shows that writing on tablets with digital pens is very accurate, and benefits from additional advantages such as having access to different colours for emphasis purposes and being able to save the annotation in electronic format for distribution to students and colleagues.

In order to enable teachers and students to use freehand movements during face-to-face sessions, interactive whiteboards were created, and became popular because they had the look and feel of a regular whiteboard with the additional benefit of storing the freehand-drawn content as digital files. Despite their many advantages, interactive whiteboards unfortunately also have a series of disadvantages, among which are their fixed position, which does not make them very accessible to users with motor impediments, and also the position of the presenter who needs to be writing on them with his or her back to the audience.

As a result, and thanks to evolving technology, touch screens are making a comeback by being integrated into flatscreen monitors attached to presenter computers at the front of many classrooms. These monitors are cheaper than interactive whiteboards, more portable, and allow teachers to operate them using just one special pen and a combination of annotation software functionalities. For example, teachers can use this

FIGURE 4.5 Writing on a tablet

technology to build mind-maps live in the session with input from their students, working through maths equations at their students' pace, tracing nerves and pointing out tumours on medical scans, or generally highlighting elements of interest on relevant subject diagrams or illustrations.

Moreover, touch screen monitors can be installed on flexible stands which allow easy and convenient repositioning to suit user requirements, so that eye contact with the audience is never lost and handwritten content is accurately captured. As already mentioned, a key advantage is that this digital content can be stored as images, PDF files, or PowerPoint slides, and circulated to the audience immediately after the session.

Visualisers

Visualisers are an even cheaper way of displaying content created by hand to the audience. A visualiser is made up of a camera which is pointing downwards from a relatively small height at a flat surface on which the speaker can place objects that need to be shown through a projector. Such objects range from a piece of paper on which the speaker writes as he or she presents, to Post-it notes collected from the audience following an individual or group task, to three-dimensional objects which the speaker or the audience want to present to everyone.

Visualisers enable speakers to zoom in on particular areas of the objects they are sharing, and because of the wide range of objects that can be displayed using them, they allow for much more interactive face-to-face sessions. This means that, for instance, a teacher can spot a useful and relevant article in the morning newspaper and bring it into class to share with students without needing to turn it into a slide.

Smart pens

Interactive whiteboards, touch screens and visualisers, all allow the use and projection of handwriting or drawing to an audience. However, they are not ideal in terms of portability – especially in terms of engaging the audience in the process of creating dynamic content. Should a teacher want to involve the students in annotating relevant graphs or illustrations, in most cases the students would need to come to the front of the class, which might be intimidating, impractical and time consuming. A more effective way to achieve the same result is to use a relatively cheap option provided by a recent technology called *smart pens*.

There are two main types of smart pen: one which allows the live display of content, and one which, at the moment of writing, does not. We will mention both, starting with Papershow.

Papershow uses a battery-operated pen, as well as special writing paper which has microscopic dots printed on its surface. The pen has a built-in camera and uses Bluetooth technology to broadcast its exact position on the page. A USB Bluetooth receiver, which needs to be plugged into the presenter computer, comes with specialised software that will display on the projected screen the exact position of the pen on the page. The special writing paper has additional areas on its side which act like buttons, and which enable users to change the colour and the thickness of the stroke, as well as erase content from the screen or draw predefined shapes such as arrows, rectangles or circles – Figure 4.6 illustrates what

FIGURE 4.6 Freehand content created with Papershow is displayed live on a connected presentation computer

83

Papershow looks like and how content authored on the special paper is displayed on a connected computer.

If the user chooses *Papershow for Teachers* instead of *Papershow for Office*, he/she will also have access to a zoom functionality, mathematical symbols and a calculator, as well as a wider range of colours.

In addition to the ability to create live content from scratch, Papershow allows the import of existing PowerPoint presentations, which the teacher can print on the special Papershow paper and annotate live in the session with a very high level of positional accuracy.

The obvious advantage of such a technology is that, for a fraction of the price of a tablet PC or an iPad/Android tablet, it allows the presenter to create dynamic content live in a face-to-face class, or work on pre-prepared content. When necessary, the speaker can pass the smart pen and paper to the audience – within a range of six metres from the presenter computer – for the audience to continue creating live content. This can enhance the sense of a learning community and collaborative learning (see also the constructivist account of knowledge in Chapter 1). Sessions can therefore become a lot more interactive through this way of using technology to foster audience participation.

 CASE EXAMPLE

Replacing PowerPoint presentations for medical students with Papershow sessions

Steven Sourbron, School of Medicine, University of Leeds

Steven had been looking for ways to make his face-to-face PowerPoint-based sessions more interactive and engaging. Among the challenges he was up against, teaching in a variety of lecture theatres which did not have the same technological setup was a significant one. He was an advocate of live slide annotations, but the absence of touch screen monitors in all the lecture theatres he was using meant that, in order to achieve the same result consistently, he would have had to carry around a laptop everywhere in order to author, edit and deliver his sessions.

Steven agreed to pilot Papershow in his discipline after hearing encouraging reports of how this technology had been used successfully by Dragoş Ciobanu in the Staff and Departmental Development Unit and Samar Al-Afandi, Programme Manager for Arabic and Islamic Studies.[4]

After a short and successful pilot period, Steven has replaced his PowerPoint-based sessions with content that is being created collaboratively with his audience. This approach had proven successful in staff development sessions, as well as Arabic language lessons, and it became apparent quickly that medicine was another area well-suited to this approach. However, Steven did not stop at just changing his own practice. He has acquired several Papershow kits and actively encouraged several colleagues to adopt this way of presenting, too. The results have been praised by the students who appreciate the slower pace of delivery and the fact that they can influence and participate in the creation of content.

For more information on the use of smart pens in education, see: http://goo.ql/Ne3L5

 PAUSE FOR THOUGHT

Consider the different examples of technology introduced above, e.g. visualisers, smart pens, tablets. Which would be most suited to your discipline and style of teaching and why?

FINDING OUT IN REAL-TIME WHAT THE AUDIENCE IS THINKING

Presenting to large groups of students is a rather daunting task for most teachers. Without opportunities for meaningful discussions and similar types of interaction, it may seem almost impossible to identify what the audience is thinking and whether the message the speaker is trying to get across is achieving its goal. However, there is a very effective piece of technology which can assist with this task of making sure that the audience is with the speaker: *interactive voting systems*, also known as *personal response systems, audience response systems, e-voting systems*, or more commonly as *clickers* or *crickets*.

These are individual battery-powered devices whose size varies between a slightly thicker credit card and a small TV remote control.

They have buttons with numbers or letters on them – ranging from six buttons (1–6 or A–F) to ten buttons (0–9) – which the audience can press in response to a question from the speaker. After the audience finishes voting in the allocated time, their responses are broken up, centralised by question choice, and displayed automatically in the form of bar or pie charts, thus giving an immediate and accurate graphical interpretation of what the audience thinks in relation to the speaker's questions.

Thanks to a combination of hardware and software that integrates with PowerPoint, but can also be used independently, teachers can ask questions at any stage in their sessions and receive answers back from their students instantly summarised as graphs. Available question types range from multiple choice questions to multiple response, true or false, numeric, or short answer ones.

What the speaker needs, in addition to voting devices to hand out to the audience, is dedicated voting software (which is mostly free and comes with the voting devices) and a receiver (which is generally no bigger than a USB memory stick, operates using radio frequencies and, depending on the brand of voting devices, can handle hundreds or even thousands of concurrently voting devices) – see Figure 4.7 for an example of setting up a clicker (slide 2 in the Figure), displaying the question and options (slides 3 and 5), and viewing the resulting graphs (slides 4 and 6).

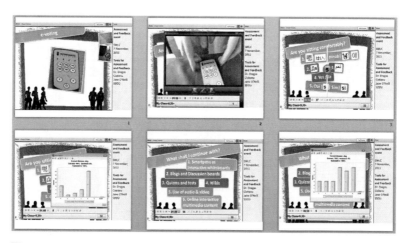

FIGURE 4.7 E-voting process: setting up the clicker, and displaying the questions and the resulting graphs (twice)

Teachers can use this technology together with slide hyperlinks (already detailed in this chapter) in order to allow the audience to drive the course of the presentation. Figure 4.7, for instance, has all the options shown in slide 5 hyperlinked to different sections of the presentation and, based on the results of the anonymous voting session, the presenter will start with option 4 or 6 instead of the first three, which seem to be less relevant to the audience.

Had there not been this anonymous e-voting session at the beginning of the presentation, it would have been almost impossible for the presenter to acquire this very important information by alternative means.

As technology progresses, some interactive voting systems now allow the audience to vote using a mixture of individual clickers, web interfaces on their laptops, SMS, or dedicated software on their smartphones in order to answer the speaker's questions anonymously or in an identifiable manner.

It is now possible to run such interactive e-voting sessions using smart-phone apps and institutional wireless networks rather than purchase individual clickers.[5] However, not having separate clickers limits the range of settings in which the activity can take place to areas with good wireless or 3G/4G coverage, and also assumes that students have smartphones and are willing to use them during the learning activities.

Having said all that, until the final stage of actually using the technology, one still needs to plan the activities carefully. This technology is quick and easy to use, and can be an effective teaching tool rather than just an information recall-measuring instrument. A few carefully crafted questions at the beginning of sessions can stimulate discussions and encourage students to apply their knowledge and explain why certain options are correct and others incorrect. In order to make the most of the interactive voting technology, presenters should:

- Not move on to additional questions without having given the audience the opportunity to analyse and discuss the results of the e-voting sessions.
- Reserve an appropriate amount of time for these discussions and appreciate fully the valuable formative role of the feedback exchanged then.

In addition, there are also the accessibility considerations highlighted in Chapter 2 which need to be taken into account.

CASE EXAMPLE

Using interactive voting in face-to-face lectures with Healthcare students

Paul Arnold, Lecturer in Medical Imaging, University of Leeds, UK

At the beginning of the 2009–2010 academic year, University of Leeds Healthcare lecturer Paul Arnold was looking for a solution to several challenges:

- How to make his face-to-face sessions more interactive, and have a better understanding of how much of the content covered in class his students were acquiring.
- How to check whether the study resources he was providing before the class on the module VLE area were being consulted by his students.
- How to get his students' opinions on what additional support resources they needed after each class.

After discussing his challenges with then University of Leeds staff development officer Dragoş Ciobanu, as well as the learning outcomes of his module and the other online and face-to-face activities that he was offering, the solution was the introduction of e-voting clickers in Paul's face-to-face sessions.

Throughout his whole module, Paul would start his teaching with three or four multiple choice questions relating to the pre-sessional reading that the students were meant to have done. The students would answer these questions using the e-voting clickers anonymously, then the resulting bar charts with their centralised responses would be analysed and explained.

Following these discussions, new content would be introduced and discussed for around 30 minutes, and then three or more anonymous multiple choice questions related to this new content would be asked and the students' responses debated. The same process would be repeated in the second half of the session, and the session would end with a reiteration of the learning outcomes presented in the beginning, and an invitation to the students to vote anonymously on which specific

Clicker Session Review Question 1

**Which of the following areas do you feel
MOST comfortable with?**

1. Production of US images
2. Role of US in medical imaging
3. Applications of US
4. Safety issues in US images

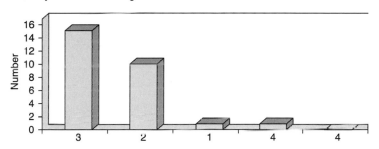

■ **FIGURE 4.8** Summary graph of student responses submitted
through an ARS

learning outcomes they felt they needed more support with (see
Figure 4.0).

End-of-module feedback questionnaires and focus groups indicated
that this use of technology was rated extremely highly by the students
because it made clear links between the online and face-to-face session
content, and it gave them a voice during the session itself through voting
anonymously and then discussing the results of the votes in order to
clear up any misunderstandings there and then. The students also felt
they had a say in what online resources would be made available to them
following the face-to-face sessions, and they perceived the module as
being personalised to their needs.

As far as Paul was concerned, he very soon discovered that he was
no longer able to cover as much content in the face-to-face sessions as
before. However, the quality of the interaction and discussions was
much higher, and he found he was in fact teaching a lot more by
discussing the results of the anonymous voting sessions, and inviting the
students to motivate or explain possible misleading interpretations of
the new content, than by using the examples he had prepared on his
presentation slides. He consequently prepared online resources to cover
some of the content that he chose to leave out from the face-to-face

sessions, and checked the students' understanding through clickers and subsequent discussions.

The ALT-C 2010 presentation on this topic is available at: http://goo.gl/uAR5W

BROADCASTING PRESENTATIONS ON THE AUDIENCE'S OWN DEVICES

Sometimes, either because of accessibility reasons (e.g. because of the room layout some participants will not be able to see the projection screen easily) or because of limited resources (e.g. the university may not be able to provide e-voting clickers to all students), presenters will want and need to engage the audience even more by broadcasting their presentation to the audience's own devices – be that a smartphone, tablet, laptop or desktop.

Moreover, the session tasks may also require the audience to use such devices in order to contribute actively to the session through a live chat functionality, by answering a variety of question types, or by creating and sharing hand-drawn annotations or content.

Such an approach to the use of technology for face-to-face interaction can also be advantageous from an accessibility point of view, as illustrated with the case example on combining technologies to provide access for deaf and hard-of-hearing students in Chapter 2.

Technology has evolved to make it significantly easier for teachers to have several of the functionalities we have already discussed at length in this book (e.g. e-voting, remote presentation control, live presentation annotation, live integration with social networks such as Twitter) in one application, on one device. Nowadays teachers can choose between using dedicated web conferencing software or dedicated presentation-sharing apps.

Using dedicated web conferencing software

Using a web conferencing application, a presenter can use the Internet to share their computer screen with a number of audience participants who have access to the same web conferencing application.

These applications are most often web browser-based, and may require the installation of additional web plug-ins such as Flash or Java.

Some of the current biggest players in this sector are the extremely flexible Adobe Acrobat Connect Pro,[6] the education sector-orientated Blackboard Collaborate,[7] and the very capable free and open-source initiative BigBlueButton.[8]

In terms of interacting with the audience, web conferencing platforms differ in the number of functionalities they offer users. However, most will allow participants to interact with presenters via text chat, audio and webcam. They will also allow, in addition to presentation and screen sharing, the sharing of a whiteboard to which participants have access, in order to annotate or create fresh content. More platforms now support multiple choice and multiple response questionnaires, with statistics presented in a similar way to the e-voting solutions already discussed, and the sessions can be recorded and made available to participants and guests for subsequent watching. In addition, just like a regular face-to-face classroom, online session participants can be split into groups, each of them with an individual break-out room featuring a range of collaborative functionalities such as a common whiteboard; text, voice and video chat; presentation and application sharing, etc.

Moreover, web conferencing applications are increasingly available on mobile devices such as tablets or smartphones, thus allowing for a more convenient interaction with the audience. Of course, keeping an eye on the audience backchannel discussion – i.e. the one taking place in the chat area – while also delivering a lecture can be a challenging task, and a skill which needs some time and effort to be acquired and refined. Yet the results of engaging the audience and seeing in real time how much of the presenter's message is getting through is invaluable.

 CASE EXAMPLE

Using Adobe Acrobat Connect Pro at the University of Leeds

Alina Secară and Dragoş Ciobanu, Centre for Translation Studies, University of Leeds

The benefits of using online classroom technology became obvious to the University of Leeds Centre for Translation Studies (CTS) upon looking for effective ways to engage with overseas prospective students, as well as finding ways to bring external experts into the classroom without the administrative and financial inconveniences associated with such an initiative.

Given the range of specialisms of the staff involved in research and teaching, as well as the variety of professional software applications taught as part of the MA programmes available in the CTS, in-country events were challenging to organise: any HE department would find it impossible to send all its staff to meet and discuss with prospective students in their home countries.

After assessing the pros and cons of the many online conferencing tools available, Adobe Acrobat Connect Pro was chosen for its increased flexibility, wide range of functionalities, and modest demand on local computer resources. Successful online sessions have been organised regularly with our external applicants, and have been a significant component of our enhanced recruitment.

Moreover, Adobe Acrobat Connect Pro has also been implemented successfully as a teaching, research and collaboration tool. It has been used to record teaching sessions, foster collaboration between students attending practical sessions in our computer clusters, work with peers on research projects, as well as exposing our students to the expertise of external experts who have kindly agreed to present to and interact with our students from the comfort of their offices.

As already mentioned in the Chapter 2 case example on combining technologies to provide access for deaf and hard-of-hearing students, we have just piloted an initiative to provide synchronous note-taking and same-language-subtitling alongside the recording of the lecturer's video and presentation, with extremely positive feedback from all our students.

Not only have the teaching session recordings been popular with our students, but also the face-to-face Professionalisation Lecture Series organised by Alina Secară. Being able to record national and international experts talking about the art of translation, subtitling, interpreting and translation project management, and more importantly, being able to release these recordings online almost instantly after minimum editing, enables our students to continue to refer to and benefit from such expert interventions throughout their MA programmes.

Between 2009 and 2012, Adobe Acrobat Connect Pro was also a key technology at the European Articulate Conferences organised by Dragoş Ciobanu at the University of Leeds. Expert interactive demos from all the Articulate E-Learning Heroes were some of the highlights of this event. Moreover, when e-learning guru and inspirational instructional designer Tom Kuhlmann joined the 2012 conference, being able to broadcast the main presentation screen onto the audience's devices enabled everyone to follow closely all the demonstrations, and have an excellent conference experience overall.

As a result of these success stories, it did not come as a surprise that other University of Leeds colleagues became interested in benefitting from the advantages of Adobe Acrobat Connect Pro. A university-wide pilot project was therefore initiated in order to enable staff in all other faculties and services to use the many functionalities of the tool for teaching, research, open days, interviews and numerous other collaborative tasks.

An illustration of how Adobe Acrobat Connect Pro has been used in a live session dealing with several uses of web conferencing software, including live lecture broadcasting, is available in this recording of a demo by Dr. Dragoş Ciobanu, Dr. Neil Morris and Alina Secară al ALT-C 2010: http://goo.gl/zpLpk

As the case example mentions, this technology can be a cheap way of bringing an external expert into your face-to-face sessions. One important aspect, nevertheless, is to bear in mind the vital importance of seeking and obtaining prior approval from session participants before recording their contributions. Failure to do so can result in participants requesting entire recordings or parts of them to be removed. Moreover, it is also worth bearing in mind that, because classes are recorded, any content teachers are showing is essentially republishing it. Therefore it is very important to have the permission of the original content producers for such republishing, or simply to ensure that presentations only contain copyright-free resources – for more on this see Chapter 6.

In practical terms, once all the legal formalities have been addressed, you will need a webcam, at least one microphone – a wireless one if you needed to pass it around so that the audience can ask questions that are recorded and heard by the external participants – and loudspeakers. As already mentioned, most of the available web conferencing applications can be run within a web browser, without the need to download and install any client software. You and your invited speakers will need to click on the same web link to access the same virtual room at the same time.

You will also need to ensure that you allow for slightly more time in your session. There may be slight technical issues at the beginning, and your audience will benefit more from such a session if they have the opportunity to interact with the invited speakers. One cannot overstate the benefits of such activities despite the relative complexity of organising them to involve several active participants: apart from strengthening your own relationships with members of your research community, you could also easily expose your students to global issues presented by international experts.

Using dedicated presentation-sharing apps

Web conferencing software applications are very capable, but they do require some getting used to. An alternative is dedicated presentation sharing apps, an excellent example being Nearpod.[9] This is the iPad app which was recently ported to Android, and which allows educators to broadcast interactive presentations containing static slides, videos, interactive questionnaires, as well as hand-drawing and annotating activities to their students, as well as to collect their responses and annotations and share selected results back with the group.

Content authoring in Nearpod is done online, and the app is free for students, but not for educators in its most functional form. A strong community is growing who wish to share engaging and interactive educational content.

What is useful to know is that, as illustrated by Figure 4.9, Nearpod presentations can accommodate a good range of content and interactive

FIGURE 4.9 Some of the Nearpod functionalities

tasks: from static content (slide 1 in Figure 4.9) to videos (slide 2), live hand-drawn annotations that can be shared individually with the rest of the class (slides 3 and 4), and interactive quizzes with feedback which allow teachers to keep an eye on their students' levels of understanding (slides 5 and 6).

TECHNOLOGY FOR FACE-TO-FACE INTERACTION IN LABORATORY AND PRACTICAL TEACHING

Depending on the size of the laboratory classes (labs), all the technologies and activities already mentioned could also be applied there. However, of particular interest may be the use of visualisers, hand-annotating techniques and web conferencing tools. These allow the recording of sessions involving teachers demonstrating why and how to use various lab-specific equipment, as well as the use of audio and video recording technologies for groupwork tasks.

Live broadcasting and recording of lab sessions

Given the hands-on and practical features of the kinds of interactions which happen in these environments, recording demonstrations and interactive tasks will be very valuable indeed to the students for consolidation and revision purposes.

 CASE EXAMPLE

Recording interactive hands-on translation studies sessions

Dragoş Ciobanu, Lecturer in Translation Studies, University of Leeds

All the sessions of the University of Leeds' MA in Applied Translation Studies core module on Computer-Assisted Translation take place in a computer lab, where students become familiar with translation project management concepts and skills, as well as numerous translation technologies.

Given the challenging and technical nature of the module, I decided to use the web conferencing tool Adobe Acrobat Connect Pro in order

95

to record all the staff and student presentations, set group-based collaborative tasks to the students and record those interactions, be able to share the presentation screen, as well as – when appropriate – individual students' screens, and conduct in-session interactive voting activities very similar to the ones described in the e-voting subsection above.

The recording of the variety of activities that take place during these hands-on sessions was considered even more important, as this module is team-taught by a group of professionals with different backgrounds in translation studies, translation project management, technical writing, software localisation, subtitling and search engine optimisation. As students do not have permanent continuous access to all of these specialists, it was considered very important to store in a shared online space their contributions to the module, as well as the students' presentations indicating their progress throughout the year.

In addition to capturing the lecturers' demos, I have also used this technology to coordinate and involve the external participants – who take part in our international student projects – in the regular student feedback presentations which are scheduled at the end of each project.

Initial feedback from students and staff highlighted the usefulness of these lab activity recordings, both for revision purposes on the part of the students and for ensuring consistency of message on the part of the staff.

The tool was chosen after careful consideration of available options; deciding factors were user-friendliness, flexibility and modularity of the tool, wide range of functionalities, availability on several mobile platforms, as well as price.

We have already discussed how online conference and collaboration tools can support shared learning tasks. The following Case Example is another example of how technology can be used creatively to encourage collaboration in labs.

CASE EXAMPLE

Using collaborative environments to encourage collaboration in highly specialised technical classes

Jack Armitage, School of Electronic and Electrical Engineering, University of Leeds

This Case Example relates to a first-year, two-semester undergraduate module in Electronic Music Creation and Production in the School of Electronic and Electrical Engineering. The aim of the module is to introduce students to the techniques of music production using Apple's Logic Pro software. The module is studied in the Multimedia Lab, where each student has access to an Apple Mac computer with a Roland MIDI keyboard and Edirol desktop monitors.

The technology used in this module creates a dichotomy of attention between the multimedia lab environment and the computer environment. Students are necessarily immersed in a multisensory way – eyes are glued to screens, ears covered by headphones, and keyboards and mice occupy hands.

They occasionally rejoin the lab environment momentarily to ask each other for help, which necessitates physically alerting each other to win attention. There are set intervals where work is shown and discussed, and students have to totally disengage from their own computer, which is difficult for some and impossible for others! Subverting this opposition is awkward – in a supposedly highly interactive environment, it is very difficult to instigate an activity where multiple people are interacting with the same thing at the same time.

In an attempt to challenge this problem, all the learning resources for the sessions were transferred to a collaboratively editable document platform in order to enable a wider range of interactive activities. The hypothesis was that students' active participation in curating and discussing the learning resources in both lab and computer environments – before, during and after scheduled sessions – would enable them to learn from and about each other, and catalyse internal feedback.

Before the sessions, students were given brief preparation tasks, which involved collecting resources and adding them to the collaborative document. As an example, for one session students were asked to provide commentaries and YouTube links for songs whose production techniques they would like to emulate or discuss.

After a few sessions it became clear that the dynamics of certain activities made them better suited to being preparation tasks or in-session tasks. This was one of the most challenging aspects to engineer, and there is much still to explore.

The prepared content, along with learning activity content added by the lecturer, formed the structure of the sessions, but what the interactions revealed along the way allowed the session to be diverted towards the most pertinent topics. An instance of this arose out of a learning activity in which students, together in real time, filled in a table of production techniques, depending on whether they: (a) knew how to do it, (b) knew what it was but not how to do it, (c) did not realise they already knew how to do it, or (d) had never heard of it.

Immediately some techniques revealed themselves to be well covered and some completely unheard of, and the session could proceed accordingly. What was most exciting was that if only one student knew how to do something and no one else did, they could share their knowledge with the class.

Experiments in these learning techniques are ongoing, and there has been no official evaluation data generated as of yet. However, some observations and future directions can be made and suggested. A lot of care has to be taken to consider the nature and value of the various interactions between students and staff throughout the lifetime of the collaborative document.

During the session, timing is important for guiding the transitions to and from interactive, collaborative work and individual focused work. The next stage in blurring the boundaries in computer-based learning environments is to decouple the student and the computer, in order to promote a collective sense of ownership of the entire learning environment. Following the writings of Mark Weiser on what he calls Calm Technology, I would like to suggest that only then will computers 'disappear' and learning will take centre stage.

For inspiration on future-proofing your use of learning and teaching technologies, visit the Horizon Project – http://nmc.org/horizon-project

TECHNOLOGY FOR FACE-TO-FACE INTERACTION DURING FIELDWORK

Fieldwork is generally an intrinsically stimulating activity for students. Depending on the availability of 3G/4G, or even wireless coverage in that particular location, some of the technologies mentioned already in this chapter might be used to enable certain relevant activities.

However, fieldwork also opens up the possibility of making the most of three additional technologies which allow the audience to experience and learn more about the environment they live in, and the object you are talking about, through their mobile devices: quick response (QR) tagging, geotagging and Augmented Reality (AR) – for more on this, see Chapter 10.

QR tagging

In practical terms, QR codes are square, two-dimensional images which can be created for free from URLs, short paragraphs of text, phone numbers or automatic SMS. They need to be scanned by smartphones and tablets using specialised – but also free   software in order to reveal the additional data. Similar to the barcodes on product packaging that are scanned in supermarkets in order to bring up their price and any offers associated with them, QR codes bring up websites/text/phone numbers and SMS messages containing more information about the objects in question.

For instance, using traditional methods one cannot include too much detail   and very limited, if any, multimedia – about exhibits in a museum. However, this information may already exist on a website. A QR code placed next to the exhibit enables visitors to access all that wealth of additional multimedia instantly by simply scanning the code, instead of manually having to type in long web addresses or having to go elsewhere, find a computer, and look up recommended websites.

QR codes can also be used to tag and annotate points of interest around the campus, allowing visitors to discover interesting information about buildings and people as they travel around the site. The process for taking advantage of this technology is simple: mobile-friendly websites with written, video or audio content are created. The web links to these pages are copied and used in a QR code generator.[10] The resulting image is printed and displayed next to the object or building it refers to. Any visitor with a mobile device able to read QR codes will be able to access the web page behind a QR code by simply scanning it using the smart-phone camera and free downloadable QR scanning software.

You have been exposed to QR codes throughout this book because they represent such a convenient way to take you to the reference websites we had in mind compared to having to type in long URLs manually. (Had we not all been camera-shy, we could have also turned links to videos of us talking about the topics close to our hearts into QR codes. We decided to shelter you from such an experience, but you can easily imagine how you could use QR codes to make additional information available to your students in an electronic format.)

From an accessibility point of view, it is still advisable to provide both URLs and QR codes in your electronic resources, because not all screen readers handle QR codes as well as they handle URLs.

Geotagging

A more complex implementation is the use of GPS information regarding the location of the mobile device in order to enrich the metadata of a piece of content such as an image or a video clip. The point is to be able to create graphically discoverable content on the move, as opposed to a rather more static content-creation approach implied by the use of QR codes.

The geotagged content can be published to online collaborative platforms such as Google Maps or Google Earth, which will display it as an additional layer on the original map data. While this approach no longer relies on printing and displaying QR codes in public places, it does assume users are happy to share their GPS location in order to produce, as well as access, multimedia information about the place they are in.

The vast majority of mobile devices now come with GPS and geotagging functionalities, and it is therefore possible to conduct a field trip during which specific elements of interest are photographed and geotagged using the students' own devices. All of this ad-hoc created content will be displayed online as a chronological and visually annotated path of the fieldwork.

TECHNOLOGY FOR FACE-TO-FACE INTERACTION IN TUTORIALS

Tutorials are the epitome of personalised interaction. Ideas are exchanged, arguments are debated, and future plans are drawn up. Given the nature of this one-to-one face-to-face situation, technology does not tend to feature highly.

However, educators can still employ some of the tools we have already mentioned in order to enhance the quality of this type of interaction – for instance, by keeping an accurate record of the ideas covered, as well as the action points and who is responsible for what. While setting up a full lecture capture system for tutorials or using a video camera are clearly a bit much, portable interaction capture alternatives such as smart pens or tablet note-taking apps will be perfectly adequate.

If it is necessary for the success of the task to capture the audio interaction between students and teachers participating in the tutorial together with handwritten notes, and if tablets which can be very suitable for this kind of activity are not available, the second variety of smart pens could be used. We have already mentioned the first variety – Papershow – which allows live handwriting to be displayed on a projected screen. Now consider the second variety, which records audio in sync with the handwritten notes for subsequent display, replay and dissemination of multimedia resources created using this technology.

Perhaps the most popular smart pen in this category is Livescribe, which uses special paper and its own internal microphone and flash storage to record and synchronise audio and handwritten content. Figure 4.10 details how the pen can be used with the special notepad in order to capture both sound and handwriting (slides 1–4), and then be connected to a computer (slide 5) in order to export the recording as an interactive PDF with both synchronised animation and sound.

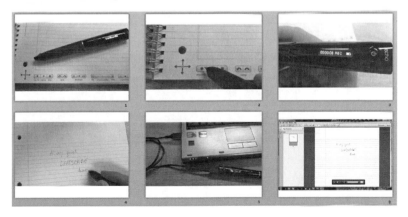

FIGURE 4.10 Livescribe pen workflow

Such technology will enable participants to access the context which surrounds the notes they have taken, and thus ensure that the action points and the delegation of tasks accurately reflects the tutorial discussions.

Personal experiments have shown that the Livescribe microphone is adequate for a range of 2–3 metres, and that the resulting interactive PDFs are extremely useful beyond the tutorial setting, for record-keeping, minute-taking, groupwork documenting, supervision meeting notes and even teaching session capture.

CONCLUDING REMARKS

The constantly evolving technology will always offer new functionalities for teachers and students. However, the key aspect to bear in mind is to ensure that the technology chosen for face-to-face sessions enhances the interactions and supports the tasks. Individual pieces of software will have several applications, and very often the answer to particular student engagement challenges can be found on personal devices such as smart-phones and tablets.

Teachers should start building effective working relationships with instructional designers and learning technologists, who will be keen to help design exciting and engaging activities using a range of technologies.

Moreover, one should also remain open-minded about the source of such interactive technologies: many companies advertise themselves as offering bespoke educational solutions, yet more effective alternatives – both in terms of functionality and price – can often be found in the free and open source, as well as non-education-specific commercial sectors.

Given the fact that we are training our students with a view to equip-ping them with real-life skills, we should also be open to technologies that are prevalent in the workplace, and which our students will therefore need to become familiar with in their professional careers.

All in all, regardless of the technologies we use, we need to make the most of our face-to-face time with our students, and create meaningful learning opportunities to inspire them to collaborate and engage more deeply with the subject matter that we care so much about.

NOTES

1 As the pace of such app development is impressively fast, any recommenda-tions here are bound to become outdated very quickly. However, should you

need such functionality for your smartphone, you can always ask the Twitter #edtech community for recommendations. An alternative is typing 'presentation remote app' into your preferred search engine, which will return several useful results complete with user ratings.

2 http://www.nationalnetworkforinterpreting.ac.uk

3 http://www.articulate.com/

4 A very brief video of their work is available at:
   http://lutube.leeds.ac.uk/smldc/videos/5717

5 As in the case of the PowerPoint presentation apps, development in the area of clicker apps is also extremely fast, so our suggestions are likely to become outdated quickly. However, one can look into stand-alone apps such as Socrative, web-based services such as the Banxia Interact HE, or even more complex solutions such as Poll Everywhere. Whatever your final choice, give serious thought to where your students' data is stored, how safely, and how easy it is to retrieve it should the service provider discontinue the service.

6 http://www.adobe.com/uk/products/adobeconnect.html

7 http://www.blackboard.com/platforms/collaborate/overview.aspx

8 http://www.bigbluebutton.org/

9 http://www.nearpod.com/

10 Such as: http://www.qrstuff.com/

USEFUL RESOURCES

The NMC Horizon Reports have been very useful sources of information regarding the evolution of learning technologies. In addition, they also include numerous short case studies of teachers using these technologies in innovative ways. These reports are certainly worth reading carefully. See: http://www.nmc.org/horizon-project

Chapter 5

Technology for assessment and feedback

INTRODUCTION

Technology can give the teacher the chance to build assessments that can be taken by hundreds of students and which can be marked immediately, so it seems the potential for reducing workload is great. This point alone has proved to be very alluring to many in HE, particularly at a time when staff-to-student ratios are declining and resources are increasingly limited.

However, it is also important to consider *how* using technology might change how we view assessment, and how it will impact on the ways we use it to support and measure student learning. Technology can provide a range of opportunities to assess different things in different ways, as well as doing what we always have but just on a computer. Technology has therefore become a 'driver' for change, a prompt for reflection on practice, as well as being a way of responding to change.

Providing prompt, high-quality feedback is also much more likely when using technology to assist assessment. However, its use should be measured and sensitive to developments in research, as how students actually use such feedback and how it might impact on their approaches to learning is still an under-researched area. Nevertheless, it is clear that students do place a very high value on good feedback – even though what they mean by this isn't always clear – and according to National Student Satisfaction Survey data they have not always felt that they have received it.

Technology also provides a number of ways in which assessment can be personalised to enable better alignment with individual student choice and individual pathways of learning, as well as personal circumstances and needs. These mesh well with new developments in social media discussed in Chapter 3.

For example, the use of ePortfolios and journals, blogging and discussion boards, provide a range of ways of capturing learning at a distance, and over time and space. Technology can help a teacher monitor and support student progress *through* an assignment, during a work placement, or while they are undertaking individual or group projects. The technology helps the educator move away from traditional forms of assessment, and better link assessment with the intended learning that is being fostered and promoted through the course.

Finally, when it comes to cheating on assessments, technology can help in the *detection* of both unintended plagiarism, poor citation and referencing practice, and plagiarism proper. However, it can also help those who wish to gain academic credit without the hassle of actually doing the work. 'Cheat' Internet sites, where students can purchase essays or employ someone to do their assignments for them, are now commonplace. So much so that universities are developing their own policies and legal frameworks to deal with such cases (Walker and Townley, 2012).

Using examples from different disciplines and current assessment development projects, this chapter will address these and other related issues.

ASSESSMENT MODES

The purposes of assessment

To fully understand how technology can be relevant to assessment and feedback, a framework needs to be in place in order to talk meaningfully about assessment. Assessment can be considered in a number of different ways; for example, it can be categorised in terms of its purpose(s) and defined as being *summative*, *formative* or *diagnostic*.

Summative assessment represents a summation of the learner's achievement and results in a mark or a grade that contributes to the final award. Formative assessment is focused on the ongoing development of the learners, and is the feedback provided to them while they are learning – if this does include a mark, this is simply as a measure of progress and it does not 'count' towards the final grade they will obtain for the award (Bloom et al., 1971). Usually, summative assessments take place at the end of the module or course – for example, the end of year examinations. Formative assessments take place at several times during the period of study – for example, giving feedback on essays or reports, or comments received after giving a seminar presentation or homework. Diagnostic assessments are usually timed at the beginning of a period of new learning in order to assess the students' starting points and judge their aptitude for new study. Sometimes students are subsequently streamed or allocated further support on the basis of their initial, baseline assessments. This type of assessment can also provide a benchmark against which to judge learning, in terms of the 'value added' or 'distance travelled' for an individual learner.

Frequently, individual assessments have multiple purposes – for example, a piece of coursework may be conducted during the module in order to provide continuous feedback, but also contribute a small percentage towards the final, overall mark, thus combining formative and summative properties.

The importance of the assessment

The outcomes of assessments that are crucial to the success of the student are usually referred to as being *high-stakes assessments*. Assessments can be high-stakes in two key ways: learners have to pass the assessment to be able to progress to the next stage of the course or, more commonly, the marks that they achieve contribute significantly to the overall qualification that they will obtain.

Either way, they are very important for the student and, because of this, assessment setters are very careful that the assessment is *fair* to all learners, is *valid* in terms of the alignment with the course goals, can be *reliably* and consistently implemented, and is *transparent* in both process and quality assurance mechanisms (QAA, 2011).

Many coursework assessments and second-year (Level 2) assessments can be *medium-stakes assessments* – for the student the consequences of failure, or of poor performance, will be more modest. It may be that a weak result on one element of the course can be compensated by a strong result elsewhere, or the weighting of the assessment is relatively low, with only a small number of marks 'counting' towards the final result.

The key focus for the assessor is that the assessment helps improve learning, supports the student in building on their existing understanding, and helps them to progress to new material and concepts. It is also recognised that making the assessments 'count', even in a small way, can have a significant impact on how seriously the students engage with the assessment.

In the majority of undergraduate programmes, the learning that takes place in the first year (Level 1) is often subjected to relatively *low-stakes assessment*. These assessments are designed to improve learning, and indicate if there are any gaps in the student's knowledge and under-standing. They also enable learners to experience and practice different assessment methods, and determine their own levels of progress against the course goals. Because they are 'low-stakes', assessors are often much less concerned with ensuring absolute reliability around assigning grades, and are more focused on ensuring that the assessments support learning, act in a formative or diagnostic capacity, and help students adapt to university-level study and assessment processes.

To this end, it is important that first-year assessments model the demands and requirements of assessments in later years. For example, recent research has shown that the strongest indicator predicting whether students will plagiarise on high-stakes assessment is if they have plagiarised before – perhaps on low-stakes assessments – and effectively got away with it (either it has not been detected, commented upon, or penalised). Therefore, although assessments in early years of the programme may not affect the classification of the final degree directly, it is still important that they are treated as rigorously as later high-stakes assessments. There is a clear role for technology in this regard, too – for example, in the use of software such as 'Turnitin' (which is discussed below), which finds matches between submitted work and existing online sources (including other submitted coursework), and so helps educate, deter and ultimately detect plagiarism.

The nature of the assessment

Assessments can also be categorised in terms of the response they require from students; these can be *convergent* or *divergent* (or a mixture of the two). Convergent assessment questions have right answers, and test the learner's knowledge of facts and procedures. Divergent assessment anti-cipates a range of different responses, and rewards academic skills such as analysis, critique and evaluation. So, to put it crudely, convergent assess-ment is more likely to be found in the sciences where there are lots of facts to learn, whereas divergent assessment is more likely to be found in the arts and humanities.

PAUSE FOR THOUGHT

Please consider the assessment in your discipline, and put them into the categories of 'summative', 'formative', 'divergent' and 'convergent'.

This distinction between convergent and divergent assessment has big implications when choosing the ways in which technology can contribute to effective student assessment. The majority of technology-supported assessments have so far been developed to provide *convergent* assessments types, and this has led to the development of many different forms of objective testing – in which students must select correct answer(s) that have been predetermined by the examiners.

Assessing whether a student knows the right answer(s) to pre-set questions is fairly straightforward, and can be done in a number of different ways – for example, true/false, multiple choice tests, multiple response, matching pair questions, labelling diagrams or plotting graphs. Software can handle all aspects of this type of assessment because the answers can be pre-set.

Things get more complicated when technology is used to support divergent assessment, where the computer cannot be programmed to recognise the right answer because there are several possible 'right answers' that could be presented by the student in many different ways. For such assessments, the computer can support some of the assessment processes (e.g. submission of the essay, passing on the feedback and grade to the student, etc.), but it is currently unlikely to be able to handle the assignment of marks or the production of student feedback on all possible inaccuracies.

This gives rise to another way of categorising assessment that considers the involvement of technology: *e-assessment*. e-assessment is defined by JISC as the 'end-to-end electronic assessment processes where ICT is used for the presentation of assessment and the recording of responses' (JISC, 2007). Nevertheless, within this description a further division is helpful: between *computer-based assessment* (CBA), in which the assessment is communicated to the student and marked by computer, and *computer-assisted assessment* (CAA), which only relies partially on computers (typically to deliver the assessment to the student or record results, but not to carry out the marking). Currently CBA is used to assess convergent assessment, and CAA is more commonly used to help human markers with divergent assessments.

In this chapter we will explore the ways in which computers and computer software can be used to assess and aid the assessment, including feedback, and we will use the term e-assessment to represent the diversity of these activities.

DRIVERS FOR CHANGE – WHY USE TECHNOLOGY IN ASSESSMENT?

Why change current practice?

There are a number of reasons why we might want to change current practice:

■ To find effective new and improved assessment methods that align with innovative teaching methods; such innovations are often brought about by other developments in technology (see, for example, Chapter 4).
■ To broaden the skills and abilities that can be tested.
■ To respond to the changing goals of HE, which frequently include those of academic, professional, vocational and work-based learning.
■ To emphasise deep learning and personal reflection, rather than surface and instrumental learning.
■ To provide more frequent formative assessments, and increase the quality and timeliness of the feedback that can be provided.
■ To promote self-study and self-assessment so that students can engage with learning and testing in their own time, at their own pace, when they are ready.
■ To increase student confidence.
■ To reduce the likelihood that students may be awarded grades that they do not deserve (e.g. by reducing plagiarism).
■ To address the need for greater cost effectiveness and to save staff time.
■ To provide quality assurance mechanisms, and to track and maintain the standards of assessment.

Goals in e-assessment

Good e-assessment, like all assessment, should aim to:

■ Engage the students with the assessment criteria so that they understand the standards they are being judged against.

109

- Support individual and personalised learning.
- Ensure feedback can lead to improvement.
- Focus on the students' development and progress.
- Stimulate constructive dialogue.
- Consider staff and student effort and workload (JISC, 2010).

Implementing e-assessment

For an individual considering adopting a different kind of assessment and one that makes greater use of technology, there are a number of factors that will affect the decisions made:

The context

The institutional strategy and culture together with the normal assessment procedures and operations, including the quality-assurance protocols, will influence the choice and implementation of assessment. In reality this is a major consideration, as certain forms of hardware and software will be adopted and supported in the institution, and the assessment policy and procedures will encourage or inhibit assessment innovations. For example, the ways in which peer assessment or self-assessment elements can be used in summative assessments are often limited by assessment policy, and quality-assurance protocols are likely to require the provision of 'safety' backups to replace technology in the event of its failure.

Available technology and support

At the heart of any adoption of e-assessment is the computer infrastructure and its delivery systems together with, for summative assessment, the levels of security that are available. The technical support that the institution provides and the training that is available are also important factors.

Pedagogy

The use of the technology has to match to learning outcomes (knowledge/skills) and the teaching and learning philosophy of the particular teacher, course and institution, ensuring that the assessment remains valid and fair.

People and resources

Making any change usually involves a staff cost in both time and effort. Furthermore, using technology places specific demands on space and IT equipment that is likely to require additional investment.

The adoption of an e-assessment approach needs to take into account a variety of factors that will vary hugely from one teaching and learning context to another.

 PAUSE FOR THOUGHT

What assessment approach – assessment method, assessment timing, need to provide feedback, etc. – is appropriate and relevant to the module aims and learning outcomes of your courses?

Can the assessment happen when it needs to, and provide learners with good quality and timely feedback?

Are there any accessibility, ethical or health and safety concerns to be taken in account? For example, are all the students able to access the technology, read from a computer screen, view video clips, etc. (see Chapter 2)?

Are there any intellectual property rights (IPR) and copyright issues to be addressed – for example, when using photos, audio, quotations, etc.?

What institutional or professional quality assurance processes need to be adhered to?

Will the students and staff require any guidance or training in how to use the technology?

How robust and reliable is the technology? What backups are needed? What testing needs to be done before the technology could be used for large-scale, high-stakes assessment?

Is plagiarism a concern? What can be done to avoid it and detect it?

If something does 'go wrong', how can university appeals and griev-ance procedures be adhered to – is there a need to enable human remarking?

Ways in which assessment can be 'e-ed'

When thinking about technology and assessment, many people first think about providing e-based tests to students, perhaps in the form of an online quiz or multiple choice exam (for example, using Rógo). However, it is worthwhile remembering that there are many ways in which technology can support assessment processes:

- Question generation – for example, random generators, building question banks, etc.
- Question/task presentation and delivery to learners – for example, students sit at the computers to take the test.
- Development of standalone, self-study and self-assessment tools such as RLOs (reusable learning objects) – these may take the form of self-assessment quizzes or problem-solving tasks.
- Submission of student responses.
- Marking/grading answers.
- Providing automated feedback and further guidance.
- Detecting plagiarism.
- Analysis of (class) grades and generating statistics and evaluation reports.
- Recording and monitoring learner achievement – for example, using ePortfolios.
- Storage of assessments and student attainments for quality assurance purposes.

 PAUSE FOR THOUGHT

In what ways does assessment in your subject lend itself to being 'e-ed', and what issues would you need to take into account to achieve benefits for you and your learners?

OBJECTIVE TESTING

In some disciplines, teachers need to test students' knowledge of facts and procedures, set questions with right and wrong answers, and be able to test for the achievement of competencies. These disciplines can embrace quiz-style computer assessments on a large scale and, with care and investment, can produce banks of questions that also allow higher-level cognitive skills to be tested – for example, how to analyse data.

Multiple choice questions (MCQs) are the most commonly recognised form of objective tests, in which the learner is invited to select one response from a possible list of four or five given responses. Typically, these will include:

- A stem: the core questions (which can be just text or can include other multimedia elements such as video or audio recordings).
- The options: the set of alternative responses.
- The key: the 'right' answer; the best match to the stem.
- The distracters: the 'wrong' answers that don't match the stem.

In addition, there should also be *feedback statements* – the response students will receive after submitting their answers, either to confirm their correct choice or to correct wrong answers and provide further guidance. Good general advice for writing MCQs is provided by McKenna and Bull (1999) and Haladyna et al. (2002).

An important limitation of this form of 'traditional' MCQ is that they give very little insight into the thinking that lies behind the student's response – the student could be simply guessing or have misguided reasoning (Crisp, 2007). Providing sets of grouped or linked questions on a topic can provide the tester, with a pattern of student responses that gives further information about a student's abilities in different areas of the curriculum. These are sometimes referred to as 'matrix' or 'composite' MCQs. The tests can be constructed so that students effectively 'unlock' the next set of questions upon getting correct answers in earlier groups of questions. This method can help pace students through test material, and supports the notion of 'building in progression' through more complex topics or themes.

There are a growing number of ways in which technology can be used to design and set objective tests, which may align more effectively with the learning outcomes of a module and give better insight into the reasoning processes of the learners.

Types of objective tests

Objective tests include:

- Drag-and-drop: click and drag images or words into position on a diagram, map, table, photograph, etc.
- Multiple choice question: a 'stem' statement or question that has one or more 'correct' responses.
- Fill-in (or select) the blank: missing key words (possibly selected from pull-down list).

113

- Hotspot: clicking on a picture or diagram to indicate the answer.
- Knowledge matrix: several MCQs grouped together.
- Matching pairs: matching items in a list of words or statements with items in a second list.
- Pull-down list: a set of statements that are matched with items in a pull-down list.
- Ranking: a list of choices that must be ranked in order numerically. For example: in priority order, which are the more common causes of a subarachnoid hematoma?

The building of well thought-out banks of questions is clearly very time consuming, and it is sometimes possible to join syndicates to share ideas and generate a larger pool of questions more quickly; this more commonly happens for very large courses that involve many teachers, such as in medicine. Computer software such as 'Question Bank' can be used by departments to build up and manage question banks, by setting up databases of questions for all the courses and modules they deliver, requiring that they are formatted similarly and are stored in one place – Rhein Parri, a lecturer in pharmacology at Aston University, describes this very clearly in his YouTube clip.[1]

However, for individuals, a staged development, over a number of years, is usually needed to build up a good question bank. Because of this, online objective tests are more commonly used in large, introductory level, first-year modules, where the time invested in development is worthwhile, and the material being taught is fairly static and does not require regular updating.

Views on the value of objective testing vary – some researchers fear that they encourage surface learning and memorisation (Biggs, 2002), while others argue that it is very possible to test higher-order cognitive skills if the questions are carefully designed and the test is constructed with this in mind (Nicol, 2007). Providing learners with several opportunities to take tests and gain feedback is recommended, to help them orientate effectively to the test conditions, and to better understand what is expected in terms of the range of knowledge and skills being tested and standards they need to achieve (Rust et al., 2003).

A module could therefore have a set of formative tests, set at intervals during the course, and a summative test at the end, which follows the same format. Such a structure is known to motivate and help pace learners, and it encourages students to adopt a 'study as you go' approach rather than leaving it all until the last minute.

In well-constructed tests, students choosing an incorrect answer can be given instant feedback that points them to the learning outcomes and elements of learning that they have not yet mastered, rather than simply giving them the right answer. The built-in incorporation of different feedback responses is often cited as a key benefit of running MCQ-style self-assessments or computer-based examinations.

One interesting strategy, that is being facilitated by technology in some medical sciences multiple choice examinations, is that the students are also asked to attach a confidence measure to each of their answers. In practice this means that incorrect answers tagged with 'high confidence' will lose the student more marks than incorrect responses with 'low confidence' tags (Gardner-Medwin and Gahan, 2003).

Another approach used to discourage 'guessing' is that of negative marking — where incorrect answers result in the loss of marks or partial marks — and the inclusion of 'abstain' or 'don't know' responses that score zero but do not carry the penalty of lost marks. The literature is very divided on whether this is a good approach: some argue that it favours risk-takers, and that in fact informed guessing is a valid strategy in many disciplines [2]

In actually running the e-assessment tests, there are some practical considerations to take into account, including load testing the server to make sure it can cope with the volume of students (depending on the size of the class, it maybe necessary to run phased exams). This can prevent overloading the server, but does of course create the challenge of keeping the student groups apart between test sittings.

If the exam room has banks of test-ready computers next to each other, this may mean that the computers are 'locked down' to prevent users accessing other applications, particularly search engines. It might be desirable to produce exams that have the same questions, but which are presented in different sequences for each student, making it very difficult to copy answers from neighbours and giving each student a unique experience. Moreover, it is also possible to generate unique tests with random questions for each student using large question banks, and in quantitative disciplines randomly generating different number combinations in mathematical problems is also possible. However, the literature does not favour these tactics, as it is very difficult to be sure that every question poses an equal level of difficulty and, in effect, each student is sitting a different test. Having said that, what is clear is that this is something that would be almost impossible in traditional paper-based exams, but is relatively straightforward within e-assessment.

When scheduling online assessments, you may wish to consider:

- How will students log in to take the test? Can they use their individual university ID or will they have to use a randomly generated password, which might only be valid for the duration of the test?
- Could tutors or invigilators have a spare set of log-ins, set up in advance for use in emergencies?
- Could access to the test only be permitted for the test period to ensure fairness for all users?
- Is there any need to limit the number of attempts the student makes?
- Is there any need to limit the frequency with which students can revisit earlier submitted answers?

Objective testing – limitations and barriers

For some teachers – particularly in the arts and humanities – objective testing is never going to be a large part of what they do. On the other hand, automatic computer assessment of essays and reflective work is still in its infancy, and is still seen by many as an unpopular development. Just consider, for example, how one might design computer software to mark a question on Descartes' conception of the self.

That said, there are examples of short-answer questions being assessed through a process of matching content to keywords (see the case example below). However, for longer, more variable, essay-style submissions, it takes considerable effort to 'train' the computer by feeding through hundreds of example answers to refine the marking accuracy (Valenti et al., 2003).

This is an investment which might be sensible if you are marking thousands of scripts, but not if you are marking tens of answers. One particular challenge is to train the computer to recognise words that are correct, but which may be spelt wrongly. This is a difficulty that is clearly of particular importance for non-native English speakers and dyslexic students. The general worry here is that computers are unable to distinguish between syntax and semantics.

CASE EXAMPLE

Pattern matching short answer questions
OpenLearn LabSpace

The OpenMark, *pattern match* question type, developed and used by the Open University (OU), tests if a short free text submitted by a student matches a predetermined response pattern.

Pattern match is a more sophisticated alternative to many *short answer* question types, and offers the ability to cope with a range of misspellings and word ordering. It also checks for the proximity of words in the response.

For certain types of response it has been shown to provide an accuracy of marking that is on a par with, or better than, that provided by a cohort of human markers. *Pattern match* works on the basis that you have a student response that you wish to match against any number of response-matching patterns. Each pattern is compared in turn until a match is found, and feedback and marks are assigned.

The OU provide question writers with extensive advice, and are clear about the scope of questions best suited for use with the software: '*Pattern match* works best when you are asking for a single explanation that you will mark as simply right or wrong. You will find that dealing with multiple parts in a question or apportioning partial marks is a much harder task that will quickly turn into a research project'.

The Moodle VLE have developed a question type called PMatch based on the Open University's free text questions.[3]

Visit the OpenLearn LabSpace website for more information: http://goo.gl/wJZ1p

The fact that the technological development for assessment also moves at a relatively fast pace can be a barrier, leaving teachers often wondering which the best software is to 'invest' in and use. In the UK, JISC is a key organisation that aims to guide practitioners on the effective use and integration of technology in HE. JISC has a long track record in advising on the use of technology-enhanced assessment, and funding long-term projects that evaluate various technology tools and test their interoperability.[4]

In institutions where there has been a large-scale adoption of objective testing (e.g. Dundee and Loughborough universities), appropriate frameworks and structures also needed to be developed in parallel to ensure quality standards – for example, codes of practice and policies. These institutions have invested in specialist personnel – having e-assessment officers who support the schools and departments to develop and implement e-assessment – and they have put in place a range of different training provisions, not only in the use of the technology, but also in 'good practice' in writing effective questions.

Space appears to be a common barrier for institutions wishing to expand the use of computerised assessment. The space that is best suited for summative assessment is rarely the best kind of space for learning, so having flexible space is desirable. Moreover, space is at a premium during the end-of-module exam season. One response is to use laptops rather than a fixed computer suite, and to run assessments that can be taken at different times rather than those that need to be sat by all students at the same time. However, this would raise worries about a range of security issues. Practitioners report that their big concerns in practically running summative e-Examinations are around security, and what to do if the technology fails for any of the students (for examples, see King et al., 2009).

Imagine a student being able to 'book in' at the computer test centre to take a test. They might be asked to log on to a website and type in their password, and then sit the timed test – of course, in some ways this is already happening with the International English Language Testing System (IELTS), and the Clinical Aptitude tests taken by those wishing to apply for medical school in the UK. From a security perspective, Apampa et al. (2009) suggest that we need to be concerned about three different questions:

1   Is the student present to take the test or is he/she able to log onto the site from elsewhere?
2   Who is the student taking the test?
3   Is the student who you think they are?

CASE EXAMPLE

Objective testing – developing a public assessment

Cambridge Assessment has been investigating e-assessment for the delivery and marking of public examinations for many years, and was asked by Cambridge University to develop a generic university admissions test.

The resulting TSA test is a timed, multiple choice examination with 50 questions for each test. A large question bank has been devised to examine 'A' level thinking skills. Candidates can answer the questions in any order and submit all their final answers at the end of the test. The test score awarded consists of a critical thinking score, a problem-solving score, together with the total score.

The TSA is a Java application that runs over the Internet in real time. The software manages the online registration of the candidate prior to sitting the test, then the delivery of the randomised set of questions to the candidate, and finally the real-time marking of the test.

The software ensures that the overall level of test difficulty is the same for each candidate. The test sessions are booked at timed intervals, they are invigilated, and students only occupy every other workstation as an added security protection. TSA is now administered through a set of central test centres, and is used as part of the selection and admissions processes by a number of disciplines (e.g. medicine) and colleges.

If e-assessments are considered 'coursework' rather than 'examinations', some of the challenges do reduce. The students can take the tests at different times, they can use their own computers, and they do not need to have invigilators present. However, as with other coursework assessments, it is not always possible to be 100% sure who actually did the work. Currently the use of e-invigilators (anti-cheat packages which include 360-degree video webcams, finger print log-ons and locked-down browsers) remains a cumbersome and costly response to this problem.

PAUSE FOR THOUGHT

Would objective testing be a useful assessment method in your discipline? If so, what do you think would be the benefits and difficulties of introducing it or expanding its use?

Assessing knowledge – not as simple as it first seems

Considering the different kinds of knowledge a teacher may be interested in, 'assessing knowledge' is more varied than it might first appear. The literature on knowledge types and stages of knowing is considerable. As a useful example, Anderson, Krathwohl, et al. (2001), in their adaptation of Bloom's taxonomy, refer to four kinds of knowledge:

- *Factual*: terminology, specific names, dates, facts and details.
- *Conceptual*: classifications, principles, theories and structures.
- *Procedural*: how to do things and when to do them; subject-specific techniques and methods.
- *Metacognitive*: strategic understanding, self awareness and reflection.

It is possible to write objective test questions that demand each of these knowledge types, but ePortfolios and blogs are probably a better way of assessing metacognition (see later sections in this chapter).

Technology improving traditional assessment

A range of e-assessment software and approaches have been produced to support staff handling workload-intensive assessments, such as:

- The examining of oral presentations through digitally recording them – so that they can be reviewed at any time and accessed by external examiners.
- The use of tablet computers that allow a tutor to annotate work with an electronic pen. As already mentioned in Chapter 4, the resulting annotations are electronically stored and can be shared with others – for instance, capturing handwritten comments on

design drawing in architecture and engineering, or corrections on complex mathematical calculations.[5]

■ The inclusion of a range of digital media in questions, which enables certain skills and knowledge to be much more cheaply and validly assessed. For example, the inclusion of breath or heart sounds in MCQs, or the inclusion of video clips in performance arts, business and geography.

■ The use of blogging to monitor, assess and provide feedback for students studying away from campus or on long-term projects (see Chapter 3).

■ Peer assessment tools that facilitate the grading of individual contributions in groupwork can reduce staff time and provide a transparent system that students have faith in.

Alternative assessment products

Much of the assessment in HE seeks to judge the quality of 'things' that the learner has produced as a result of their learning. In a traditionally taught module, the product might be an essay, a report or a design drawing. Technology increases the range of products that we can ask our students to evidence for assessment purposes, and the range of learning artefacts that they can be asked to produce.

The creation of different assessment products can enable different skills to be developed and different processes to be assessed. Students can be asked to develop a website or produce a podcast, rather than write a standard report. For example, Cane and Cashmore (2008) explain how they introduced a podcast task in a genetics module taken by second-year medical students. Thirty students, working in groups of six, researched and produced 5 to 10 minute podcasts on a range of topics that explored the ethical issues surrounding genetics.

 CASE EXAMPLE

When technology offers a helping hand – language teaching

Patrizia Lavizani, Teching Fellow in Italian, University of Leeds

I teach Italian to undergraduate students as an elective subject, and our beginners' modules are very popular and generally full, with up to

18 students in a group. In language teaching, this is considered a large class and so, to maximise the time we spend in teaching and practising the language, we conduct our speaking assessments via the VLE. In the past the speaking assessments took over three hours of precious class time.

At present, students work in pairs to prepare a role-play. They develop, practise and record it over a two-week period. They then upload their recording to the module assessment area provided in the VLE (Blackboard). They follow specific instructions regarding the maximum length of the recording and the type of file format that they need to use. Students are responsible for their own role-play, are asked to clearly state the part that they speak, and to produce a transcript of their work. They also post a rationale and reflection on their work.

The students demonstrate many skills via this activity. Firstly, they construct and design the content of the work, which means that they need to make choices and derive clear ways of demonstrating their knowledge (language functions, vocabulary, links and progression). They need to practise and develop good pronunciation, so they record and listen to themselves speaking several times. They have to work collaboratively with others, promoting peer learning and feedback.

The teacher listens to all the recordings, and assesses and gives feedback to each student. One possible drawback is that students do not get immediate, in-class, oral feedback, but they do get more accurate grading and specific written feedback returned to them via the VLE.

Inevitably, this adds to the tutors' workload, so in future I intend to explore the possibility of using a programme called 'Screencastomatic'[6] to record and post audio and video feedback. Here the VLE provides the mechanism to share the recorded role-plays, and for the assessments and feedback to be given to the students, producing a revision resource that students can always go back to in order to enhance their learning.

ALTERNATIVE ASSESSMENT PROCESSES

Self-testing and diagnostic testing

Providing learners with self-study online packages and self-testing tools has become commonplace in many fields of continuing professional development. The flexibility they offer means that busy people can access and self-monitor their learning and progress at a distance, and in ways that suit their lifestyles and personal contexts. The popularity of this has been seen recently with the world-wide development of Massive Open Online Courses (see Chapter 8).

At university, such self-study packages are often used as part of a blended curriculum design, and in ways which support face-to-face teaching. For example, as part of a pre-laboratory preparation task, students may be asked to access an online introduction to the experiment that they will be carrying out, and will only be admitted to the laboratory when they have successfully completed and passed the quiz-style assessment that demonstrates they understand the theoretical underpinnings of the lab session, and the health and safety requirements necessary to conduct the experiment.

Diagnostic assessment needs can also be met frequently through the use of testing packages aimed at discovering a learner's current ability level or range of knowledge.

For example, Diagnosys[7] is a basic maths diagnostic instrument developed at the University of Newcastle Upon Tyne, that helps tutors check which topic areas their new students are already competent in and familiar with, and which are new to them. The test is adaptive which means that, based on whether a student answers a question rightly or wrongly, the computer subsequently selects the next question in order to further test that student's particular skill level (see also the discussion of many-to-many teaching in Chapter 10). Students are therefore not faced with lots of questions that are too hard and they cannot answer, or a whole set that are trivial to them. Diagnosys can then produce a diagnostic report (either for the student or the tutor) to help shape the future course of study needed.

ePortfolios and assessing progress and reflection

Portfolios are collections of selected materials, feedback and reflections that relate to a student's development and learning. They provide a place to record and evidence achievements. Portfolios have long been the assessment vehicle of choice in continuing professional development, as they provide a way of structuring very different sets of experiences and individualised learning. They are particularly widely used in healthcare and education. Such collections are much easier to compile, manage and share with others if they are in electronic format – thus the development of the ePortfolio.

Not only do ePortfolios provide a repository for captured data and reflections that can be used to 'make a case' for the achievement of specific learning goals and outcomes, but they also provide a prompt for planning, goal-setting and review, as well as collaboration and personal reflection.

> An e-portfolio is a purposeful aggregation of digital items – ideas, evidence, reflections, feedback etc., which 'presents' a selected audience with evidence of a person's learning and/or ability.
>
> (Sutherland and Powell, 2007)

Technology provides a very effective way of compiling, constructing and sharing portfolios, and enables the inclusion of a wider range of digitised items (e.g. video and audio clips, links to existing web material, and blogs). ePortfolios also feature a number of tools and mechanisms that allow the author/compiler to give full or restricted access to their work. This means that the same ePortfolio can potentially be used for different purposes (e.g. qualifications, personal reflections, promotion applications, etc.). Making the portfolio electronic also means that it is easier to transfer it between contexts – it can be possible for a portfolio started in school to move and develop with a student into university, and then into the workplace. This clearly requires coordination in the availability of software and systems, and is a long-term goal for many who research the area.

All in all, an ePortfolio gives a very high degree of control to the students who can choose how to build it, can tell their stories in the way they want to, and can allow them to select their audiences and what they share with them.

Assessing student blogs and wikis

As discussed in Chapter 3, blogs are usually a series of web postings made by an individual to provide a commentary, news, views, or personal insights on a particular topic or experience. They are frequently interactive, in that they invite readers to add to and comment on the original posting. The majority are text-based, but increasingly bloggers are using photos and videos, music and audio to enhance their postings.

Like the ePortfolio, blogs can show how a learner's ideas and views have developed over time, and so can be used as a vehicle to document and track development over the course of a module or a year. Blogs can be assessed diagnostically, formatively or summatively – for example: to ask students to post what they know already on a subject, before they attend a class (diagnostic); to share their thoughts after the discussion seminar and to receive additional feedback comments from peers and the teacher (formative); and as part of a final submission for an assignment (summative).

Students can be asked to submit several short blog posts on different topics or themes – perhaps that they have explored as part of the research they have undertaken to complete an essay or a report – or they can submit a 'continuous' diary-type blog that tracks their progress through a group project, illustrating what they have learned from the process of collaborative working. Please see Tables 5.1 and 5.2 for two examples of assessment rubrics to aid the grading of blog postings.

On the other hand, a wiki provides an electronic approach to assist co-authorship and collaboration. It is a web page, or set of pages, that can be edited by several users at the same time, giving all the users access to the writings of each other. It can be a very useful tool to support student group projects, and it can also be a product that can be assessed – see Chapter 3 for a more detailed discussion of this.

So how can blogs and wikis be used in relation to assessment? The very personal nature of many blogs suggests that they could be a useful vehicle to 'see into' a process of development and a longer period of learning. They could enable a teacher to see the skills development of their learners over time. They provide an outlet for personal critique, review and reflection – high-order cognitive skills, such as *metacognition*, *evaluation* and *synthesis* can be observed through a well-written blog or wiki.

Wikis can be produced by student groups or teams undertaking collaboration or group projects. They can be used to assist the processes of working together and aid communication flow. They can also be used to monitor the sharing of workload and help control against free riding.

Teachers can comment on the blogs and wikis as the students are adding to them, thus providing ongoing formative assessment and encouraging dialogue between students and teachers at a distance. In the same way, students can be asked to peer-assess and provide feedback to each other.

However, it is one thing to set up blogs and wikis for students to use as they are studying, and quite a different matter when it comes to using them for summative assessment. For example, deciding *what* can be

125

assessed well through this format is a challenge, and establishing clear assessment criteria requires careful thought. A quick online search shows that educators are using blogs to assess a range of intellectual skills, such as:

- Critique and reflection
- Analysis and problem-solving
- Creativity and ideas generation
- Data gathering and evaluation

Teachers are also using a range of quantitative and qualitative measures to judge the quality of the actual posts themselves, for example:

- The number and frequency of posts
- The quality and accuracy of the writing
- The use and relevance of any links or embedded media
- The response to comments provided by teachers or peers
- The number and quality of comments posted on other people's blogs (see Tables 5.1 and 5.2)

TABLE 5.1 An example of a simple blogging assessment rubric

Criteria	Poor	Satisfactory	Good	Excellent
Frequency of posting	>0–2 posts	3–5 posts	6–10 posts	More than 11 posts
Blog content	Unoriginal, confused and disconnected from topic	Limited originality, not always clear, some connection to topic	Some originality, clear and connected to topic	Clearly original, very clear and always connected to topic
Response to comments	No response	Some response	A good, thoughtful response	An excellent response
Links and embedded media	No embellishments	One or two links	Links and media	Excellent integration of links and media

TABLE 5.2 An example of a more complex and descriptive blog assessment rubric

Criteria	Unsatisfactory – 0%	Limited – 80%	Proficient – 90%	Exemplary – 100%	Rating
Content and creativity Weight for this criterion: 40% of total score	Postings show no evidence of insight, understanding or reflective thought about the topic	Postings provide minimal insight, understanding and reflective thought about the topic	Postings provide moderate insight, understanding and reflective thought about the topic	Postings provide comprehensive insight, understanding and reflective thought about the topic by: building a focused argument around a specific issue; asking a new related question; or making an oppositional statement supported by personal experience or related research	
	Postings present no specific viewpoint and no supporting examples or links to websites or documents are provided, or the links selected are of poor quality and do not add any value to the information presented	Postings present a specific viewpoint but lack supporting examples, or there are links to websites or documents, but not all links enhance the information presented	Postings present a specific viewpoint that is substantiated by supporting examples and links to websites or documents, but not all links enhance the information presented	Postings present a focused and cohesive viewpoint that is substantiated by effective supporting examples, or links to relevant, up-to-date websites or documents that enhance the information presented	
	Postings do not stimulate dialogue and commentary and do not connect with the audience	Postings are brief and unimaginative, and reflect minimal effort to connect with the audience	Postings are generally well written with some attempts made to stimulate dialogue and commentary	Postings are creatively and fluently written to stimulate dialogue and commentary	

(Continued)

■ TABLE 5.2 Continued

Criteria	Unsatisfactory – 0%	Limited – 80%	Proficient – 90%	Exemplary – 100%	Rating
Voice Weight for this criterion: 20% of total score	Postings do not reflect an awareness of the audience and it is difficult to identify the author's voice	Postings are written in a style that does not fully consider the audience, and the author's voice is difficult to identify	Postings are written in a style that is generally appropriate for the intended audience and an attempt is made to use a consistent voice	Postings are written in a style that is appealing and appropriate for the intended audience, and a consistent voice is evident throughout	
	Postings do not reflect the author's personality and word choice does not bring the topic to life	Postings reflect almost no personality and little attempt is made to use effective word choices to bring the topic to life	Postings reflect a bit of the author's personality through word choices that attempt to bring the topic to life	Postings reflect the author's unique personality through expressive and carefully selected word choices that bring the topic to life	
Text layout, use of graphics and multimedia Weight for this criterion: 20% of total score	Does not insert any graphics, or uses only low-quality graphics and multimedia, which do not enhance the content	Selects and inserts many low-quality graphics and multimedia which do not enhance the content	Selects and inserts graphics and multimedia that are mostly high quality and enhance and clarify the content	Selects and inserts high-quality graphics and multimedia when appropriate to enhance the content's visual appeal and increase readability	
	Does not acknowledge any image or multimedia sources, either with a caption or an annotation	Acknowledges only a few multimedia and image sources, and uses incomplete captions or annotations	Acknowledges most image and multimedia sources with captions or annotations	Acknowledges all image and multimedia sources with captions or annotations	

Criterion				
Timeliness and tags Weight for this criterion: 10% of total score	Does not update blog within the required time frame	Updates blog when reminded, posts are often missing a date stamp	Updates blog when required, most posts are date stamped with the most current posting listed at the top	Updates blog as often or more often than required, all posts are date stamped, and the most recent posts are placed at the top of the page
	Does not categorise and tag the topic appropriately	The post is not categorised and tagged appropriately	Post is categorised and tagged	Post is categorised and topics are tagged appropriately
Citations Weight for this criterion: 5% of total score	No images, media or text created by others display appropriate copyright permissions, and do not include accurate, properly formatted citations	Some of the images, media or text created by others do not display appropriate copyright permissions, and do not include accurate, properly formatted citations	Most images, media or text created by others display appropriate copyright permissions and accurate, properly formatted citations	All images, media and text created by others display appropriate copyright permissions and accurate citations
Quality of writing and proofreading Weight for this criterion: 5% of total score	Written responses contain numerous grammatical, spelling or punctuation errors. The style of writing does not facilitate effective communication	Written responses include some grammatical, spelling or punctuation errors that distract the reader	Written responses are largely free of grammatical, spelling or punctuation errors. The style of writing generally facilitates communication	Written responses are free of grammatical, spelling or punctuation errors. The style of writing facilitates communication
Total				

CASE EXAMPLE

Using public and private blogs for continuous and summative assessment

Dragoş Ciobanu, Lecturer in Translation Studies, University of Leeds

I have been using blogs very successfully on the Computer-Assisted Translation core module of the MA in Applied Translation Studies to foster student collaboration and encourage critical self-reflection and peer feedback.

Since the beginning of this academic year I have been managing a public blog in the VLE to which staff and students contribute either new blog posts, or comments to existing entries. The scope of this blog is to set new challenges to the students and encourage them to discuss how to solve them, as well as to create a space where students can ask their own questions about the concepts, techniques and software we assess in this module.

So far, in six months of teaching, the blog has been accessed 1,150 times by the 37 students enrolled in this MA and the five members of staff contributing to it. The blog exists in parallel to a Facebook group the students set up themselves, and a LinkedIn community I set up for all our alumni. The module staff only interact with the students on the VLE blog and the LinkedIn community.

I did not subscribe to the drive to seek interaction with students at all costs on all their social networks. I trust them to organise themselves both socially and professionally on their Facebook group, or whichever other social media platform they decide as a group to adopt, and they all know that the VLE blog is for all course-related discussions and continuous feedback.

Moreover, they are all aware that the LinkedIn community gives them access to the alumni group, and therefore needs to be approached in an even more professional manner, with well-formulated and well-researched questions and answers.

In addition to this blog, which is run for formative purposes and which has been so popular thanks to a very large extent to the members of staff contributing to it regularly and nurturing the student inter-action, I also require students to reflect critically on their performance, as well as that of their peers on separate, private blogs. These blogs are each linked to the regular international student projects which we run, and which our students rate very highly.

During these projects, our students get to experience all the components, challenges and joys of managing or working on international, multilingual translation and localisation projects. At the end of each project, and with reference to a list of performance criteria also available in the VLE, for a percentage of their final grade, students need to reflect critically on their performance and also grade themselves. The success of this task is also based on the fact that, when I return the final grades through the VLE, I also pick up on their self-reflection in my written feedback, in which I suggest ways in which they can improve based on their project deliverables, project performance, self-reflection and peer-feedback.

These private blogs are also consulted before each project feedback presentation given by the staff in response to the student project managers' own feedback presentation to the whole group; we are therefore able to make useful feed-forward general comments very soon after the end of a project, and our students see that their reflections are taken seriously by the teaching staff, and are reflected fairly in their project grades and general, as well as individual, feedback they receive.

Assessment of simulations, role-plays and scenario-based learning

Technology can help teachers to simulate the experience of working in some difficult learning environments that are maybe dangerous, unpredictable, complex or too time-consuming or expensive to access – for more on this see Chapter 9 on immersive 3D online environments. How students learn in these simulated situations can be tracked with a variety of (usually) formative assessment tools. For example, these can check how the students make choices, justify their decisions, tackle new problems, apply their knowledge and understanding, evaluate their situation, etc.

For example, in Geography, students may prepare to undertake some fieldwork by first participating in a fieldwork simulation so that they are better equipped for the task, and therefore gain more from the 'real' experience. In such a case it can be helpful to use formative assessment to highlight strengths and weaknesses in the student preparation, and to help ensure learners have realistic expectations of working in the field.

Technology can also provide preparatory learning environments in which the student can role-play various scenarios before being faced with the complexity and unpredictability of real-life human–human interactions. For example, in Nursing Education, students may 'meet' a number of simulated patients in a computer-generated ward or clinic before being introduced to real patients. Learners can be assessed regarding their interview skills, ethical awareness and the ways in which they interact with a simulated patient before they begin to work with real people.

Assessments can also be constructed online to ask learners to work through a set of linked scenarios in which their choices and actions in earlier scenarios influence and change the future situations they may face. These approaches are commonly used in online gaming when players solve puzzles, face different challenges individually and in groups, and move between different stages or levels of the game – for more on the 'gamification' of teaching and learning, see Chapter 10. Similarly, learners may be asked to manage a simulated economy, plan a set of physiology experiments, or design an interactive museum in which their earlier decisions will affect the future challenges they face.

Here we have seen how technology is reshaping the possibilities for learning and assessment, by providing more authentic and immersive experiences that require learners to apply their understanding and learning in more realistic and integrated ways.

 PAUSE FOR THOUGHT

In what ways could assessed simulations, role-plays and scenario-based learning be appropriate in your discipline? What benefits and challenges do you anticipate in incorporating such methods in your school or department?

GIVING AND RECEIVING FEEDBACK – TECHNOLOGICAL ADVANCEMENTS

Assessment and feedback practices should be designed to enable students to become self-regulated learners, able to monitor and evaluate the quality and impact of their own work and that of others (Nicol and Macfarlane-Dick, 2006).

Again, there is a clear role for technology to play in providing support and encouragement for learners to become more engaged in the assessment processes, and so be better able to understand the goals and standards that are applied in their disciplines. This is particularly apparent when we consider the ways in which formative assessments can be carried out and feedback opportunities shaped.

Many have experimented with methods to provide richer feedback to their students. For example, the JISC 'Sounds Good' project at Leeds Metropolitan University has evaluated the provision of individual online audio feedback very positively. One approach they piloted was to record MP3 audio files using a digital audio recorder. These files were uploaded to a computer and made available to the students through the VLE. Most of the teachers taking part in the project report very high levels of student satisfaction, and that more could be communicated through the spoken voice than through the written comments they had previously provided for their learners. On the issue of time economy on the part of the teachers, the jury is still out. Other similar initiatives had different results, with some students preferring traditional written feedback to audio comments. Research is still needed to identify patterns: is audio feedback more suitable for certain disciplines and certain student profiles?

A number of projects have also experimented with the development and provision of video feedback and screen-captured feedback, as the case examples below illustrate.

 CASE EXAMPLE

Using video for feedback

Anne Crook, Enhancement Manager (Teaching, Learning, Assessment and Feedback), and colleagues at Reading University

Video can represent an exciting, dynamic and engaging mechanism for providing rapid feed-forward and feedback to students. A project at the University of Reading, ASSET, evaluated the use of short video clips that staff prepare and provide to students either in advance of assessments (e.g. as a way of 'feeding-forward'), or to provide rapid generic feedback on completed assignments. The project evaluated the use of this medium to enhance the effectiveness and engagement of staff and students with this form of feedback provision.

Providing high-quality and timely feedback to students is often a challenge for many staff in higher education, as it can be both time-consuming and frustratingly repetitive. From the student perspective, feedback may sometimes be considered unhelpful, confusing and inconsistent, and may not always be provided within a timeframe that is considered to be 'useful'.

The use of video addresses many of these inherent challenges, by enabling the provision of feedback that supports learning (i.e. feedback that contains elements of 'feed-forward'), is of a high quality, and which can be delivered in a timely manner. Moreover, the visual nature of video media can enhance learning opportunities while enabling staff to 'say' a lot within a given period of time (in comparison to more traditional written methods of feedback). In particular, the pedagogic benefits of video/audio media can be exploited within a Web 2.0 context to provide a new, interactive resource to enhance the feedback experience for both students and staff.

We used simple video technology such as webcams and Flip video cameras. These are easy to use and can capture clips in a range of settings. Our experience suggests that clips should ideally be between one and three minutes long, but certainly no longer than five minutes. We found the use of generic feed-forward videos to outline the procedures for a lab practical, or the criteria for a written assignment, were particularly popular. The fact that video clips can be made and posted rapidly to provide generic feedback to groups shortly after the hand-in date of an assignment was also popular in the intervening period before students received more detailed individual feedback.

Ten tips in preparing and giving video-recorded feedback:

1 Use 'simple' video technology – e.g. webcam or Flip devices.
2 Make sure the sound is of a reasonable quality.
3 Keep the video clips short (less than five minutes).
4 Avoid editing, and don't worry about 'ums' and 'ehs'.
5 When you first use video, have a practice run.
6 Use video to convey your enthusiasm and excitement about your discipline.
7 Try different settings for recording your videos.
8 Think about using video clips to prepare students for assignments, as well as for feedback.
9 Make sure students can easily access the videos.

10 Experiment with different formats for providing feedback – e.g. 'talking head', 'screen capture', informal discussions, etc.

For further information, please see the University of Reading website: www.reading.ac.uk/videofeedback

CASE EXAMPLE

Screen capture software for feedback

Russell Stannard, Centre for Applied Linguistics, University of Warwick

Screen capture tools allow you to record the screen of your computer as if you had a video camera pointed at it. Everything you do on the screen, anything you open, highlight or write, will all come out in the video. If you have a microphone attached to your computer, then it will also record your voice. This technology is widely used for computer training, since the trainer can simply screen-capture himself/herself using certain technologies as a way of training people to learn them.

In 2006, Russell Stannard used the same technology to provide feedback to his students. He simply opened up the students' work onto his computer screen, turned on the screen capture technology, and recorded himself correcting his students' work. He then sent the resulting video to the student. Each student received a video where they could listen and watch their tutor correcting their work. A simple example can be seen here: http://www.teachertrainingvideos.com/luFeedback/index.html

Early research into the idea showed the following benefits:

■ The students liked the fact that the feedback was both visual and oral.
■ Students received much more feedback. At 150 words a minute, a teacher is able to provide the equivalent of 750 words in a five-minute video.
■ Students felt the voice was important.
■ Distance learning organisations were especially interested in the idea, as it meant close contact with students they never see.

135

- The feedback is more multimodal. There has been a major shift in the teaching and learning being more multimodal, but feedback is generally still very text-based.

The idea has attracted enormous interest. It has been covered in the national press on several occasions, and there are now extensive research projects in the UK, Norway and Canada – please see: http://goo.gl/iLfJt and http://goo.gl/KILXY

MANAGING ASSESSMENTS WITH THE HELP OF TECHNOLOGY – VLES AND OTHER TOOLS

Virtual learning environments (VLEs), such as Blackboard and Moodle, are now an expected part of a student's learning experience at college and university – they are discussed in greater detail in Chapter 7. Here we simply focus on some of the ways that VLEs can help teachers manage assessments and provide a consistent approach for all students. The goals are therefore twofold: reduce assessment administration, and improve the experience for learners.

Some universities are using VLEs to systematise and coordinate how students submit work assignments, and help to manage how assessments are processed.

 CASE EXAMPLE

The assignment handler

At Sheffield Hallam University, software termed the 'Assignment Handler' has been developed and implemented. Students submit work through the VLE (in this case Blackboard), staff read it and grade it, and post feedback comments and the mark they have awarded via the Blackboard extension.

However, the Assignment Handler requires the students to engage with their feedback and post up a set of key learning points before the system releases information about the grade awarded. In other words, the software only releases a student's grade when they have read and commented on their feedback.

It is hoped that automating the release of feedback to all the students on the module at the same time, and alerting the students to this via an email notification, will reduce any confusion about when and how to collect marked work, and therefore also promote better engagement with the feedback provided.

In addition to the management of assessment issues discussed above, the VLE can also help the teacher make better use of their contact time, and provide in-class feedback on work already produced in advance by learners.

CASE EXAMPLE

Improving 'in-class' feedback

Yuka Oeda, Teaching Fellow in Japanese, University of Leeds

The wiki feature on the Virtual Learning Environment (VLE) is a useful tool when I teach my English–Japanese translation class. In my translation class, I ask students to post their sample translations on the VLE before the lesson. I then collect their samples and go through their work using PowerPoint slides. As some students feel uncomfortable when their mistakes are highlighted and corrected in front of everyone, all samples are shown anonymously.

This system is very popular, as all students are able to receive individual feedback for the work they have done. By looking at their peers' work, students are able to share and compare their own work. Students find it difficult to choose the appropriate word from their dictionary when they translate. Explaining and discussing the nuance of words using the students' own work is valuable as feedback because it helps students connect directly with their work.

Posting their translations before the class also enables me to use my class time effectively. I used to ask students to write their samples on the whiteboard, which took some time. Now I can spend more time on feedback using the wiki.

137

CHEATING AND PLAGIARISM

There are many ways in which students can try and cheat assessments. One specific way is to plagiarise – in other words, to seek to pass off somebody else's work as if it were their own – in order to be awarded marks and credit. If the 'somebody else' is a fellow student, then this is called 'collusion'.

If students are required to submit their work electronically, a range of software tools are available to help teachers detect instances of plagiarism. One called 'CopyCatch' matches scripts with others submitted within the same cohort, and so assists in detecting collusion. The teacher can set the level of similarity to be noted, and can very quickly screen the submitted work; if collusion is detected, a human marker can then check the highlighted papers more closely.

The most commonly used text-matching tool is probably 'Turnitin', which searches the Internet for textual similarities to the submitted work. However, Hinchliffe (2000) writes that such tools have a number of important limitations. For one, they only search part of the web, and many of the essay bank sites are likely to be copyright-protected and therefore not searchable.

Moreover, the software cannot detect work on the web in different languages and translated into English by the student. It is also powerless to detect intended fraud – when a student has paid another person to complete their essay or assignment for them – see Ed Dante's (2010) *pseudonym* 'shadow scholar' article for further insight. Some cheat sites guarantee that the 'bought' work will be original and will not be detectable in this way. Finally, the software can only ever highlight matches with textual content. This is not the same as plagiarism, where further academic judgement will always be needed.

Text matching software can be used to catch those who seek to cheat, but it can also be used to guide, deter and allow students to self-check their work submissions. With the attitude 'prevention is better than cure', many teachers are now using the tools to help educate learners on plagiarism and how to avoid accusations of cheating. They are also using them to help reinforce teaching on how to reference, cite and quote from the work of others properly.

CONCLUDING REMARKS

Technology is providing educators with an expanding array of tools and platforms to assess and give feedback to learners. Not only does the

138

technology provide the potential to manage larger assessment loads more quickly and cost-effectively, and provide more timely and accessible feedback to learners, it also gives the opportunity to assess different kinds of knowledge and academic and generic skills. Perhaps most importantly, technology is forcing reflection and research on assessment and feedback practices in HE and their underlying pedagogy. However, the role of the human marker is still assured, particularly in free text, divergent assessment forms.

NOTES

1 http://www.youtube.com/watch?v=6vDx7xcPKuU
2 McKendree considers some of the evidence on this for the HEA at: http://goo.gl/vWQE2
3 http://docs.moodle.org/22/en/question/type/pmatch
4 For the latest JISC guidance, visit: http://www.jisc.ac.uk/assessment#tools
5 See for example: http://explainingmaths.wordpress.com/
6 http://screencast-o-matic.com
7 http://goo.gl/qFqvM

USEFUL RESOURCES

CopyCatch: http://www.cflsoftware.com

Engage in Assessment http://www.reading.ac.uk/engageinassessment

Engage in Feedback http://www.reading.ac.uk/engageinfeedback

Quality Assurance Agency Quality Code Chapter B6: http://www.qaa.ac.uk/publications/informationandguidance/pages/quality-code-b6.aspx

Sounds good project: http://www.jisc.ac.uk/publications/reports/2009/soundsgoodfinalreport.aspx

Turnitin: http://turnitin.com/

Chapter 6

Podcasting and vodcasting

INTRODUCTION

The terminology associated with e-learning seems, like bacteria, to grow exponentially. Worse still, the meaning of the terms keeps evolving; even when you have navigated your way through some of the ideas and can begin to converse meaningfully, the rug seems to be pulled from under your feet. One particularly good example of this 'Petri dish' is the audio and visual (AV) aspect of e-learning.

Talking to people involved in e-learning, and reading the literature and websites discussing AV, it soon becomes clear that one person's 'podcast' is another's 'vodcast', which is another's 'video capture' and another's 'screen capture'; and all might be lumped together as a *digital learning object*.

In this chapter, 'podcast' will mean *any audio* recording captured *digitally*, and 'vodcast' will mean any audio *and visual* recording captured *digitally*; these are intentionally broader than normal definitions of these terms.

In this chapter we will look at the use of AV technology in teaching, and will consider some of the possible benefits and problems. We draw on a number of case studies in order to demonstrate 'sounds and pictures' in 'real life' HE situations.

USING SOUNDS AND PICTURES: A PRACTICAL GUIDE

This section is a very basic 'how to' guide, also discussing the benefits, worries and pedagogical implications of using AV materials.

Podcasts can be made as easily as pressing 'record' on most smartphones – there are a number of apps to help which have a built-in microphone and give the user the facility to upload digital files.[1]

A better-quality recording device, such as a digital Dictaphone, can be bought relatively cheaply. However, when buying such a device, be sure to focus on the digital upload functionality, as well as the ability to record digitally.

At the top end of recording devices – and hence the most expensive – is studio-quality recording equipment such as the Marantz PMD661 Professional Portable Field Recorder, and many universities may own such devices. However, many of the cheaper versions of such equipment record acceptable-quality audio: the deciding factors in choosing a particular piece of kit will need to be – apart from price – portability, battery life, storage capacity, connectivity and, very importantly, whether the microphone can pick up what the audience is saying and not just the teacher.

Once the podcast is recorded, the teacher might want to edit the audio file. Perhaps there were some inaccuracies, or the device wasn't switched off before students asked questions after a lecture. For this task, at the time of writing, there are a number of freely downloadable and more than adequate audio-editing programmes, such as Audacity.

There are a number of ways in which teachers can share the edited recording. One easy method is by uploading the individual audio file into the virtual learning environment's (VLE's) 'podcast uploader', which is present in most VLEs used in universities. Audio files could also be shared by email, but file size may limit this – see Chapter 7 for a discussion of VLEs.

However, whatever the practitioner decides to use, she will need to decide whether to stream the podcast, allow it to be downloaded, or both. Streaming here means to listen to the audio file online rather than downloading it to one's own device. Streaming requires an Internet connection for the entire duration of the podcast episode, and may therefore be inappropriate if the aim of creating such an audio file is for students to listen to it no matter what their wireless or 3G/4G coverage.

Making the files downloadable is the most popular option among students, as it gives the ability to listen to/watch material 'on the move' rather than having to rely on Internet connectivity. If possible, both options should be provided.

Vodcasts are only slightly harder to create, although there are more ways to produce them. For example, a vodcast can be made using an in-built laptop camera or a relatively cheap digital camera. However, universities are increasingly installing highly sophisticated video recording devices in lecture rooms (e.g. Echo360). The vodcasts created from these devices – more often called *lecture captures* – are of high quality and have a great amount of functionality.

While the overwhelming majority of such resources combine an audio recording with the capture of slides or computer demonstrations, the number of recordings that also contain a video of the lecturer is smaller. Despite students informally indicating that seeing the teacher enhances the human element of the recording, some teachers become rather self-conscious when they have a camera pointed at them, restricting their freedom of movement significantly.

When it comes to the textual content though, one important feature of such high-end vodcasts is the search function: for instance, a lecture may be recorded and the slides used in the lecture synced automatically; a student who understood the first part of the lecture and remembers some specific issue, but cannot remember *where* that issue arose in the lecture, could use a built-in search option to take them straight to that part of the lecture. Not surprisingly, the vodcasts produced on such devices are very popular among students despite the fact that, due to the increased amount of information on the screen – presenter video, slide menu, slide content, slide thumbnails, slide notes – they are not suitable for viewing on relatively small smartphone screens.

If a lecture theatre has the sophisticated equipment installed, then the teacher will find it by far the easiest way of creating a vodcast. This is because there is no need to get involved in any of the technical setting-up and processing. If a lecture room has such facilities, depending on the system installed, the teacher can simply press 'record' and then 'stop': the vodcast is created, processed and the URL can then be made available to the students automatically.

A related form of sophisticated vodcast is *screen casting*. This is growing in popularity, and there is free and open-source software (e.g. *CamStudio*),[2] as well as professional licensed software such as Camtasia.[3] A screen cast offers a video capture of what is happening on the computer screen, along with an optional audio commentary and text elements such as comments, instructions, questions, etc. This is particularly useful in subjects such as mathematics, engineering and philosophical logic where audio and annotations sit well together.[4]

142

DECIDING WHAT TO POD/VODCAST

The really interesting and crucial question for the teacher to ask is *how* will podcasts and vodcasts be used? There are many different ways to answer this question, and to give you a taste and to set you thinking, let's consider a few:

- The most obvious and perhaps the most frequently used method is simply to record a lecture from beginning to end, and then release it in its entirety to the students. This is probably most often used as it requires less intervention from the teacher – if any editing is needed, it is minimal – and is consequently the quickest way of getting the material to the students.

- A less obvious method, but arguably more useful to students, is to create 'bite-size' vodcasts or podcasts – such as the online video tutorials that have made the Khan Academy[5] famous. This enables the teachers to focus on a discrete issue. For example, they might focus on a topic that has been problematic in the past, or on a subject that students have found difficult. They could then devote a 'bite-size' pod/vodcast to explaining the issue in more detail, pre-empting the worries students face. Such shortened versions have typically been reported to have a big impact on students, and they can often be far more useful for their learning than a long audio/visual record of the whole lecture (Parson et al., 2009).

- The teacher could discuss issues *outside* the set lecture topics for the course. For example, the teacher could usefully refer to current research in the podcasts, showing students that the material is evolving and is not simply a discrete packet of information, while at the same time reinforcing the idea of the practitioner as both researcher and teacher.

- The teacher could create a series of interviews or discussions about the topic with students or other teachers.

- Near exam time or essay deadlines, a teacher could pre-empt 'study-skill' questions, as well as specific questions about the essay/exam, by releasing a few relevant pod/vodcast episodes.

 PAUSE FOR THOUGHT

If you were to use pod/vodcasting in your teaching, which approach would best suit you and your students' needs?

143

HOW TO USE PODCASTS AND VODCASTS

Once the content has been decided, a further vital question arises as to *how* to use podcasts and vodcasts best. Here are a few ideas:

- It is often said that the best experiences of education are through small-group interactive discussions; and indeed the benefits of such small-group interactive teaching have been well documented (e.g. Garside, 1996). Thus, the practitioner could record a set of 'stimulus' videos which the students would be required to watch, think about, and then come to a tutorial ready to discuss. This approach has been used a lot, and under the banner of 'flipped classroom' is seeing increasing popularity – see Rhem and Glazer (2012).

- Another suggestion (discussed in the case example below) is to encourage students – as part of their assessment and ongoing engagement with the material in the course – to create *their own* videos, which they could introduce in class. These videos could facilitate discussion and encourage peer feedback while developing the creative skills of the students through the production of the AV resources.

- A further way in which video/audio can and has been used is to support *distance learning* programmes. It would be of great benefit to students if they could watch lectures, or see or hear key ideas being discussed by the practitioner. Moreover, in relation to distance learning, as video conferencing and Skype conversations can be recorded, there is an obvious benefit in the live Q&A interaction being shared by other students (see Chapters 4 and 5) – a good example of this is Blogging Heads TV.[6]

- Universities are also using video more and more as marketing tools. These videos are often released as open educational resources on channels such as YouTube, EDU or iTunes U.

- Video can also be used to bring the 'outside' world into the classroom. For example, they can be used to make assessment more realistic through recorded interviews in medical objective structured clinical examinations (OSCEs); or perhaps a practitioner is teaching a course on animal ethics and uses a short clip from an abattoir to infuse the topic with more realism.

- The growing importance of feedback, especially with the focus on clear, high-quality feedback, might suggest the use of vodcasts and podcasts as a way of developing university practice in this area. This could be done by a teacher discussing issues regarding the general problems students have encountered and the general ways in which they could improve. Particularly when providing timely, individual feedback might be difficult (e.g. soon after summative examinations, see Chapter 5).

 CASE EXAMPLE

Student-created video in seminars

Jonathan Tallant, Philosophy, University of Nottingham

In response to student requests for some form of assessed presentations, we trialled video presentations in a Philosophy of Language module. The aim was to generate a flexible, formative mode of assessment that allowed students to acquire oral and presentation skills, while also reinforcing key learning outcomes.

By making the presentations through video – rather than live – we aimed to provide a safe space for experimentation, and to relieve the tension of having to deliver a public presentation. For instance, some students had remarked in advance: 'They [the presentations] terrify me. I don't like to talk in front of people'. We also hoped to allow for students to reflect critically upon their own performance, which watching the presentations back would allow.

In outline, students were required to work in small groups of four to five to answer set questions. Each group had to record a series of short films to be shown in a seminar. Each member of the group had to deliver some of the content. Students were told that the seminar questions would closely mirror the exam questions. All presentations were then to be used to stimulate seminar discussion of the topic(s). After the seminar, each group received feedback from the rest of the seminar group – via anonymous feedback forms – and also from the seminar leader.

The trial was moderately successful: 'well thought out and supported – makes a change from more basic and nerve-wracking presentations'. A large number (60%) agreed or strongly agreed that constructing the presentations was an excellent way of learning the subject.

The median mark improved from 59 to 61.

However, the project also brought out a number of challenges we need to overcome in order to implement this strategy more widely. Contrary to our expectations, students found the video presentations *more* nerve-wracking than straightforward oral presentations: 'It may seem that recording the presentations prior to the seminar would take the pressure off. I think it actually puts the pressure on more'. There was also a good deal of concern from within the groups about peers not 'pulling their weight': '[My main concern is that] . . . people won't pull their weight'.

In sum, we took the trial to be a moderate success. Students agreed that the presentations helped them to learn the subject and the marks improved. However, the format still requires sensitivity to the issues of student nerves and worries about lack of collaboration.

When giving AV feedback, teachers also need to pay attention to their tone and general manner, as students do pay close attention to these aspects, too:

the impact of the podcast feedback was perceived [by students] as being harder-hitting, in a form less easy to ignore; and the tone of voice of the feedback provided a clear context to the critical comments, that is unavailable in traditional written feedback.

(France and Wheeler, 2007: 10)

POD/VODCASTS FOR THE TEACHER'S OWN CONTINUOUS DEVELOPMENT

In addition to providing useful feedback and clarifications to students, vodcasts can also be a highly valuable educational tool in terms of the *teacher's* own development. Once a teacher moves past the 'cringe factor' of seeing and hearing him/herself, then videos can be a real revelation which may lead to an improvement in style, approach, understanding and delivery. It is no surprise that teacher-training courses routinely use video in this way (e.g. Gray et al., 2012). Moreover, as videos are generally easy to access, teachers may even watch each other and give feedback, while picking up some useful hints at the same time.

When viewing videoed teaching practice, two very different approaches can be adopted: first of all, a problem-centred approach, in which things that could be done better are highlighted with a view of putting them right; secondly, an appreciative approach, in which the positive and beneficial actions of the teacher are noted, with the view to being able to build and transfer these positives to other aspects of teaching, and thus grow confidence.

A related issue here is that if the teacher decides to pod/vodcast a lecture, then they ought to think hard about its nature and content. If, for example, a lecture includes interactive group exercises, a question and answer session, or the use of student response units (see Chapter 5), then the pod or vodcast will need editing or, in an ideal scenario and given the right technology, pausing to avoid post-editing, as there will be periods where nothing is happening.

Another important factor is to remember that, if a student asks a question during a lecture, it may not be picked up in the pod/vodcast. So either the teacher needs to use a wireless microphone which they could pass around the lecture room, or they need to repeat the question before giving the answer. Having said that, it is good presentation practice to rephrase or repeat questions from the audience so that the entire audience hears them before hearing the answer.

Finally, and extremely importantly, if the lecture is recorded with the intention of being broadcast, teachers need to ensure that they have the permission of all the session participants to record and release it, and they also need to ensure that their teaching resources do not include any copyrighted materials for which they have not obtained permission to republish. Releasing a lecture recording is in effect republishing the content it contains, and teachers could find themselves being sued if they do not check that their images, videos, animations and any other content not produced by themselves, are properly referenced and republished according to the strict instructions of the original publisher.

Pre-empting some of these issues will help the end-user experience significantly, and will also ensure that teachers do not have to deal with unpleasant legal matters.

WILL STUDENTS LIKE POD AND/OR VODCASTS?

It is clear from research and anecdotal evidence that the simple answer is 'yes' and 'yes' – we could not find one set of results in which the predominant view among students was against their use (Barker and Greeff, 2011; Vajoczki et al., 2011; Govender and Mkhwanazi, 2012). The reasons why students like them are quite easy to ascertain. First, it is worth noting that students prefer vodcasts to podcasts (Traphagan et al., 2010). The most obvious explanation for this is that a vodcast will pick up many non-verbal elements of the lecture. Depending on the quality of the camera used, if a practitioner raises her eyebrows or shrugs her shoulders after making a statement, it may be possible to record these non-verbal elements clearly, as they would send the students a very distinct message.

Lecture capture techniques are popular among students because of the varied ways in which the AV material can be accessed. Once the *lecture cast* is created, the student can typically receive the material in various formats. They can simply listen to the audio, or can access slides and audio, or if they want they can access video, audio and slides.

Another reason that pod and vodcasts are so popular among students is that they give them the chance to be wholly engaged in the lecture rather than trying to take (legible) notes, as well as listen carefully at the same time. They have a 'safety net' and so they are able to enjoy the lecture and concentrate on understanding it, knowing that they can always revisit it at a later date.

Of course, related to this is the immensely useful resource for *revision* that lecture recordings, as well as vod and podcasts, provide. Rather than relying on a set of notes, students can revisit lectures or listen to an explanation of a key concept again and again. Furthermore, vod and podcasts can allow for greater flexibility for students in terms of *when* they learn – related to this point, it is interesting to note that tracking the usage of pod and vodcasts shows that the access statistics peak near assessment times (Nicholson et al., 2010).

Both vod and podcasts can help students manage their workload more effectively, which in turn helps teachers to manage their workload better, particularly in relation to the footfall and email traffic they receive. For example, if a teacher creates a podcast where they talk about how to write an essay/lab report/exam, and if this is done well, it will pre-empt many of the duplicate emails/visits from students asking 'how do we write this essay/lab report/exam?'

Moreover, non-native speakers benefit greatly from the chance to revisit lectures and listen to concepts, terms and ideas as much as they need – indeed, pod/vodcasts can be particularly useful in learning languages (e.g. Rogan and Miguel, 2013). The reverse is also true: if the teacher's first language is not the language of the course, or if the teacher's accent is particularly challenging, having access to session recordings will benefit both the teacher – to review continuously his or her delivery and clarity – but also students who may find it difficult to follow and understand lectures.

Last, but not least, podcasts and vodcasts are also very helpful to students with learning difficulties. Dyslexic students would benefit from being able to learn and understand at their own pace, which in turn would help the quality and depth of their educational experience (Leadbeater et al., 2012), and students with cognitive impairments will also benefit from being able to replay more challenging parts of the lecture in order to take in their meaning.

POTENTIAL CONCERNS ABOUT USING POD/VODCASTS

Despite the apparent benefits of pod and vodcasting, practitioners are typically reticent to use them. Although this is sometimes due to technical worries, the concerns most frequently expressed are pedagogical, and relate to how practitioners perceive themselves and their relationship with students.

The first concern is that of attendance. If a whole lecture is podcast, does this mean that students will simply stop turning up to lectures? Why would they turn up? The jury is still out on these related questions, although some research does seem to suggest that this worry is well-grounded. Traphagan et al. (2010), Bell et al. (2001) and Harpp et al. (2004) note small reductions in attendance, while others have not found any connection between attendance and podcast use (Grabe and Christopherson, 2008; White, 2009). One could also ask provocatively – what is the value-added in attending the lecture if the students can get all they need from watching a pod/vodcast instead?

In contrast, students often talk about podcasts being a *supplement* to a lecture rather than a replacement. Students are actually sensitive to the lack of 'live interaction' that *podcasts* afford, and so they see a need to keep attending the lectures.

A second cause for concern among practitioners is that their own role could apparently come into question. If, during a module, the teacher creates a complete collection of pod/vodcasts, then why are they needed at all? Isn't the practitioner doing themselves out of a job by pod/vodcasting lectures? This is a genuine concern we have heard expressed many times, but we would like to offer a number of arguments to allay this fear.

We know that courses do become outdated and require refreshing. For instance, a pod/vodcast series on the role of banks in the world economy would have to be rerecorded year on year. The teacher's

149

presence is therefore crucial for the creation of updated resources. In addition, as already known to those familiar with the criticism of the passive receptive mode of using Khan Academy instructional videos, pod/vodcasts on their own do not encourage active engagement. Consequently, from a pedagogical point of view, replacing teachers with instructional videos may be a step forward in terms of technology use, but will be a giant leap backwards in terms of educational practice.

Having said that, it is important at all times to reflect on the *context* in which pod/vodcasts are presented. In particular, if pod/vodcasts are used as a way of facilitating discussion in seminars/tutorials, then the 'audience' certainly won't be 'passive'. In fact, far from encouraging 'surface learning', you might think that pod/vodcasts would encourage a 'deeper learning' (e.g. Lakhal et al., 2007). After all, they encourage and allow material to be revisited, which in turn allows the students more space to ask whether they really understand what is going on.

Moreover, the use of pod/vodcasts can make interactions between educators and students more meaningful. To put it another way, the use of pod/vodcast allows the practitioner to be valued more and develop as a teacher. In particular, pod/vodcasting can make teaching more personal through increasing the use of group interactivity. We mentioned earlier the notion of the 'flipped classroom', describing the situation in which content that would normally be delivered unidirectionally by the teacher can be recorded and watched by students in their own time before the session, ensuring that the full face-to-face session can be spent on interactive activities that add real value to the learning experience. For instance, an economist working on food production may want his students to study the moral issues surrounding food. If he had access to pod/vodcasts about these issues, he could simply direct his students to listen/watch them and thus engender a sense of working within a community of learners for both the students and practitioner.

Third is an issue about how the nature of lectures might change, and in particular the issue of self-censorship. Lectures are organic and sometimes controversial. For example, if a practitioner was lecturing on the Middle East and wanted to put forward a pro-Israeli view, or was lecturing in an American university in the deep south and wanted to put forward a pro-abortion stance, they might be less inclined to air their views if they knew there was going to be a permanent record of what they said; not only that, but also a record that could be shared with the public.

This particular point is fascinating, and a number of things can be said

150

about it: more often than not, the vod or podcasts *are not* in the public domain, but are password-protected. Therefore, the worry about curtailing or self-censorship may be less pressing than one first thinks. However, there is still a worry here: after all, a student could download a lecture and then share it in the public domain, and that is certainly something that the practitioner would be aware of. Moreover, as highlighted in Chapter 8, there is a growing move towards open-access materials that are freely available via the web.

In addition, if the teacher has to change what they are going to say based on whether the lecture is recorded or not, then perhaps they should not say it at all. If it isn't defensible and is perhaps more of a rant, then those points may not belong in the classroom, except perhaps to start a justified debate. One could argue therefore that pod/vodcasts can be seen as a way of pruning lectures of unnecessary and unjustified content and attitudes. Again, this is controversial and is an issue on which the practitioner should seriously reflect.

Another important concern, which has been implicitly highlighted in other chapters and discussed by other researchers (e.g. Oblinger and Hawkins, 2006), relates to the teacher's view of the relationship between students and technology. The teacher needs to be sensitive to the fact that the students' technological competencies are distinct from informational competence: students can embed, blog and use a wiki, but this does not automatically mean that they know how to filter and engage with the important parts of the blog or wiki (see Chapter 10, where we discuss curatorship as a new and important skill for students). There is nothing in technological competence which gives students the ability and skill to process the presented information in an effective or efficient manner. The practitioner should then work with students to help them gain the skills required to benefit fully from the use of technology in their learning.

How might they do this? Well, practitioners could contextualise the recordings by directing students to further resources, and encouraging comments/tags on the material she has released. For example, the pod/vodcast could be built around a course webpage.

There is also the difficult issue concerning the legal ownership of these vod and podcasts – see, for example, Schnackenberg et al. (2009). Can the teacher take her pod/vodcasts with her if she wishes to move to another university?

The answer to all the legal questions will probably lie with the institution, but very often there is no explicit directive. For this reason the practitioner should ask the very specific questions which concern them at

151

university level. A typical sort of response given by institutions is outlined by the University of Nottingham (UK), which says:

> where a member of staff moves to a new institution, the University will normally, in its discretion, be willing to grant rights to use existing Course Materials to the member of staff concerned and/or the host institution. Authority to grant such rights is delegated to the Head of School. Any such grants must be in writing and may be subject to terms and conditions.[7]

Continuing with the legal theme, there is also a concern about what happens if a student appears on camera without having given their explicit consent. This and other related issues, such as copyright and those relating to ownership, do become very complicated, and we would like to refer the reader to the JISC legal resources[8] for detail and accuracy.

We believe that an important development for vodcasting, and one that will quickly increase its popularity, is the increased availability of editing software. Students could then be encouraged to annotate and develop videos to demonstrate their understanding. This would further demonstrate to the teacher a level of informational competence, as well as the assumed technical competence.

Finally, another popular application is a series of pod/vodcast episodes to help students make more informed choices about modules/courses. Often students are not quite sure what a module or course involves, so it can be very useful in their decision-making process to listen to/watch either a lecture from the module, or see/hear the teacher talking about the key ideas in the course.

CONCLUDING REMARKS

Given the user-friendliness of emergent technologies, and the way pod and vodcasts can help students with learning disabilities and satisfy growing student expectations, the use of pod and vodcasting is increasing rapidly in universities. We suggested that this requires the teacher to think carefully about the accompanying pedagogical and legal issues we have specified. That said, the use of AV media in teaching can enhance teaching and enrich the student experience significantly.

In this chapter we have also highlighted that the best way of using audio and video is not necessarily simply to record whole lectures, but to think more inventively about how they might be used – for example, by creating study-skills support resources, or bespoke supplements to lectures.

We also suggested that encouraging students to create audio and video for themselves will not only support peer-to-peer teaching and group-work, but would also help teachers get a better sense of how the students are dealing with the course material. As with all the technology in this book, podcasting and vodcasting should not be thought of as something with inherent value, but should mainly be considered as something that can supplement and enhance student learning.

NOTES

1 For instance, Cinch: http://cinchcast.com/
2 http://camstudio.org/
3 http://www.techsmith.com/camtasia.html
4 For an excellent blog on the use of screen casting in mathematics, see: http://explainingmaths.wordpress.com/
5 https://www.khanacademy.org/
6 http://bloggingheads.tv
7 http://www.nottingham.ac.uk/hr/guidesandsupport/universitycodesof-practiceandrules/documents/copyright,databaserightsandassociatedissues.pdf
8 http://www.jisclegal.ac.uk/

USEFUL RESOURCES

Guide to podcasting: http://www.bcs.org/content/ConWebDoc/20217

Article discussing some legal and ethical issues: http://www.scientificjournals.org/journals2009/articles/1461.pdf

Guardian article 'Will podcasting finally kill the lecture?' http://www.guardian.co.uk/education/2006/sep/19/elearning.highereducation

Good slide show on pod and vodcasting: http://www.slideshare.net/sedsall/converting-lectures-into-vodcasts-podcasts-for-mobile-devices-options-for-pc-mac-users

Chapter 7

Virtual learning environments

INTRODUCTION

Virtual learning environments (VLEs), also known as 'learning management systems' (LMSs), are a natural progression in the use of online technology for educational purposes. Their architecture generally follows the constructivist learning theory (see Chapter 1), and they offer password-protected – but also openly available if necessary – online spaces in which students are enrolled to complete tasks, access course information and scaffolded learning resources, and receive feedback and grades for their activity.

Some readers may be slightly suspicious of our decision to include such a chapter, given the recent growing talk of the 'death of the VLE'.[1] Despite that, we still think that there is a place for the VLE in contemporary education, and we will endeavour to illustrate with examples throughout this chapter what that place is.

First, one may be surprised to find out that VLEs/LMSs extend far beyond the well-known platforms Moodle, Sakai, Blackboard or Desire2Learn. In fact, sources place the exact number of systems out there between 150[2] and 429.[3] That is more than enough to turn the task of choosing a VLE into a very daunting exercise. A lot of teachers, however, are not likely to be involved in deciding which VLE is better for their institution. What is important, nevertheless, is to be aware of effective applications of VLE tools because, although technology will keep evolving, good teaching practice will continue to depend on sound pedagogical design first, and clear and purposeful use of supporting technology second.

The arrival of VLEs – starting with the PLATO[4] system in 1960 – was initially hailed for their student management functionalities (which grew to include easy student enrolment and self-enrolment, dissemination of information to entire cohorts of students or to predefined groups, storing of grades and feedback, management of complex weighted grading formulae, tracking of student access to online learning resources, and automatic alerts to course tutors regarding students whose performance would fall below a customisable threshold). They were also popular for allowing tutors to make password-protected learning resources available to entire cohorts or to customisable groups, as well as for additional time-saving assessment functionalities such as automated marking of quizzes and plagiarism checking.

In recent years, however, as a result of progress both in the area of what online learning technologies can do, but also in no small part what they can look like, VLEs have been criticised heavily for being inflexible, unintuitive, difficult to navigate, slow to integrate with popular external collaboration and interaction tools, and even 'boxy'.

While these points are founded to various extents, we would like to emphasise that VLEs still have significant benefits for learning and teaching. We view some of these criticisms, especially the ones dealing with the aesthetics of a VLE, to be of secondary importance while educators everywhere are still grappling with much more important dilemmas, such as how to identify, track and properly acknowledge the importance of online and offline informal learning, and how to motivate and reward students equitably for engaging in collaborative blended learning.

WHICH VLE?

As with any other type of learning technology, the nature and price of VLEs continues to be a significant point of debate. We discuss the implications of free and open source vs proprietary software in the next chapter, but here is a preview.

Free and open source, proprietary, or free but proprietary?

Institutions can choose free and open-source software which has no initial direct cost and no additional tie-ins, but still requires specialist installation, maintenance and customisation – examples are Moodle and Sakai. The advantage is that such VLEs tend to be more agile and more quickly integrated with the latest popular file, image, video, audio, slide

155

presentation, and any other content-sharing platforms, because their development is continuously carried out by a community of experts and enthusiasts who modify code and re-release it under the same license as the original system.

This advantage can also quickly become a disadvantage as, without some project management in place, individually installed updates can be incompatible with and can affect adversely the entire VLE installation. Given this predominant community support model, if things go wrong much rests on the shoulders of the in-house VLE team – unless external dedicated support had been contracted for the VLE installation and maintenance.

At the opposite pole are the proprietary systems – such as Blackboard and Desire2Learn – which fairly often come with dedicated support in return for what can in some cases become a significant financial investment. Such systems also have certain requirements and limitations, potentially tying institutions into lengthy contracts and requiring additional funding for updates and extensions of functionalities, such as mobile device support. Updates are not always quick to appear, the vendor's priorities are not always the same as the individual institutions', and this has an effect on the VLE's integration with new learning platforms and social media tools. In short, proprietary systems are less nimble and slower to respond to change, but can be more stable and reliable.

The model which is becoming increasingly popular is that of outsourcing the installation, configuration and management of a VLE, and therefore looking for hosted and cloud-based solutions – meaning that the VLE does not 'live' on campus, but rather in 'the cloud' and is accessible via a web interface. This model can be more cost-effective and also offer the peace of mind of knowing there is someone to call if anything goes wrong – although the terms 'hosted', 'cloud-based' and 'Software-as-a-Service' are quite often used interchangeably, they differ in the range of applications that can be supported by these models, the degree of built-in redundancy ensuring fast access for users, as well as the influence of their architecture on the end-user cost.[5]

Locally-hosted or cloud-based?

Another approach, which is proving increasingly attractive to educational institutions worldwide, is the use of existing free cloud-based tools to initiate and manage the online aspect of their blended learning activities. However, it is important to note that educators must not assume: that everything that is free has been built with the end users' best intentions in mind; that it adheres to the principles of the free and open-source community; that it will be around forever; and that it will be considerate towards protecting personal data (more details in Chapter 8).

The Google tools – Gmail, Calendar, Drive, Docs, Sheets, Slides, Sites, as well as the numerous additional free or paid-for apps in the Google Apps for Education repository – are an example of how such free tools can be combined into an interactive, collaborative, up-to-date and visually engaging online experience.

All these tools and approaches have their advantages and disadvantages, and at the time of writing it is mainly issues of data protection and data security which are preventing educational institutions from migrating en masse towards free cloud-based tools. Is online education therefore 'stuck' with traditional VLEs, even in their cloud hosted incarnation? From a certain point of view, yes, but one should not be too pessimistic about this, as there are plenty of effective learning activities which can be supported by the VLE, as our examples will illustrate.

VLEs AS CONTENT REPOSITORIES

One of the most basic applications of VLEs – which is also the one that seems to be generally responsible for their unfavourable reception – is acting as content repositories. Tutors can easily create content folders and subfolders for their students, and make available within them a wide range of resources in almost any file format imaginable.

Depending on the structure of the VLE, these resource files can be stored in shared, central areas rather than in individual modules, thus being available at the same time to several courses/modules/organisations (depending on what the VLE-specific terminology may be). This has obvious benefits, from content sharing to preventing duplication and keeping the total file size of resources in check.

Built-in multimedia tools

As with all respectable content repositories out there, VLEs have the capacity to host video and audio files. Not only that, but some VLEs also enable users to create content using dedicated VLE plug-ins – although admittedly this is mainly audio content so far.

For instance, tutors can ask their students to contribute audio responses to online discussions. This is particularly helpful in the case of language teaching, but it also has merit from the point of view of offering a viable alternative for contribution and interaction to participants with motor impairments.

Depending on the specific VLE and its respective plug-ins, teachers and students can do more than just leave each other voice messages. They can also vocally annotate resources such as external websites, and then have a full conversation with both voice and text messages about that particular resource.

A practical example of such a use of VLE tools comes from the University of Leeds' Department of Russian and Slavonic Studies, where the Wimba Voice Presentation tool was used extensively to introduce a website with Russian TV news clips and their corresponding transcripts to students. These students would then practise delivering the same content using the transcripts available on the external webpage with a speed and intonation similar to the original resource.

Integration with external services

In addition to built-in multimedia functionalities, the large majority of VLEs also integrate with popular multimedia hosting websites such as YouTube and Vimeo for video, Flickr for images, and SlideShare for presentations.

Such integrations enable educators and students to reuse valuable resources available on those global websites much more easily than before – provided, of course, that copyright restrictions allow it. In practical terms, having such integrations available means that the user no longer needs to find the embeddable code for the particular resource, and then wrestle with the VLE to convince it to accept that code; all that is needed now is just the web link to an individual resource, customised playlist, or relevant resource channel.

Dynamic content through RSS feeds

We mentioned content channels briefly in the previous section, but it is certainly worth investigating them closely because they constitute a very easy way of keeping VLE content up-to-date automatically.

The technology behind making this dynamic content appear in the VLE automatically is called RSS – which originally stood for 'really simple syndication', and now is developing new meanings. The advantage of using such a technology is that users can subscribe to an RSS feed in their preferred news reader, and there are a whole host of options out there: starting with the less exciting, but still adequate Microsoft Outlook; to fashionable mobile and tablet apps such as Flipboard which turn your newsfeeds into very attractive digital magazines; and ending with a variety of podcast applications which are suitable for audio and video content published via RSS. As we have already mentioned in Chapter 6, RSS is the dynamic content technology which can turn a collection of separate audio or video files into a podcast or vodcast in the strict sense of the terms.

Once subscribed to such a dynamic content feed, the user no longer needs to visit the website he/she is interested in, in order to check for updates. Instead, these updates will be automatically pushed to the user in a manner similar to email. When a user opens their newsreader appli cation or service, the new content – be it text, audio files, audio and images, or videos – is automatically displayed.

For instance, http://www.nmc.org/rss.xml is the news feed address for the New Media Consortium (NMC), who are behind the very useful Horizon Reports we have already mentioned at the end of Chapter 4. NMC look at relevant emerging learning technologies, and we would therefore strongly encourage all readers to visit this resource.

While the in-browser layout of the content available at the above-mentioned address may intimidate some users, the good news is that this address is to be pasted into your favourite news reader or aggregator rather than be viewed online 'as is'. The presentation will improve radi-cally as a result. Experiment using the same address in your VLE RSS feeds tool in order to see how the content appears there.

 PAUSE FOR THOUGHT

Would there be a use in your discipline for automatic news items or podcast episodes being refreshed automatically via RSS?

VLEs AS LEARNING MANAGEMENT AND TRACKING SYSTEMS

Tracking the statistics, and 'policing' the usage of learning resources like the VLE, is often viewed as counter to the larger and fuller meaning of education. However, there are situations in which it is very useful to have automated tools capable of doing all the monitoring and collating of usage data for educators.

For instance, although many will consider counting the number of times individual students access a particular resource as tantamount to a Big Brother attitude, certain educators use these functionalities in order to anticipate knowledge gaps or misunderstandings.

Two relevant questions, which can be triggered by a quick analysis of how often students access the VLE content, are:

1   Is a particular resource accessed more because it is very engaging and effective, or is it because it is poorly put together and difficult to understand in one go?
2   Is that particular resource used to support learning in other areas of the module that are perhaps less explicit or poorly understood?

The answers are important in order to determine the effectiveness of the current VLE content, and to plan for future resource development.

In other scenarios, the VLE tracking tools are considered to be extremely useful, and can even contribute to the building of an online community through providing the instant feedback that is occasionally necessary in such an environment. For example, being able to see straight away how many times a particular blog post has been viewed, how many comments have been made, how much activity there was on any given day, or how many subscribers there are to a particular discussion board does have a motivating effect on participants. Sound collaborative learning principles are therefore supported and enhanced by statistics tracking.

Also valuable is the option to have automatic alerts sent when the performance of students falls below a certain threshold. This is particularly the case when modules are team-taught, or when teachers are acting as personal tutors and need to know as soon as possible if a student starts to fall behind.

Not only is collaborative learning supported by VLEs, but group-based tasks are also easy to set up and manage using this technology. Entire content and interaction areas can be made visible just to particular groups of students, while tutors can view the work that all the groups are doing.

In addition, VLEs do away with the need for tutors to use spreadsheets to track the grades of their students and work out a final grade. The large majority of VLEs have a dedicated area – called, for instance, the Grade

Centre in Blackboard – where tutors can specify the extent to which different activities contribute to the final grade. It is also worth noting that these activities are not restricted to exams and quizzes only, but can also include marks given for contributions to blogs, wikis or discussion boards.

Speaking of grades, when it comes to marking essays, many tutors have to deal with issues related to plagiarism and it is useful that external text matching and plagiarism detection tools, such as Turnitin, integrate readily with VLEs.

 CASE EXAMPLE

Video-enhanced feedback through the VLE for language learning

Bettina Hermoso Gómez, Spanish, Portuguese and Latin American Studies, University of Leeds

First-year students on Spanish or Latin American courses have a compulsory module that builds on their Spanish A-level language skills. The objective of the project was to provide these students with quick meaningful feedback on a written assessment – a written portfolio of activities – within 24 hours of submission. On average the module has 180 students that receive their written formative feedback two weeks after submission. In the past, students' performance was disappointing and they had complained that, quite often, they could not remember clearly what they were trying to express when they wrote the assessment. Furthermore, they felt that the written feedback did not give them a clear idea of what was expected of them.

As soon as the assignment is submitted via Turnitin, the module coordinator would examine a significant proportion of scripts and identify the most common mistakes throughout the cohort. Individual written feedback is provided via Grademark, Turnitin's own marking programme. Using a web-based screen capture programme (Screenr), a five-minute video was produced per submission. The video showed the correction of the mistakes previously identified, accompanied by a voice-over providing more detailed feedback. The video link would then be made available via the university's VLE, only visible to those students enrolled on the module.

161

The project was very well received by students. They felt that they were receiving individual feedback straight after their submission, and paid attention to both the written and audio feedback provided. While aware that they would receive further individual feedback at a later stage, they welcomed the opportunity to identify mistakes they had committed within a day of submission, and act upon them in their next submission. In some cases learners approached their individual tutor to apologise for mistakes they had made in the assignment, and hoped the tutor would not think badly of them when the assignment was marked, demonstrating that students have taken advantage of the process.

Following the project's success, other language-related modules have adopted the methodology used in these assignments and adapted it to their own needs. In subsequent academic years the recording can be reused as preparation material for the next set of assignments to help students identify common errors.

VLEs AS INTERACTIVE PLATFORMS

In addition to their functionalities as content repositories, VLEs also feature a useful range of collaborative tools that allow teachers and students to interact, create knowledge and share experiences.

The blog, wiki and discussion-board tools are three of the most popular technologies used by teachers to engage with their students outside contact hours. They provide safe and accessible spaces for participants to reflect on their learning experiences, complete tasks and engage in two-way feedback.

Apart from the three types of collaborative interactive tools mentioned so far, VLEs also have functionalities enabling students to interact with pre-defined content. One such example is the possibility for educators to set up online quizzes, tests or surveys for their students. While these tools can be used for data gathering, they also have significant potential to enhance the learning experience: quizzes and tests, for instance, can be created with extensive relevant feedback, which transforms them from automated grading tools to progress-checking and learning-through-feedback mechanisms.

PERSONALISED LEARNING EXPERIENCES

Perhaps one of the more exciting applications of VLEs is the possibility of creating individual learning paths for students, based on their performance at key stages during a course. Thanks to the ability to track students' grades for various activities, such as exams, tests and quizzes, as well as for their involvement in more collaborative tasks, appropriate resources can be made visible automatically to students in order to support their progress.

There are two reasons why VLEs are used as sizeable repositories rather than agile and stimulating learning environments: (1) first of all, there are some teachers who use the VLEs to provide all the available supporting resources to all the students, regardless of their individual level; (2) secondly, there is also the misconception that you cannot address individual needs through an environment such as a VLE. In fact, by using simple built-in tools, teachers can easily display or hide information as needed from students, depending on the progress they are making through the course.

Collaborative activities

 CASE EXAMPLE

Virtual rehearsal space: using online resources in collaborative devised theatre processes

Scott Palmer and David Shearing, School of Performance and Cultural Industries, University of Leeds

Problem: what are the best ways to document, share and extend the evolving creative process in a devised theatre ensemble?

Around 80 undergraduate students in the School of Performance and Cultural Industries at the University of Leeds choose to create a large-scale public performance as a significant aspect of their final-year studies. The task involves the synthesis of practice and research to create a devised collaborative performance for a public audience. Students often create work that is not initiated by a previously published written playscript, and begin with fragmented starting points. A signifi-cant amount of the students' study and rehearsal time is spent in small groups exploring the potential of material, and this needs to be docu-mented to create a shared resource for further creative development and for reflective analysis, both during and after the process.

163

Solution: the use of a wiki or group blog creates a virtual rehearsal space which can be accessed during rehearsals if necessary, and also becomes an important resource for students and staff outside of the rehearsal room, as ideas develop between taught sessions.

The University of Leeds' Blackboard VLE provides a secure area in which material such as images, video clips, script excerpts, minutes of production and planning meetings, as well as devised scenes and evolving ideas can be shared online. The deposited materials are then open for discussion as part of an ongoing reflective process.

The Dream/Play group were adapting Strindberg's 'unstageable play' to create an immersive playful experience for their audience.

The Into the Dark group used the blog to assist in developing key ideas and to establish a common group focus through the development of a group manifesto.

Evaluation/feedback: this has proved to be a useful tool in deepening students' understanding of the content, key concepts and response to stimulus material, often by providing new insights which stimulate responses from other members of the group. The process of reflecting on performance material in this way can aid in the understanding, value and impact of potential performance moments. As McKinney and Iball observe, '[p]ost-hoc reflection on the shared experience helps explicate tacit understanding and feeds back into further iterations of the practice, contributing to developing insights about knowledge which is embodied' (McKinney and Iball, 2011: 123).

Reflective tools such as blogs can be used to reflect on the impulsive material generated during taught sessions.

Students are able to share clips from relevant sources such as performance companies working in similar ways, and to link to and discuss relevant academic articles. Tutors are able to comment, provoke and support online discussions between taught sessions.

Students can archive key moments and ideas in the process. In a recent project, the posting of a group manifesto was vital in focusing the groups' key artistic intentions. Material shared in this way, through the process, becomes an invaluable resource for later reflection on how ideas developed. Students use this evidence to assist in a post-performance essay task. Tutors can also monitor individual students' online activity within the larger group, and observing the frequency alongside the level of their contributions to the creative group endeavour also informs the assessment process.

The use of a blog in the creation of performance is 'messy', mirroring physical anxieties and fragmented processes. In this way the blog and wiki tools can be seen as an extension of the more traditional creative process that takes place in the rehearsal studio, while in addition opening up shared space for considered, ongoing reflection.

CONCLUDING REMARKS

Whether they are free and open source, or commercial products, VLEs have numerous sound applications for learning and teaching. Their capabilities to track and manage the administrative side of the learning experience are extremely useful, and their file-storage capacities beneficial, too.

Unfortunately, many teachers tend to stop at this content repository and file-storage application. They believe that there is not much more that could be done with an online learning management platform. As we have seen through the case examples, this is false. VLEs can become dynamic environments where students can follow personalised learning paths, can take part in collaborative learning activities, and can express their creativity. Additionally, teachers can keep an eye on all this activity and can be automatically alerted if intervention is needed. Student activity can also be captured and evidenced, which may be important for both formative and summative assessment.

As with most other learning technologies, though, for students to engage seriously with the tools, there must be a solid and transparent pedagogic reason to use them, and teachers must endorse the technology by engaging with it almost as often as the students. The alternative, which we have seen only too often, is to create a number of VLE interactive spaces and expect students to be self-sufficient, as well as constantly motivated to interact effectively with these spaces. We have not seen this approach work so far, and it is reasonable – due to the flaws in the instructional design approach – to expect it never will.

NOTES

1 http://goo.gl/Xe5ch
2 http://goo.gl/Tkv2y – page date: 16 August 2011
3 http://goo.gl/WZ07u – page date: 1 August 2012
4 http://goo.gl/PRtLu
5 http://goo.gl/nFQt7

Chapter 8

Open source

Throughout this book you will have seen many examples of using technology effectively in one's learning and teaching. However, quite a few of the solutions presented involved using proprietary – also known as *commercial* – software and hardware; both of which will have a financial impact on your institution, and will come with different licensing terms. But is there another way? Is it possible to deliver an inspirational experience to your students without having to break the bank?

The phrase *free and open source* has become extremely popular in education circles. However, few people realise the historic inaccuracy of this phrase, as well as the ethical, philosophical and social aspects behind the free software movement.

A LITTLE BIT OF BACKGROUND

There is a saying that enjoys a certain amount of popularity in business circles: 'there is no such thing as a free lunch'. In the education sector, that certainly used to be the case. Ever since 1986, and the beginnings of the free software movement, one needed to have a significant background as a programmer in order to be able to run the free software available, as it often lacked a graphical user interface (GUI), making it difficult for most teachers to use.

Related to the development of the free software initiative, two philosophies evolved in parallel.[1] On the one hand, the *free software movement* was driven by the view that access to technology is a human right and should be provided to everyone for free; on the other hand, the *open source* movement started to emerge and gain popularity. This was less ideologically motivated, but was still interested in the collective creative power of the community. At the risk of popularising this hybrid concept, we will keep using the phrase *free and open source* throughout this chapter. We simply ask the reader to be mindful of the distinction.

One simple way of demarcating these labels is via the type of license under which both software and content are released. The GNU General Public License (GPL) is the most widely used license for *free* software. This license allows users to study and modify free software, as long as any modifications to the software are re-released together with the source code under the same GPL license. This means that there are no restrictions on further modifications and re-releases. For a much more in-depth discussion of the history and implications of the free software initiative, see Deek and McHugh (2008).

IMPLICATIONS FOR TEACHERS

Apart from the obvious philosophical and ethical aspects, most institutions and individuals will find the financial connotations of *free* extremely appealing. However, again you need to be aware that not everyone is using the term to mean the same thing. More often than not, you can end up handing over valuable personal information to commercial organisations without even realising it. In addition, the teacher's ignorance can lead to students also handing over personal data.

Services such as Twitter, Google Apps for Education, and most other social media services are free (at least at the time of writing), but only in as far as there is no payment on the part of the common user. In return for making it easy, and sometimes even fun, for users to collaborate and satisfy some of their communication and sharing needs, such companies keep gathering information about people's preferences and profiles, with a view to selling these to online advertisers and marketers. Of course, some people are happy to hand over such information, and do not care about their digital footprint. Others, on the other hand, are quite shocked to discover the truth. It is vital then that these issues are recognised and discussed among students, teachers and others in HE.

In addition to data protection considerations, teachers need to be very careful about which so-called *free* applications and services they are using, for the very practical reason that the publishing company can simply turn them off. For example, the popular free social bookmarking platform Delicious was very nearly closed down following Yahoo's change of priorities; more recently it was announced that the popular RSS reader Google Reader was withdrawn.

Lastly, not everyone in the world speaks only English, and once you start browsing for free and open source software you will soon discover that much of this software has been translated and localised into many other languages. This makes acquiring satisfactory levels of computer literacy a much more achievable goal in those parts of the world where English is not spoken, and of course ties into the deeper philosophical, political and ideological issues hinted at above.

PRACTICAL APPLICATIONS OF FREE AND OPEN SOURCE SOFTWARE

Teachers and students can do pretty much everything with free and open source software. So far in this book we have seen several applications of using technology in the classroom. Let's see whether we could achieve the same results using free software.

Running computer clusters or lecture room computers

Let's start with the operating system: most readers will be accustomed to switching on their desktops or laptops and using a commercial system, like Windows or Mac OS, to access their favourite applications and files. They will also, unfortunately, be familiar with security scares, viruses, slow processing and system crashes – although admittedly fewer on the Mac OS.

However, for quite some time there has been another way, and that is to use the GNU/Linux distribution, as governments, banks, animation and film studios, and even Google know. Thanks to the hard work of the free software community, GNU/Linux (also commonly known as simply Linux) has come a long way, with the ability to support fast processing and networking through command-line operations or a user-friendly GUI. In fact, 91 per cent of the top 500 supercomputers in the world where running GNU/Linux in June, 2010.[2]

Not only has GNU/Linux been powering the world's fastest computers recently, but it has also made its way into the classroom.[3]

Intrigued? You can also give GNU/Linux a try straight away by downloading and running your choice of several free GNU/Linux distributions.[4] In fact, you can have desktops or laptops which run two, or all three available options out there if you want to draw comparisons between them: GNU/Linux, Windows and Mac OS.[5]

You may argue that it's all well and good to have a free operating system, but what can you do with it in an education sector historically dominated by packages such as Microsoft Office or Apple iWork? The answer is, an awful lot with the free OpenOffice suite which, at the time of writing, had been downloaded and installed over 67 million times.[6]

OpenOffice will allow you to complete word processing, presentation and number-crunching tasks just as easily as its competitors would. As a matter of fact, OpenOffice had the functionality to save documents as PDFs long before any of the commercial packages did.

 PAUSE FOR THOUGHT

If you or your colleagues have never used such free packages, think why not? What are the worries and risks that people might associate with using such packages? How much do you think your institution could benefit from such software?

Setting up websites

The Apache HTTP server project has resulted in possibly the most successful, powerful and reliable web server software known to date. At a basic level, you can create webpages and make them available to the world on such a server. It is fashionable to talk about accessible webpages, but it is less clear to educators how to easily create them. Apache HTTP makes this a genuine possibility.

However, not everyone is keen on building websites from the ground up. If that is the case, you could use popular blogging platforms such as WordPress, as well as popular content management systems such as Joomla, which are easy to install and are extremely powerful and capable of supporting your students' activities. In particular, they can allow them to create content in user-friendly WYSIWYG ('what you see is what you get') interfaces.

Running your own VLEs

If you want more control over your students' progress, then you may want to install and configure a free VLE such as Moodle. Moodle is nowadays the choice VLE for numerous universities, colleges, schools, national bodies, and public and private institutions throughout the world, some supporting over 30,000 users such as the Open University in the UK, the Austrian Federal Ministry of Education, Universidade de Brasilia, University of Rome La Sapienza, and more[7] – see Chapter 7 for more information on the practical advantages of using VLEs.

Educational software

The Free Software Directory has a truly impressive list covering lots of domains, ranging from mathematics to geography, and from chemistry to art.[8] It is definitely worth consulting, because there is a strong possibility that you will find software relevant to your teaching practice.

Given the applications of technology already mentioned in this book, we thought it would be useful to list several that are relevant here:

- It is possible to record lectures using *free* software such as Opencast Matterhorn.[9] Not only is the software capable of doing most of the things that other proprietary lecture capture systems can do, but there are also funded initiatives to create accessible repositories of lectures, such as the Translectures[10] project led by Universitat Politècnica de València, and looking at the automatic transcription and translation of lectures.
- It is also possible to use the *free* software Audacity[11] on all three platforms (GNU/Linux, Windows and Mac OS) to record, edit and publish audio files. Audacity will allow you to record audio feedback for your students, as well as edit and refine the audio of your lecture or perhaps of an invited speaker's presentation.
- For those keen to edit images and videos, *free* software such as Gimp and LiVES may lack some of the advanced features of more popular Adobe or Apple products, but will enable most users to achieve their goals. It is important to reiterate at this stage that, thanks to its underlying philosophy, *free* software can generate a variety of file formats. You will therefore not be in a situation of creating a learning resource in one application, only to find out that users can access that resource on one device alone.
- One of the most exciting developments in this area in recent years has been the Xerte[12] project initiated by the University of Nottingham in the UK. Xerte is a suite of tools that allows teachers to create learning resources which combine images, videos, interactive questions, news feeds and YouTube channels, all in an accessible wrapper which users can adapt to their own access needs.

In terms of convenience, few other software tick as many boxes: Xerte can be installed and run either from a memory stick, or from a web server which can be present on the user's own machine, or on the institution's web space. Furthermore, in Xerte teachers and/or students can work collaboratively to create accessible and engaging content.

 PAUSE FOR THOUGHT

What kind of software and services have you been using? Are your applications *freeware* such as Skype or Adobe Reader; *shareware* (demo or limited versions of more complete software packages) such as ActivePresenter; or *free and open source* tools such as CamStudio for screencasting, BigBlueButton for online conferencing, or Audacity for audio editing?

FREE CONTENT

OERs

We hope that in the first part of this chapter we have established the fact that you can realistically expect to be able to run your normal activities involving ICT using exclusively *free* software. It gets even better: depending on the strength of your subject-specific global teaching community, you may find that there is relevant and high-quality free content which you could adapt and reuse in your teaching.

However, do watch out how you go about sourcing resources. We all know someone who thinks that just because some content can be found on the Internet, it can automatically be used in one's teaching. In fact, you could not be further from the truth and, in extreme cases, such an attitude can lead to hefty lawsuits for copyright infringement. This is why it is vital to check the license under which the content you require has been released.

Remember that we mentioned the GPL license, together with its variations, when we spoke about free software. A similar initiative exists in the area of content: Creative Commons.[13] Its most permissive license allows modification of the content, as long as the resulting resources are also shared under the same license. It also allows commercial uses of the work, and is not restricted to any individual country's legal jurisdiction. However, just as in the case of the GPL license, there can be variations of the Creative Commons requirements under which content is released, and you are strongly encouraged to visit the Creative Commons website (http://creativecommons.org/) and decide which type of license applies best to the resources which you want to use or share.

In order to find content that allows reuse, and maybe even modification, you have several tools at your disposal. First of all, if you are looking for images, sounds, videos or RSS feeds, you should become familiar with a web-based search tool called Xpert[14] created at the University of Nottingham in the UK. Xpert looks for media assets that match your key words and that have been released under a Creative Commons license. Not only that, but Xpert automatically embeds the correct attribution together with the resource so that you do not run the risk of breaking copyright.

Secondly, you can search for Open Educational Resources (OERs) repositories, where you can browse by keyword, subject, study level, etc., depending on the complexity of the repository in question. In the UK, Jorum[15] is one of the biggest repositories, but it is not uncommon for individual institutions to set up their own OER repository in addition to listing their resources in more mainstream ones. Although finding suitable OERs can be a time-consuming activity, the result of the search can often mean time saved developing your own resources, and possibly a chance to start collaborating with the OER author.

Thirdly, and most simply, you can use the advance filter search on 'Google' to locate things labelled with the Creative Commons license.

In the true *free* software and content spirit, you should adapt the OERs that you find, and re-release these versions to the community, thus contributing to the advancement of knowledge and expertise in your field.

MOOCs

With all their advantages, OERs have been occasionally criticised for being static, as not many teachers have released multimedia interactive resources. One of their biggest criticisms, alongside the lack of multimedia, was also their lack of interaction. This meant that when MOOCs ('massive open online courses') appeared, lots of teachers rushed to hail a revolution in education. However, apart from democratizing education even more (this had already been going on with iTunes U and YouTube EDU among others), the main attraction of MOOCs is their closer resemblance to traditional courses.

Despite all the studying and interaction being carried out online,

MOOCs also feature collaborative tasks in which participants use technologies we have already mentioned (such as online conferencing platforms) to build a sense of community and share expertise. Not only that, but the teachers making these MOOCs available are also involved in running regular tutorials and giving feedback.

It has recently become a race among universities to be involved in delivering MOOCs, and at the time of writing Coursera[16] is one of the most popular MOOC platforms. Just like OERs, as well as the contributions to iTunes U and YouTube EDU, releasing open educational resources of varying degrees of interactivity serves a double purpose: on the one hand it may address a philosophical belief of the individual university or teacher in open and free education for all; on the other hand, if done well, it enhances the image of the institution significantly – so much so that numerous commercial companies have mushroomed recently to 'help' universities have more visibility on the MOOC scene.

That said, teachers should be aware before embarking on a MOOC development that it is far from being a time-saving exercise. It does require excellent instructional design; the resources need to be different in terms of length, content and interaction due to the full online nature of MOOCs; the teacher still needs to be involved throughout the course; and teachers should not be disappointed if many people enrolled simply fail to complete the course – degrees of motivation vary, circumstances change, and the consequences of failure are in most cases very low.

 CASE EXAMPLE

Free and open source use in HE

We have approached Terry McAndrew, Advisor at the UK JISC TechDis, for his views on using free and open source software and content in HE. Terry proved a strong advocate of this approach.

> Once, the only way to access affordable high-quality software and computing facilities was through the institution's provision, often in large computing clusters where students could be taught together. Licences were expensive and managed for the community, but the result was a consistent approach and community practice – good for teaching and use. However, this model has become somewhat outdated due to the rise in affordable computing devices and free

173

and open source (FOSS) alternatives – students have access to a far greater diversity of applications, and may become restricted by institutional provision alone: universities need to learn how to incorporate FOSS to enhance their teaching.

FOSS is essentially free to use, not free of cost (but is often cheaper). It can provide alternatives to common 'Office' applications for staff and students for writing documents, presentations, data analysis etc., without having to compromise on functionality. Investigate OpenOffice and LibreOffice, and you will find they have all the key features of the major commercial applications. The open source nature allows developers to freely contribute to enhancements for the products. Witness the gains: the Firefox web browser, Android mobile device operating system, WordPress blogs, etc. These have become established by complementing commerce – they sell more technologies cheaper.

FOSS enables the curriculum to be more usable and accessible. For example, students can listen to documents with free text-to-speech; useful for all students for revision, but also for dyslexics and other print-impaired users. Text can be processed to portable MP3 alternatives through free online services like Robobraille, or on the computer with Dspeech and Balbolka. Staff and students can prepare dynamic alternatives to boring PowerPoint presentations by using Xerte Online Toolkits (XOT) to create reusable e-learning and building resources for the discipline. They can do this anywhere (even from a memory stick of portable software to use on university IT) because learning is far more flexible and inclusive with FOSS.

With the development of FOSS, it is clear the genie has left the bottle – it is pointless to try and control it, so why not make a wish instead, and discover a FOSS solution to integrate into the student experience and bring greater freedom for your learning and teaching?[17]

CONCLUDING REMARKS

In this chapter we have shown that *free* software is nowadays a valid alternative to commercial applications. At the same time, we also hope to have highlighted a number of potential issues, and in particular motivated you to check the licensing details of the services and software you have been using. In addition, we hope to have prompted you to investigate the available exit strategies to port your data to other environments.

We have discussed OERs and MOOCs from a more complex perspective than they are often presented, and highlighted both the advantages and hidden limitations of these resources. In general, we hope to have increased your understanding and set you thinking about how you might employ 'open source' in your teaching.

NOTES

1 http://goo.gl/7C1UW
2 http://goo.gl/TqLQr
3 http://goo.gl/sFgFp
4 http://goo.gl/acl9U
5 While you are at it, and if you have an Apple desktop or laptop with Bootcamp (a free and open source application) or Parallels (a commercial one) installed, you can experiment with Mac OS, Windows, Linux and even Google Chrome OS (Chromium). At the time of writing, Chromium was easiest to install via Parallels.
6 http://www.openoffice.org/stats/downloads.html
7 http://goo.gl/YTy6q
8 http://goo.gl/LyN0m
9 http://opencast.org/matterhorn/
10 http://goo.gl/Jz9aq
11 http://audacity.sourceforge.net/download/
12 http://www.nottingham.ac.uk/xerte/
13 http://creativecommons.org/
14 http://www.nottingham.ac.uk/xpert/
15 http://www.jorum.ac.uk/
16 https://www.coursera.org/
17 OSSWatch: http://www.oss-watch.ac.uk/

Chapter 9

Immersive 3D online environments

What's the appeal [of using virtual worlds]? . . . Well, when it comes to our current existence, video games are even better than the real thing. We're talking digital salvation here, digital transcendence. As Jane McGonigal, game designer and futurist, puts it 'Where in the real world is that gamer sense of being alive, focused and engaged in every moment?'[1]

University is an immersive environment in which the students have probably moved away from home and started to define their identity through the educational choices they make, their interactions and their relationships. However, in our ever-developing HE world there are now many different types of immersion. Due to the increase in broadband Internet access, the rapid growth in computing power and the ever-growing availability of computers, immersive worlds with no physical boundaries and no geographical location have developed. These environments exist online in an entirely virtual space.

In principle, such virtual worlds can be used by anybody with Internet access. Students can immerse themselves in an almost unlimited number of different environments, such as First World War trenches, birthing pools, rainforests, Shakespearean theatres, underwater kingdoms and Mars space stations.

A user can become completely immersed through a few clicks of the mouse. In fact, 'you' can have a unique and distinct online presence completely unlike your real world identity: users can vary their characteristics, looks, fashion sense, size, gender, religion and even species. These different online presences are called avatars, and it is these that inhabit the virtual worlds.

FIGURE 9.1 Picture of an avatar at the University of Nottingham site

As in the real world, these virtual worlds persist and change whether a particular avatar is present or not. Some virtual worlds, such as World of Warcraft, NeverWinter Nights, Star Wars Galaxy and Happy Farm are *goal-directed*, and have set narratives, tasks and puzzles as part of the online environment. In such cases, individuals construct an avatar against the backdrop of these tasks, puzzles and narratives, working out their place within them.

Furthermore, communities, groups and clubs evolve and have specific and exhaustive goals set by the rules of those particular virtual environments. For example, a group may form to storm an enemy's trench, or an avatar may be created with the express function of acquiring the skillset to fly the Millennium Falcon. Furthermore, because the tasks in these virtual immersive environments are often finite – for example, once you've secured the airport, it is secured; or once you have destroyed the Elven lord, he is dead – the identity and value of the avatar is finite and will consequently have a natural 'shelf-life'. These types of online worlds are called 'massive multi-player online games' (MMPOGs), where the key emphasis is on 'games'.

They are immensely popular, and given the growth and ease of web access through various means – in particular games consoles – their popularity can only grow. This chapter will not be concerned with this type of environment, although they have been used by educators[2] and we talk about 'gamification' in HE further in Chapter 10.

However, there is another category of online immersive environment called the 'online multi-user world' (OMUW). Crucially, such worlds have no overarching narrative, story, task or puzzle. To put it in an overly negative way, there simply is no intrinsic point to such an environment; rather the 'point' is imported by the users, educators, facilitators and the hosts of discrete areas of the environment.

For example, part of such an environment might require reflection on types of music, and the user is asked to answer questions in a quiz; or a facilitator in a group may ask users to reflect on and respond to issues concerning disability – we talk about technology and interactive quizzes/ assessment in Chapter 5. Alternatively, a group of people may create an area with the sole aim of discussing and collating evidence of unsolved murders.

The key point is that in these types of worlds, once you remove the users and the various aims and desires they bring, the world – although it would continue to exist – does not have any point in itself. This is the main contrast with MMPOGs, where there is a virtual story, characters, rules and predetermined pathways waiting for players to engage with them.

It follows that when constructing an avatar to inhabit this non-game type of environment it does not need to be really good at a particular skill – for example, to enable it to reach different levels. There is then freedom to be who you want, and do what you want, when you want. Furthermore, in these types of environment it is usually the case that the users are able to change and manipulate the environment they inhabit rather than simply responding to it. With just basic computer knowledge, users can construct, move and alter things in the shared environment.

We start with this because not recognising the distinction between MMPOGs and OMUWs is one of the stumbling blocks to using OMUWs in education. This is because first-time users will be inclined to ask 'what's the point?' without recognising that, strictly speaking, there is no point. From now on when we talk of 'virtual worlds' we will simply be referring to OMUWs.

There are a large number of these types of virtual worlds, and given the increased move to allow the nuts and bolts of computer programmes to be freely available (with source code becoming open source, see Chapter 8) and growing computer power, together with the falling costs of mobile computing devices, these worlds will continue to grow in size and in number. Some examples of OMPW include: Active Worlds; Croquet Consortium; Project Wonderland; There; Olive and Twinity. However, by far the most popular, and the one which will concern us, is called Second Life.

SECOND LIFE – THE BASICS[3]

Although originally conceived in 1991, Second Life (SL) only went live in 2003. It now has over 100 university campuses, and in 2010 had over 23 million registered users. SL is by far the most popular OMUW for educators, and there are a number of reasons for this:

- The basic elements, such as downloading the SL software, registering, orientation and a basic avatar appearance, are all free.[4]
- SL is the most widely adopted virtual world by educators, with universities such as Harvard, MIT, Nottingham, New York State and Oxford choosing to have campuses there.

- There is a plethora of resources: a dedicated SL education website with a large databank of FAQs, a support community and email lists to join.
- If you wish to teach something where real-life profit and loss are possible – economics or marketing for example – then SL has a working economy which allows conversion of Linden Dollars (the SL currency) into any currency you want.
- It is relatively simple to adapt and build in SL. This means that students can be asked to do creative tasks, compare work from different environments and create their own learning spaces.
- There are a lot of research articles written *about* SL, enabling students to research issues such as the different social norms, gender identity and privacy, *generated by* SL (e.g. Schechtman, 2012; Boon and Sinclair, 2009).
- There are a large number of case studies and papers outlining many different educational projects in SL, so a teacher need not 'go in blind' to a project (see the Case Example below).

 CASE EXAMPLE[5]

Providing geographically dispersed students and faculty a place to meet and learn together: the open university in second life

Executive summary

The Open University campus in Second Life offers something completely new and invigorating for this varied and widely dispersed student body – a chance to meet, work and live together in a virtual community.

How it began: delivering immersive distance learning without driving the distance

For decades, OU staff have been at the forefront of innovation in distance and e-learning. It was the visionary instructor Jacquie Bennett at OU who first discovered a new dimension for education – Second Life. Two years later the first OU island was unveiled.

Teaching fellow with the Centre for Open Learning in Maths, Science, Computing and Technology, Anna Peachey, said her friend and colleague believed the discovery was an important emerging technology with enormous potential to impact traditional education. 'Jacquie kept telling me I should go and look at Second Life, so eventually, in October '06, I did. I had an epiphany moment as soon as I logged in. Safe to say that I incorporated Second Life into my teaching from that point forward.'

Before she taught in Second Life, Peachey, who lives in rural Devon, would drive up to one and a half hours each way to spend a Saturday morning in a physical classroom. Of 18 students, three or four might show up. In Second Life, Peachey now reaches nearly triple the student attendance, at ten and 15 students per session, and can forgo the commute.

Thoughtful planning to ease students into the virtual world

Dr Shailey Minocha, Senior Lecturer of Human–Computer Interaction at the OU, has been conducting extensive interviews in Second Life. She has discovered that a gradual transition from familiar to fantastical is the path to building spaces that put students at ease initially.

New visitors to the OU campus are greeted at The NOUbie Center (an OU take on 'newbie', or a person new to Second Life). Student volunteers help 'NOUbie' students learn how to function within Second Life and familiarise themselves with the six OU environments. Open Life, Open Life Ocean, Open Life Village, FIT Island and Deep Think I and II.

Peachey explained, 'Students volunteer to be buddies, and there is usually at least one student buddy in-world, so if you show up at the newbie building needing help, you just click on an active picture and it sends an IM and the buddy comes over.'

Minocha leads student tours of spaces beyond the OU campus, such as the Virtual Hallucinations Island, where psychology students can experience first hand the phenomena of mental illness or disorders as described by patients.

'If island themes match with what you are teaching', Minocha said, 'then they are a useful instrument for getting over skepticism and triggering creativity'.

The open life village: virtual student residences to foster social interactions

The OU's virtual campus programme has caught on with such zeal that Peachey constructed Open Life Village, which officially opened in April 2009, to accommodate demand for student housing. 'I noticed that when people come in-world they often feel the need to have a home, a house or an apartment. So I decided to offer "halls of residence" that students could rent for free for a short period when they first start in SL'. This quickly became the focus for a community who wanted longer-term rentals, and the new island was built to accommodate this. Sixty spots were quickly leased, and there is a waitlist of students lobbying for more.

The students have not only adopted Second Life as their classroom and their home, but also their venue for student-planned events. In fact, there are now over 200 OU events and conferences held in Second Life each year.

Of course, education is not just about classrooms or lecture halls. It's about establishing friendships and future professional networks, and those relationships flourish best in a social setting. For OU students, many of whom are physically disabled, are care-takers or work full-time, the ability to participate in a social community of peers from the comfort of home is invigorating. The village green, the 'Open Arms' English pub, personal residences and beach area have become vibrant hubs of activity and persistent places for students to just 'hang out'.

Even teachers can learn in second life

After seeing the success of student interaction in Second Life, the OU's Human Resources Department realised that it could also be used for staff training. Steph Broadribb, OU assistant director of HR Development, works with HR project officer Chris Carter on a programme aimed at developing staff skills necessary to effectively give and receive feedback.

'One of the major impacts has been the ability to get groups of staff practicing role-play skills in a confident manner', Broadribb said. 'This had been a problem for us in real life as many staff would disengage with the activity and often refuse to take part. With Second Life, participants get very engaged, with a high level of energy. Often they don't want to stop at the end of the activity!'

After the pilot workshop in September 2008, participants said they have never been prompted to 'think so much' about the way they say things and approach delicate situations. Three more staff development events have been conducted since, and several more are in the works.

182

Fertile ground remains for OU advances in contextual learning curriculum

Role-playing could also facilitate a curriculum to train humanitarian workers. Peachey and Helen Yanacopulos, a senior lecturer in international development, have collaborated on a paper entitled 'Integrating Second Life in Humanitarian and Development Training'. It examines the opportunity for mixed-reality learning in Second Life for humanitarian and development workers in direct relation to their Open University course 'Working with Conflict: Tools, Skills and Dialogue'. They believe that role-playing in Second Life can help students develop sharper and more effective negotiation and collaborative skills to thrive in difficult real-life conditions.

Training workers to manage in combat or natural disaster situations is prohibitively expensive and logistically challenging. Peachey and Yanacopulos suggest that training programmes in Second Life can foster a new form of deep, cost-effective learning: 'by enabling students to suspend their own attitudes and beliefs, well-managed role plays can encourage exploration of attitude and actions beyond the personal and familiar in a safe environment'.

Now entering its fourth year in Second Life with plans for further expansion, the OU continues to prove that learning in the virtual world has resulted in tremendous real world success for students, faculty and administrators.

Links

Summary of the OU's programmes in Second Life: http://www.open.ac.uk/opencetl/?itemId=478b5caf2c3f7

Case study: http://community.secondlife.com/t5/Learning-Inworld-General/Announcing-OUtopia-Open-University-s-Innovative-Experiment-in/ba-p/650792

HOW MIGHT YOU USE VIRTUAL WORLDS IN HIGHER EDUCATION?

Before doing anything in a virtual world such as SL, it would be wise to take some time to build an avatar that you are happy with and to get a feel for the environment. You certainly should not expect to be able to simply log on and teach in SL, but rather you should take time to orientate yourself in this new environment and have a go – you need to learn how to fly after all (yes this is possible in SL).

One of the best things you can do to help with this orientation is to search out those who are *already using* SL, and chat through your concerns and get answers to your questions. Just as travel hints and tips are most useful coming from someone who has had first-hand experience, someone who has an avatar and has taught in SL will be an excellent person with whom to talk. The SL site has a number of blogs and discussion boards, which would help if you don't have a colleague who has taught in SL.[6] In part, this chapter will help with thinking through the things that you will encounter, but this is no substitute for having a go.

Given the need for orientation and avatar construction, and in some sense for adjusting to a different culture, if you plan to use SL in a course, time should be set aside to *explain* to students what it is, how to get the software, and to field questions. In particular, it is worth stressing to students the difference between OMUWs and MMPOGs. We'll address a number of points you'll need to consider when we talk about the potential problems in using virtual worlds. So, assuming you're in, and your students are not too lost, what are you going to do? One possibility is simply to *give a lecture in the virtual world.*

Many campuses have their own space, which can be used to give a traditional lecture. PowerPoint can be directly imported. You can then arrange a place and time, and give a lecture as you would in the real world. With this option, your avatar stands at the front of the class and talks through your slides as you normally would.

There are a number of things you will need to consider before giving a traditional lecture. For example:

- Should you field questions?
- Will you require all students to submit their avatar names, because otherwise there is no easy way of identifying your student from their avatar name?
- Will you have the same ground rules as in the real world – for example, will you allow talking during your lecture?
- Should you allow avatars to come to your lecture that are not on the register? You can create 'restricted' areas in SL such that only the students you pick can come to the lecture. Do you want this in place (universities often already have such restricted sites in place)?

184

Compared to a real-life lecture, there are a number of *benefits* to giving a didactic lecture in SL. Perhaps the most obvious one is that you are not constrained by geography or time. Where space and time is at a premium in universities, and students are sometimes unwilling or unable to travel to campus, a 'virtual world lecture' can be an attractive option.

Another possible way of using SL is to facilitate *small group discussions*. Again, this involves copying what is done in the real world. In using such an approach the same questions should be asked – for example, are you going to require users to disclose their avatar names? What about setting the ground rules?

The real benefit here is the case of setting up the seminar and the accessibility of it. For example, it may be that the day before an exam you receive lots of emails about a particular topic; you could then email the class to explain that you will be in SL to give an impromptu seminar in an hour. Given that SL is designed to enable social interaction, and given that SL allows for anonymity, running a seminar in SL would probably give a bigger overall benefit than conducting an ordinary lecture.

However, just transferring real life teaching methods to SL would be to miss out on its full potential; you should also consider the unique learning opportunities that OMUWs can provide. This is perhaps the most important point to think about before you plunge into teaching in any virtual world. There are too many cases where SL universities have limited themselves by importing ideas from real life – for example, some online campuses have tiered lecture theatres, classrooms with rows of chairs, or have even built lifts.

In order to make the most of SL, you should first consider what SL does well. Warburton and Perez-Garcia (2009: 421) sum up such affordances very well:

- Extended or rich interactions: opportunities for social interaction between individuals and communities, human–object interaction.
- Visualisation and contextualisation: the production and reproduction of inaccessible content that may be historically lost, too distant, too costly, imaginary, futuristic or impossible to see by the human eye.
- Exposure to authentic content and culture.
- Individual and collective identity play (i.e. taking on different roles).

185

- Immersion in a 3D environment where the augmented sense of presence, through virtual embodiment in the form of an avatar and extensive modes of communication, can impact on the affective, empathic and motivational aspects of experience.
- Simulation: reproduction of context that can be too costly to mimic in real life, with the advantages that some physical constraints can be overcome (e.g. very large engineering structures).
- Community presence: promoting a sense of belonging and purpose that coheres around groups, subcultures and geography.
- Content production: opportunities for creation and ownership of the learning environment and objects within it that are both individual and owned.

What does this all mean when it comes to teaching practice? How might these affordances be exploited to make the most out of them for teaching? Here are a few general suggestions and reflections.

Teaching in HE can include potentially *dangerous situations*. Of course, although no substitute for the real thing, SL can be used to teach about these dangers in a safe environment. For example, imagine you are training someone to scuba dive for an underwater archaeology course; or explaining how to distribute and administer drugs to patients for a pharmacy course; or giving tips on how to deal with wild animals for a veterinary course. In these instances, SL gives the teacher the chance to recreate these environments so as to test the student's skills and get some of the basics right before training in real life. Obviously this is not meant to be a replacement for real-life training, but it does allow the student to practice without incurring the real dangers.

Teaching may often require students to think about key historical events and figures, and these can be recreated through design and role-play. If, for example, you wanted students to empathise with the different opinions voiced at the trial of Oscar Wilde, then you could recreate the courtroom, design avatars that fit into that historical period, and ask students to assume the characters of different avatars so that they understand the variety of views that were put forward at the time.

Teaching may often involve theories which students are unable to put into practice because of time and money. For example, architecture students can simulate building space in large corporate buildings, or can simulate the flow of people over a bridge[7]; engineers can practice techniques, skills and measurements by building things countless times, without the need for planning permission or material costs; students studying drama can learn about lighting and set design by constructing sets; students studying fine arts can get a chance to display their work in a virtual public space with the click of a mouse.

There is also growing interest in how SL can directly help in the teaching of languages. It is said that immersing yourself in a culture is the best way to learn a language; however, this is often too expensive and time-consuming (just ask anyone trying to organise and administer work-based placements or language students' 'year abroad'). On the other hand, with a virtual world like SL, a virtual space that mimics certain features of a culture can be created. For example, you could create the whole ambience of a Moroccan market, with the items for sale labelled in Arabic, and the avatars only being allowed to speak in Arabic. SL could also be used to help international students become familiar with the language and cultural norms that they will encounter when arriving at their new university. To take this point further, they could even attend some virtual lectures at the institution before arriving, or have an induction tour.

SL gives the possibility of simulating *impossible* and/or rare situations. For example, when learning about schizophrenia, SL can give the student a chance to experience to some extent what it is like to experience visual and auditory hallucinations (see http://secondlife.com/destination/virtual-hallucinations). SL can also give the student the opportunity to study extreme weather, such as tsunamis, or to experience and interact with long-lost cultures, rituals and practice – for example, students may want to walk around the long-destroyed Great Temple in Jerusalem to give vivid context to their theological studies.

Real teaching is often hindered by the time and effort required to obtain ethical consent. Teaching in SL does not need this. For example, if you wanted to teach about counselling victims of crime, or about maternity care, or what it is like to work in an accident and emergency department, such simulations can be built in virtual worlds without requiring patients to sign consent waivers, or to go through timely research ethics boards – the onus is on the teacher to ensure the environment built will foster the acquisition of sensitive and appropriate approaches by the students.

CASE EXAMPLE

Maternity care in Second Life

Jenny Bailey, Midwife Teacher, University of Nottingham

In recent times there has been an explosive development in multimedia technologies, which has enabled universities to create a diverse range of learning resources. Second Life (SL) is a virtual world where everyday life can be simulated, and unique learning opportunities may be created in situations that would otherwise not be physically possible. Most UK universities have a presence on 'islands' in SL. The virtual maternity unit was developed on Nottingham University's island.

The joy of SL is that the students are immersed in the environment, and so learning is contextualised, with students having a feeling of 'presence' even if they are not physically there in reality (McKerlich et al., 2011). Avatars have been created to represent both the woman in labour and the midwives. It was important that pre-made avatars were available to students, as the whole idea of the project is to get students engaging with the role-play and not the technical knowledge of using SL per se.

The virtual birthing room can have either a pool or bed setting; the avatars can be made to adopt various positions in and around the pool, on the bed, or using birthing balls and mats. Simulation of the labour, birth of baby and placenta, and care during and after the birth can be engaged with by the student. Immersive learning through role-play in a virtual environment allows students to develop communication and reflection skills, and to rehearse management of care issues for women in labour. Through constructivist learning, students can analyse and evaluate the scenario as it unfolds in a contextualised environment (Bailey, 2011).

Creating such a virtual environment as a learning tool is not without its problems: teaching commitments can impede and delay the development of complex learning tools such as virtual reality. Creativity requires spontaneity, and time restraints on teachers certainly curtail this. One also has to consider the technical abilities of the teacher, and collaboration with graphic designers is almost essential. The technological capabilities of institutional and home PCs, technical support and maintenance, and SL technical issues are also areas that need

188

addressing. A further issue is students seeing the value of such learning tools, particularly if they are not embedded in the curriculum. Although they enjoyed using it and thought it was a dynamic innovation, none were proactive in attending SL sessions or the club in their own time.

Students engaged in using SL found the controls relatively simple, and enjoyed using the interactive elements of the immersive environment. Those students who participated in helping pilot the innovation felt able to answer questions/address management issues without feeling threatened by a midwife teacher asking them directly, as might happen in the classroom environment; because the learning was immersive, answers came naturally to them, and they felt that they were in the real-life clinical arena and that the practice/theory gap had been bridged.

You can use *SL itself* as a way of teaching, researching and investigating issues. For example, you might set psychology students a project to study the way people interact in SL; a philosopher might require an assignment on issues of identity and the avatar. The forum of SL in itself can therefore be used for research and teaching. More generally, students will get excited and feel liberated when given a specific shared space where they can explore the functionality and ever changing environment of SL. The fact that this happens in an environment which is perhaps more familiar than a lecture theatre only adds to the experience.

Finally, the potential benefit SL affords with regard to accessibility should not be overlooked or underestimated. Students with learning and physical disabilities can greatly benefit from SL. For example, students with autism who might find social interaction daunting and therefore miss lectures/seminars, may well feel liberated by being able to attend lectures as an avatar. Furthermore, dyslexic students often find it hard to plan and organise where their teaching is and how to get there. SL would also make this easier, as all they would have to do is log on at the correct time.

Even given this brief survey of functionalities and practical applications, it is apparent that the scope of SL is vast and potentially extremely useful. That said, there are a number of issues and problems that are worth highlighting.

ISSUES AND PROBLEMS TO CONSIDER

Available technologies and potential time costs are the biggest potential problems with using virtual worlds.

189

There are still genuine concerns regarding computing speed, congestion in Internet traffic, graphic card compatibly, the compatibility of firewalls, etc. One of the most frustrating things that can happen, and the one which could demotivate a whole class faster than any other, is if a teaching session is disrupted by 'lag'. In such a case the teaching will lose momentum and probably grind to a halt. If a student asks a question and has to wait two minutes for an answer, they are very quickly going to stop asking questions.[8]

It is vital then to investigate issues regarding compatibility before you start by asking your students to try out SL on their computers, and by testing whether SL will run smoothly on the University hardware. The SL home page has a list of known compatibility issues and a good set of FAQs regarding these technological concerns. One way of getting around the issue of 'lag' is to pick an 'off-peak' time to meet up with your students. After all, they do not need to travel anywhere, so you do not have to consider public transport, travelling at night, etc. However, this might challenge traditional teacher–student boundaries (something which has been stressed throughout the book), so it is worth considering carefully.

 PAUSE FOR THOUGHT

How else might using SL challenge teacher–student boundaries? Would this be a problem for you if you were going to use SL in your teaching?

Communication can also be an issue. From the outset you will have to decide whether to use *audio* in SL, or to communicate through typing. Using audio is quicker and can make the immersive experience even more immersive. However, the speed of the audio as compared to the speed of the graphics can sometimes create a mismatch between what the avatar is saying and what is happening on screen, making communication confusing and disjointed.

The alternative to audio is a small message board that appears when typing (like instant message boards). Apart from removing some of the accessibility advantages, using the message board over the audio approach will require a new set of rules to overcome the problems of long, wordy contributions that are bound to crop up. Students are inclined to interrupt or not finish sentences and will get bored when waiting for long replies to be written.[9] You and your students will therefore need to work out the 'rules' of when to 'publish' what you say. For example, a good tip might include breaking up long sentences by 'publishing' every time you would write a comma.

Something worth noting is that using the 'typing' method means that everything you say can be archived and printed out. On the one hand, this is good because students can have a record of what was said, but on the other hand it might put students off if they feel their grasp of language and spelling is not up to standard – of course, all this is true of the teacher as well.

The students need to know that it is fine to make mistakes, and that the jointly created document may contains errors, otherwise they may end up saying (or typing) nothing. Having said that, knowing that everything will be/can be recorded might also inhibit the actual exchange. Moreover, as anyone using email knows, if what is typed is what is captured it will be very hard to give emphasis, and impossible to use verbal elements such as intonation to clarify meaning.

Another thing to consider is culture shock, and this should not be underestimated. SL has its own sets of social norms and rules of behaviour. For instance, if a student started to walk on tables in real life, came to class in a disguise, or simply left the seminar without so much as a by your leave, then this would be seriously frowned upon and would certainly be a cause for further investigation. However, behaviour such as this is widespread and commonplace in SL.

In some sense then, teachers and students have to be mindful of their own set of norms and be wary of when these norms are hindering the education experiences in SL. One simple way to address this is to visit different locations in SL – perhaps different campuses or schools – and observe how people interact with each other, and get a 'feel' for what is the normal behaviour in such environments. SL etiquette even has its own term 'SLetiquette' – for example:

- Be interested in others
- Read profiles carefully before IMing (Instant Messaging) someone
- If you don't get a reply from someone it doesn't mean they hate you
- Be familiar with a group's rules before using group IM
- Don't teleport unannounced
- Don't beg for Linden Dollars

  Taken from: http://wiki.secondlife.com/wiki/SLetiquette

A further issue to consider is how to *identify* people in SL. Avatar names cannot be used to identify users, so as a teacher you will have to decide whether to collect the avatar names or retain the anonymity of the students. Of course, there are pros and cons to both approaches. Students may feel empowered by the anonymity because biases, such as those based on race and gender, can be eliminated.[10]

 PAUSE FOR THOUGHT

What other issues might arise if it is hard to identify students? What advantages might there be to this anonymity?

However, anonymity can mean that there is a lack of relationship between student and teacher. Furthermore, anonymity may engender disruptive and disrespectful behaviour, as there is a perceived lack of responsibility – responsibility being a skill we want to teach our students. Of course, university rules and regulations will still apply to the students qua students, the problem is how can you bring a student to account if you cannot prove who it was that was misbehaving? Also, anonymity means that it is impossible to track attendance and give feedback which connects with other learning outside SL.

At the time of writing SL has an open-access policy, but as the students now pay a lot of money for their education they may feel (rightly or wrongly) that their money gives them access to lectures which shouldn't at the same time be free to all and sundry. There is then an issue which you might want to consider regarding whether or not to limit who can come to your teaching sessions.

If you are encouraging students to use SL, then it is well worth making them aware of issues about cyber safety and bullying. Given the perceived Internet awareness of students, this might seem patronising or a waste of time, but the issue regarding bullying is often a genuine concern for both educators and learners. Linden Labs have a good 'getting started' guide[11] which deals with some of these worries, so it is worth giving the students a copy, or at least directing them to the right places. Of course, we should not think these are only issues facing students – they are relevant to teachers as well.

If students dislike collaborating and group work in the classroom, then asking them to get involved in problem-based or project-based learning in SL is not going to work magically simply because it is carried out in SL. Students need to be gradually taken through the benefits and what they should expect, and encouraged to think about their learning styles.

Related to this last point, there is the issue about managing students' expectations and challenging preconceptions. Students might find the whole idea of SL 'naff', 'sad' or a 'waste of time'; in fact, even you might think this. This attitude is partly fuelled by talk in the media of virtual worlds being a 'white elephant' and 'dying in popularity'.[12] Students might see SL as just one more thing they have to learn to do among a million others, as it appears that students have become much more strategic in their approach to their education. It is therefore important that the teacher pre-empts many of these issues so as to manage their expectations. Of course, this is true of colleagues who might judge that SL is not 'proper teaching and learning'. We need to be careful to explain the benefits to them as well.

CONCLUDING REMARKS

SL in particular, and 3D immersive environments in general, have great potential to add to a student's learning experience. Only a relatively short time ago such environments were the preserve of those with expensive and powerful computers, and lots of time on their hands. However, given the increase of computer power, and the availability of broadband Internet access, it is now significantly easier for teachers and students to make use of such virtual environments.

It is true that there are a number of issues which both the teacher and the student need to consider before launching into teaching in virtual worlds, yet none of these should be used as an excuse not to try out such environments; while they may not prove suitable for certain activities, they may be perfect for others, and without experience we would be running the risk of perpetuating urban myths.

What must be remembered though, and what has been stressed throughout this book, is that technology has no intrinsic value – in particular, teachers need to think about the specific affordances that such environments can provide. They should think about how their teaching materials and approaches can be supplemented and enhanced (rather than replaced) by such technology. However, the potential to add to the students' learning experience is enormous, and surely this can only be a good thing.

193

NOTES

1 http://goo.gl/jVgog
2 See: http://www.gamification.org/education for a useful selection and summary.
3 We would strongly encourage the reader to consult the excellent JISC document regarding teaching with second life: http://www.jisc.ac.uk/media/documents/publications/gettingstartedwithsecondlife.pdf
4 However, there is a cost to some necessary functions, such as uploading images which can be used to give PowerPoint presentations.
5 Adapted from: http://wiki.secondlife.com/wiki/Case_Study:_The_Open_University
6 For example: http://goo.gl/hoLCF
7 We are now moving away from the capabilities of virtual worlds such as SL into more specialised environments, and software designed for specific disciplines. The idea about the developmental importance of having access to simulations still stands, though.
8 We acknowledge that this point does not address the justified debate over the negative influence of on-demand multimedia content and impersonal web-based communication on students' attention spans. The scope of this book is to discuss ways in which technology can be used to enhance learning and teaching, and as communication is an integral part of the learning process, technological failures in supporting authentic communication patterns do undermine the educational process.
9 This is just one of the negative consequences of the always-on entertain me culture that is being encouraged from extremely early on in life by indiscriminate use of technology, to the detriment of real human contact – however, as we have already mentioned, it is not the scope of this book to contribute to this debate.
10 For a discussion and further resources, see: http://www.biasproject.org/
11 http://community.secondlife.com/t5/English-Knowledge-Base/Second-Life-Quickstart/ta-p/1087919?lang=en-US
12 http://goo.gl/gnLu7

 ## USEFUL RESOURCES

De Freitas, S. (2006). Learning in immersive worlds: A review of game-based learning. *JISC e-Learning Programme*. http://goo.gl/duhUJ

Kamel Boulos, M. N., Hetherington, L., & Wheeler, S. (2007). Second Life: An overview of the potential of 3-D virtual worlds in medical and health education. *Health Information and Libraries Journal*. http://goo.gl/Zhp8F

Chapter 10

Future developments

INTRODUCTION

Unfortunately (or perhaps fortunately) none of us has a crystal ball that can reliably tell us what is going to happen in the future. It would be futile and leave us hostage to fortune to claim to have any knowledge of how e-learning will develop in the next year, let alone five, ten or 20 years' time.

You might then wonder why we have included a chapter on 'future developments' at all? Well, because there are some trends that we can extrapolate from, and some indicators that might – might! – give us insight into the *various* possible futures that technology will give us.

Although we do mention a few sparkly gadgets and particular branded technologies, these should be thought of as examples and as possible predictors of new directions in teaching and learning. The 'wow' factor of innovative technology can grab all the attention, and we try here to keep it relevant to our main goal of improving the education of our students.

There are, we think, a number of general themes emerging as part of the massive expansion of the use of technology in HE. Technology will become less the domain of the 'experts', and will be driven, developed and even built (e.g. see rise of RasberryPi[1] and the section on 3D printing below) by the end-using teachers and students. Products will become cheaper and less Western-centric; battery life will increase; there is the real possibility of electricity without plugs and wires; and high-speed free WiFi will be the norm.

Notice that if knowledge is power, then these future developments will be about 'power egalitarianism'. In fact, we believe that it is this that will be the biggest change, but this is not about 'new' developments as such, but about the enabling conditions that arise from the democratisation of and access to the latest technology.

INTERNET OF THINGS

Perhaps the most profound development is about a reconceptualising of the Internet. The Internet is of course used in education; some teachers even joke (half seriously) about the Ctrl+C, Ctrl+V generation (copy and paste), and Wikipedia is often used as a pejorative term in HE. What current developments suggest, though, is the increased growth of an 'internet of things' (Ashton, 1999).

This means that there is a growing rise in interactive, real-time data-generating devices being connected through the web. Phones can be used to pay for parking; thermostats learn temperatures in homes and can be controlled over the Internet. Therefore, rather than just hosting connected information, the Internet is starting to connect people to things, and things to other things. How might this move to connect 'things' across the world affect teaching and learning?

What if a student wanted to learn a foreign language through touching the physical objects that are in their vocabulary list? Radio frequency identification tags (RFID) can be created and attached by the instructor for each of the physical items in the vocabulary list. When the student places this object on the RFID reader, it will say the word for the item in their native language and in the foreign language. Touching the item will give the student another sense to be engaged and may help them (depending on their learning style) learn vocabulary faster.

This example would fit well under the 'gesture and voice recognition' section below. However, that isn't the point. The 'internet of things' is a general idea which houses and holds these specific developments. It is this network of things that gives us a way of understanding the importance of many of the future developments we mention in this chapter, such as wearable technology and augmented reality (AR).

Let us now indulge in some less generic future-gazing, bearing in mind at the same time that these themes are necessarily incomplete, may even be in conflict with one another, and may even suggest different possible futures. In many ways this whole chapter is a 'pause for thought' – as we invite you to gaze into the crystal ball with us.

FUTURE THEMES

AR and wearable technology

One of the biggest growth areas of recent years is AR. One reason for this is the development of programme spec/code that allows for an easy move from Flash web interfaces to AR. AR development is further increasing because of the growth of user-friendly smartphone apps which can read QR codes (e.g. i-Nigma) and augment reality. We have also seen the continuous investment by Google in AR glasses,[2] which suggests that this will continue to be a growth area.

What is AR, though? It is the blending of technology *with* our everyday experience – adding, as it were, a 'layer of value' to our common experiences.

In contrast, *virtual* reality is a completely immersive experience (see Chapter 9) where you are physically isolated from reality in, for example, a simulator, or behind a desk staring at a screen and perhaps interacting with avatars on a virtual campus. This contrasts with augmented reality, which allows layers of information to be added/mixed with our everyday experience. Here is a useful – though necessarily incomplete – quotation from Yuen et al. (2011: 120):

> Augmented reality (AR) refers to a wide spectrum of technologies that project computer generated materials, such as text, images, and video, onto users' perceptions of the real world.

To complicate matters slightly, there is also such a thing as 'augmented virtual reality', in which it is the virtual reality that is augmented by 'real' objects; however, to avoid confusion, we will put this idea to one side (to read more about it, see Milgram and Kishino, 1994).

With AR, computer-generated content is often directly linked to specific cues in the environment, such as location. Consequently, rather than being transported to a different reality – as in World of Warcraft or Second Life – the person can still interact with real people, feel the ground beneath their feet, the rain, and the sounds of the city. It is just that users will have the ability to amplify and manipulate these experiences through various computer-generated materials.

This is rather abstract, so let's consider a few examples. Imagine the student studying architecture. The student is in the library at their desk trying to understand how to interpret a set of blueprint plans for a block of flats. Now imagine that the blueprints were primed to be used with

197

AR (using quick-access tags that are similar to the QR tags you have seen throughout this book). This would enable the plans to morph before the student's eyes into a fully interactive 3D model of the building through a specialised smartphone, tablet, or even computer app. The student could then spin the building and view it from different angles, as well as zoom in and out of areas of interest. This tangible interaction would, arguably, make learning more engaging and easier,[3] and could also have a direct impact on accessibility, opening up a world of opportunities for people who struggle with visualisation (see Chapter 2).

The way you can 'augment' reality is vast and will only increase. The experience of reality can be overlaid or mixed with audio, photos, video files, textual information, direct links to online reviews, etc. For example, imagine again the archaeology student standing at Hadrian's wall. As the student walks around the wall, he/she could have bespoke audio commentary directed at each part of what the student is experiencing; alternatively, their lecture notes or teachers' drawings could be overlaid/mixed onto their experience of the wall, or a 3D reconstruction overlaid/mixed on part of the structure that is not there anymore, thus giving the student an amazing insight into what the completed structure would have looked like.

Moreover, you can also imagine an astrophysics student working on a problem about the angles of orbiting planets. If planets were in front of their eyes, and they could be fully manipulated and measured, then this would ease learning. In general, AR has the potential to increase the learning experience of the student, and create many more affordances for learning than simple 'reality' does.

In a separate scenario, AR can be used to display on compatible mobile devices how specific specialist equipment works, thus removing the need to carry around heavy user manuals.

In one form or another, all of these examples are already available, but are only starting to be seen in the classroom and are less frequently seen in HE. Let's then allow ourselves a bit more future gazing.

Imagine a case where people's *speech* could be augmented. So, for example, an audio track is automatically overlaid onto someone's speech. This could help with language learning, where students could listen to language being spoken and could have immediate interpretation, or a commentary on their own language fluency.

Alternatively, imagine Greek or Hebrew being immediately translated from the page and projected onto the theology or history students' desk in any language of their choosing, or foreign-language research articles

198

published in Japan that the postgraduate student needs to read. Machine translation is still a long way away from replacing human translators, but it is currently good enough to get the gist in most situations – naturally, when it comes to rigorous scientific research, a lot more than just the gist of an article will be needed, but it is not unrealistic to expect that the quality of machine translation systems will continue to improve.

Of course, such possibilities raise as many concerns and questions as they do benefits. For example, should the fact that a student comes from a 'widening participation' background be something that is displayed to a tutor when they meet a student? Or, if this technology becomes more discrete, how does this affect assessment and possibilities for cheating?

What the future holds in AR is also dependent on parallel developments in the size and mobility of hardware. Put crudely, it will be about the ease with which the device that augments the reality can be carried around by the student and teacher. Developments in AR at the moment tend to focus on enhancing smartphones with such functionalities. This is just the beginning, as walking around and frequently raising one's phone to one's eye level is slightly inhibiting – not to mention it gives a clear signal that AR is being used, which may in turn be a barrier to accessibility and inclusivity (see Chapter 2). More discrete and user-friendly technology is being developed (e.g. cameras and projectors in spectacles and caps),[4] and in the future it is not inconceivable to imagine contact lenses or neurological implants as a way of developing AR – and the obligatory ethical debates will be fascinating.

In some ways, AR is reconceptualising how we see technology, and our interaction with it, by allowing us to decompartmentalise the 'technical' from the 'real'. In turn, this will have some profound implications for teaching and learning in HE, as AR has the very real potential to revolutionise physical 'teaching space': for example, if a teacher wanted to hold their class outside and present to the students, AR would allow them to use *any* compatible device as a 'screen for teaching'. The wall of the teaching building, the floor, or a statue could be used. Biology lectures could be given outside, where cutaways of trees showing fungi could be overlaid onto real trees.

We believe that this signifies a much more general issue about how future technology will gradually become ubiquitous, *invisible* and consequently allow users to get to the *substance* of electronic teaching and learning resources without having to stumble over and negotiate their *form*.

Creating AR resources

AR is at the opposite end of the scale in terms of ease of production compared to traditional resources such as handouts and lecture notes. The idea behind this technology is that users would point their mobile device's camera in various directions, and they would be able to see a dynamic layer of additional simulations and animations appearing on top of the physical reality that they perceive without the mobile device.

AR can be triggered either by special images not dissimilar to QR tags, or by the GPS position on the user's device. Specialised software/apps capable of interpreting and displaying AR content will be necessary, but the obvious advantages of superimposing additional layers of dynamic information onto reality have sparked a lot of enthusiasm among educators, as well as students.

Many-to-many technology

In the not-too-distant past teaching was simply one-to-few. A teacher would develop a working relationship with a few students; they would mark their deanonymised work and coach the students as persons, not just as students, through the trials and tribulations of academic and probably personal life. At the majority of universities, however, this is now a distant memory, which explains the recent moves towards implementing and emphasising personal tutoring by academics. Nowadays a teacher will typically teach larger numbers of students in his/her lectures, seminars and tutorials.

In fact, technology has meant that, because of the rise of open source and massive online courses (see Chapter 8) there has been a significant rise in courses where one teacher is teaching *thousands* of students via vast online materials. That is, the paradigm of teaching has moved from the one-to-few to *one-to-many*.

However, this is not the end. Technology is developing such that it is becoming increasingly easy for there to be *no* identifiable 'teacher' – that is, there are communities which have evolved without a discrete teaching lead. New developments in technology enable *collaborative learning communities* – a group of peers who learn together and teach each other. Technology is therefore strengthening the *many-to-many* approach to education.

The main reason for this is that in the past, in order to be able to share one's resources online, knowledge of programming, scripting, and how to manipulate and upload materials was required. However, advancing technology now means that the whole process has been made remarkably easy. If you feel that you have something to offer regarding, say, applied bioethics, or the history of blues guitar, or advanced calculus, you can easily create attractive online modules that get your knowledge transferred among users on the web. There is no need to go through teaching qualifications to demonstrate levels of expertise in relation to a benchmark. All you require is the material and a computer that is connected to the Internet.[5]

This illustrates another clear trend in the development of new technologies: the move to aggregation and curatorship, or what has been refereed to as 'sharing with discernment':

> Digital curation is an active process whereby content/artefacts are purposely selected to be preserved for future access. In the digital environment, additional elements can be leveraged, such as the inclusion of social media to disseminate collected content, the ability for other users to suggest content or leave comments, and the critical evaluation and selection of aggregated content. This latter part especially is important in defining this as an active process.[6]
>
> The 21st century will not be defined by the volume or speed at which you consume 'information'. (That was the old way of being smart.) It will be defined by how well you curate that information, translate it and contribute information back in a way that your community can understand it. Teaching students to be competent curators is our main responsibility as educators.[7]

The developing trend is not for students and teachers simply to observe material online passively, but to engage actively with material online in a way that maps out paths and makes meaningful connections among material. Software has been developed to give teachers and students the ability to order, rank, tag and narrate information – such tools include Scoop.it, Pearltrees, Pinterest and Storify). This means that learning material can be created by curatorship software and shared via online classrooms.

The value of such developments is moving away from mere consumers of information to people who have to reflect on material they find on the web in order to create pathways for other students, as well as for teachers. This critical and metacognitive ability is one of the key skills that we as teachers hope that students will

201

develop. Advances in technology will allow an increase in this digital wisdom.

This fast-developing technology is the ultimate in what Dewey (1933) called the 'democratization of education'. Why might this be in a book about HE? Well, because it demands that practitioners in HE reflect on what, where and why a university is, and about what 'added value' a university brings. The future of technology in HE is then arguably about challenging the very concepts of a university and a student.

Learning analytics

Related to this – and perhaps more impactful on pedagogy than anything that has been mentioned thus far – is how technology is helping create bespoke learning experiences, and allowing the development of a reviewing and ranking culture. Let's take these in turn.

Higher education is increasingly looking towards large Internet companies such as Amazon, and how they manage data to create bespoke recommendations for users. For example, if you buy items from Amazon, the data generated allow the company to recommend future purchases for you. Universities are slowly developing powerful technologies and sophisticated algorithms to create bespoke information for each individual student. This learning analytic means that universities can help students choose future courses, as well as isolate and highlight their weaknesses – after all, there is in all of us a striking lack of transparency when it comes to identifying our own weaknesses. Moreover, the university can be more predictive in how students from different demographics might behave.[8]

However, there is an associated piece of developing technology (which is also related to curatorship) which is arguably more pernicious. Consider how more and more companies are recognising the power of *reviews*. Technology is advancing to allow a greater quantity and specificity of reviews. Companies incentivise people to give reviews, as they recognise the direct impact that peer-to-peer advice has on consumer behaviours. The 'review' is arguably set to become a central part of HE as the technology advances. Without entering into a pedagogical argument about the merits of a 'rate my professor' type of culture in universities, it is worth reflecting on this (see for example Legg and Wilson, 2012).

202

PAUSE FOR THOUGHT

If all things associated with 'university' become reviewable and in the public domain, is this beneficial to education? How might it affect teaching practice? How might it affect the emphasis that universities place on things such as marketing, corporate image and courses?

Games and gamification

Gaming and gamification is one of the latest trends to take over HE. Gaming represents the use of games – also called *serious games* in professional training circles – to educate. They can be pre-existing games used for entertainment (e.g. the teaching of English via the game Skyrim, as presented in the Case Example below), or can be newly created games such as using Guitar Hero to teach economics and project management by planning a band's tour and all the associated elements that this involves.

CASE EXAMPLE

Teaching a video game as (and alongside) a literary text

Donna Beth Ellard, Post-doctoral Fellow in English, Rice University

An upper-division course on medieval Scandinavia and modern Scandinavian fantasy asked students to read and discuss Icelandic sagas in class, while playing Skyrim, a hugely popular Viking-themed video game, outside of class.[9]

Each saga reading was paired with a quest line in Skyrim, and once the class concluded its saga, it turned to a comparative analysis of the video game. Students began these comparisons by identifying moments of intersection between the worlds of the sagas and of Skyrim (inclement environments, supernatural figures, mythologies). Once they established these connections, basic readings in Freudian and Lacanian psycho-analysis were used in order to consider *how* and *why* elements of medi-eval Scandinavian culture have been taken out of historical milieu and

203

literary context, morphed into unfamiliar shapes, and appropriated towards the game's own fantastic pursuits.

Student papers were modelled on the course's intertextual dialogue between sagas and Skyrim. After reading/playing and analysing three Icelandic texts and video-game quests, students chose a scene from text and game that they'd like to explore comparatively. In the first paper, students wrote only about the saga scene, for which they received a grade and comments for revision; the second paper revised and extended this material into a comparative discussion about how and to what ends Skyrim appropriates and adapts this saga material.

Students began to see video games as not only worthy of critical evaluation, but moreover as narrative 'texts' that participate in a larger literary and cultural discourse. Likewise, they learned why and to what extent medieval Scandinavian fantasy worlds resonate with contemporary Anglo-American culture as spaces of serious 'play'.

The advantages of gaming are now clear (McGonigal, 2011). The myth that to play is a waste of time has now been rejected, and a unique set of skills and motivations are associated with games. Moreover, a large number of students engage in gaming as a leisure activity. The attraction and immersive nature of games is something recognised by gaming companies, which now lead the way with billion-dollar franchises and developments in graphics.

Of course, just because the technology exists and some companies are investing significantly in it, does not automatically mean that universities should also jump on the shiniest bandwagons around. However, the core idea behind educational games is a sound one: if games can be tweaked or built with immersive features in realistic environments conducive to human development and empathy, rather than alienation and unethical attitude and behaviour acquisition, then it would be a win–win situation where students would voluntarily enter into educational contexts. For example, 'SimArchitect' is a simulation game in which architects are given jobs by fictitious clients. Even more meaningfully, games such as Sweatshop go quite a long way to present the dark and very real consequences of the consumerist society.[10] Or games could include a simulation of the stock market, where students are pitted against other students to see who can make the biggest profit.

This is contrasted with *gamification*. Gamification uses the structures, dynamics, ideas and scaffolding from games, but employs them in education. The motivation associated with games can then – hopefully – be used to drive real-life educational interactions. Gamification is not therefore actually about games per se, but rather real-life learning contexts infused with the motifs that are found in games.

So, just as tagging, badging, ranking and completing levels is part of typical games, so these features might be imported into the classroom, which arguably might increase motivation to participate (see Leblanc, 2004; Koster, 2004). Because gamification is about rethinking the content, it can be used with the other technologies featured in this book, and we might, for example, 'gamify' AR or the use of Twitter.

Let's consider an example. Rather than grading students, and arguably students then being motivated by worrying about *failure*, the teacher could introduce the concept of levels into assessment: as a student studies, they complete tasks, gain points, and move up levels.

In such a case, rather than being driven by a fear of failure, students would be motivated by concepts of progress and advancement. Moreover, progress motivates progress and draws the student through the learning tasks. There is a sense that, by employing this type of 'gamification' in learning, the student is building towards a goal. Moreover, once a general level/point system is introduced into a module, it would be relatively easy to introduce other game 'motifs' – for example, awards and bonuses. Notice that one good thing about gamification is that it is primarily about reconceptualisation rather than developing new content.

 CASE EXAMPLE

Shawn Graham's blog[11]

I find myself teaching 'The Historian's Craft' this term. There are 100 students registered in the course, which unrolls over 13 lectures and tutorials. The course is one of our required courses, and introduces the second year student to the nitty gritty of being an historian – archives, transcribing documents, building arguments from documents; that kind of thing. Of course, with me being an archaeologist, I also slipped in quite a lot about material culture, visual culture and landscapes.

Full disclosure: I was terrified to teach this course. My main concern was, how could a student ever hope to engage with the full gamut of tools, techniques and approaches from a single class? I decided I would set up a social network for my class, and build achievements around the tools and techniques of being an historian. I'm using WordPress and Buddypress to handle the social interaction, and the Achievements plugin to create the reward system. Participation on the site is completely voluntary; it is entirely separate from the formal assessment exercises in the course. The name of the game: he who gets the most points, wins. Top quarter (more or less) on the leaderboard will see a (very) small bonus on their course participation grade. So all in all, the 'gamification' of this class is a pretty simple mechanic: a gold star, in essence.

Each week, I create a few more achievements which relate to the course lecture. I've assigned one TA to monitor the course site, verify achievements, and facilitate discussions on that site. Verifying achievements does take a bit of time, but once we showed students how to share screenshots, the process became much quicker. Some achievements are one-offs; others can have multiple levels. For instance, the National Archives in the UK has a series of progressively more difficult tutorials on palaeography; they also have a series on Latin. I've found exercises on critical thinking. The most recent is on oral history. Students also get points for starting new conversation groups related to the course content, and for sustained activity in those conversation groups.

Of the 100 students in the class, so far (and we're at the midpoint now), 40 students have completed successfully at least one of the achievements. Thirty students have completed two or more; 20 have completed three or more; and the remaining 20 students have completed ten or more achievements. One student is gunning for all 40 achievements (but there are still more to come). The most popular achievements? Palaeography and Latin.

The hardest part so far has been figuring out how many points to attach to each achievement. Do more points signal a harder task, or a task that will take more time, or a task that I think more important in terms of being an historian than some other task? Should I tell the students why some have more points associated with them than others? Should achievements be designed that are of equal importance to the course objectives (and thus maintain the same point value?).

Maybe if I had definitive answers to these questions, I would have a higher participation rate. Nevertheless, 40 per cent turnout for extra work above and beyond the course work? It's worth gaming your craft to see what happens. It will be interesting to see how the final grades turn out – does participation in Historian's Craft: The Game lead to better outcomes? We shall see.

Gesture and voice recognition technology

Fitting into the idea of gamification and the use of games in education is 'gesture and voice recognition technology'. By this we mean software and hardware which recognises and responds to human interactions such as eye movements, gestures and voice. The use of such technology has developed at a pace, with the Xbox 360 Kinect and Nintendo Wii being the main examples. In fact, a number of people are incorporating the Kinect into classroom practice.[12]

The benefits of this technology are many. An obvious one is the fact that it increases the accessibility of learning materials (see Chapter 2) – for example, if a blind person could access learning materials easily via voice recognition, then this is going to open up a world of material enriching their learning experience. Another obvious benefit is the immediacy of the interaction. If the student moves their hand, or says something, then the programme responds immediately. Therefore, if a student is learning sign language, the software can recognise the movements of the hands and give him/her immediate feedback on how well they are doing. Similarly, a medic could benefit from interactive lessons and immediate feedback regarding surgery or autopsies.[13]

Related to this is that fact that such a learning experience would be more immersive (for more on immersive technologies, see Chapter 9). If there is no mediation between the student and the software via the keyboard and mouse, then the student is more likely to 'lose themselves' in the learning experience as the interaction is more instinctive, and we can assume that more immersion will lead to greater fun and a richer experience (see, for example, Kandroudi and Bratitsis, 2012).

The whole way of thinking about learning and teaching would also have to be more interactive; after all, the software demands physical interaction in some form or another. Moreover, there are fewer cultural issues to impede interaction. Gestures, in particular, are more universal than the written or spoken word.

In the future we can imagine the technology developing to such an extent that how a computer 'sees' a person will become much more sophisitcated and nuanced. For example, rather than the computer 'seeing' a hand movement, the computer would actually detect the angles of each individual finger; similarly, you can imagine a portable and affordable piece of hardware for measuring and responding to eye position. Such implementations could make their way into teacher training courses using the recognition and mapping of eye and hand movements to teach classroom techniques.

3D printing

3D printing is rather self-explanatory:

> 3D printing refers to technologies that construct physical objects from three-dimensional (3D) digital content such as computer-aided design (CAD) . . . A 3D printer builds a tangible model or prototype from the electronic file.[14]

In plain English, such printers take computer models and turn them into real 3D things. It is also worth adding that the prototypes created can have moving parts and be created out of different materials, including metals. 3D printing has already been used in the commercial areas of engineering and architecture.

The reason that this is relevant in HE is that, at the time of writing, the price of 3D printers had come down to approximately £2,000. However, two other factors mean that HE can more easily adopt 3D printing. First, the software on which 3D designs are constructed is already often installed in universities (e.g. CAD software), and second, there is a vast collection of free prototype designs that can be used and adapted.[15]

How, though, might 3D printing be used in HE in the future? First of all, there are the more obvious applications such as the architecture student printing blueprints, window designs and room structures, and engineering students printing engine parts.

Less obvious uses might include the following. Often, archaeology and anthropology students have to deal with very rare and valuable artefacts. If, however, a 3D replica could be printed, say, of a Bronze Age broach, an Egyptian mummy or an Incan fertility statue, then this would allow interaction with the artefact on a larger scale. Moreover, because the computer model can be sent anywhere in the world and then be reprinted, there is no added risk of breakage due to travel.

Moreover, imagine the art historian thinking about a rare statue; a biologist wanting to look at a skeleton of a rare species of bird; a furniture design student wanting to cheaply and quickly produce prototype furniture; or an organic chemist wanting to print out complex molecular structures. 3D printing will have valuable applications in all these scenarios.

Add to this the possible future development of bioprinters, and 3D printing is a truly revolutionary development. Bioprinters have the potential to construct living tissue artificially by outputting layer upon layer of living cells – a lung or heart might therefore be printed in a lab. This has the potential revolutionary effect on many areas of biomedical research, together with an equally significant effect on the field of bioethics. If you don't need to wait for donations, or if you don't need to use animals in experiments, the ethical and financial implications are going to be interesting, and prolonging life this way will certainly raise numerous philosophical debates.

 CASE EXAMPLE

3D printing to support engineering

Edward Pan, PhD student, University of Virginia

Dynamics is a foundational course in an undergraduate mechanical engineering curriculum, and is traditionally taught using lectures and static diagrams of moving systems. Students often fail to solve the problems correctly, and an inability to mentally visualise the system can contribute to student difficulties. Adding opportunities to help students visualise these systems, through access to physical or virtual objects (called manipulatives), may be potentially powerful for struggling students and have implications for undergraduate engineering education in general.

In a quasi-experimental study comparing the effect of adding physical and virtual manipulatives to traditional instruction, 70 students in a dynamics course were divided into three treatment groups: traditional instruction, traditional and physical manipulatives, traditional and virtual manipulatives. The physical manipulatives were physical models of machines depicted in textbook diagrams, and the virtual manipulatives were computer-aided design (CAD) models of the same machines. Students solved problems using the static diagrams and/or manipulatives.

The study found no differences between treatment groups on quantitative measures of spatial ability and conceptual knowledge. There were differences between treatments on qualitative measures of mechanical reasoning ability (student explanations of how the machines worked), in favour of the use of physical and virtual manipulatives over static diagrams alone. There were no major differences in student performance between the use of physical and virtual manipulatives.

209

Student opinions about the static diagrams and dynamic models varied by type of model (static, physical, virtual), but were generally favourable. The 'traditional' group students, however, indicated that the lack of adequate representation of motion in the static diagrams was a problem, and wished they had access to the physical and virtual models.

The results suggest that adding physical and/or virtual manipulatives to some traditionally theoretical mechanical engineering courses can help students to learn more effectively.

SOME MORE 'SCI-FI' AND DISTANT SUGGESTIONS (FOR A BIT OF FUN)

Brain computing interface

There is a growing development in using brainwaves to control computers, with the practical application of allowing paralysed individuals to function on some levels. The road is still long, but steps are being made: companies are already selling affordable headsets which allow basic gaming and controlling powers, together with additional functionalities (e.g. the companies NeuroSky and EmotiveEpoc).

It would be interesting to reflect on the possible impact of this in the classroom. For example, if a student can sit in lectures with a headset which provides real-time feedback alerting the student when they need to refocus, or recharge. This sounds rather Orwellian in many ways, yet if the education sector is not careful about jumping on various technological bandwagons, one day some teacher may monitor the class's focus from the front, or accuse a student of not really understanding the material even when they say they do; having said that, our aim in this chapter is not normative, but descriptive.

Direct brain-to-brain connection

There is even a more distant – and far less probable – development. Recent advances in technology and brain intervention have been able to connect up rats' brains over the Internet, such that they could communicate directly and hence learn from one another.[16] In the experiment a rat was taught how to get food, and the other rat, to which it was connected directly via the brain, 'learned' how to get the food. This is very much on the sci-fi end of future technologies, and it would be interesting to see how direct brain input might be adopted by education. Could teachers be directly connected to multiple students across the world? Of course, what education *could* adopt, and what it *ought* to adopt, are significantly different questions, and we aim to be as neutral as possible. All this raises a lot of interesting philosophical and pedagogical issues that we will not deal with here, but, for the sake of academic debate, please consider the question in the Pause for Thought box below.

 PAUSE FOR THOUGHT

Imagine that a teacher could have direct brain-to-brain connection with their students. Would we say that the teacher 'taught' the students? If so, why? If not, why not?

Holograms

Holographic telepresence means we can record a three-dimensional image in one location and show it in another location, in real-time, anywhere in the world.[17]

Although holograms sound very 'sci-fi', they are already being used in courses, and non-educational settings. For example, bands have used holograms of dead musicians who come on stage,[18] and famously CNN introduced a hologram to read a news item.[19]

If this is possible, then technology could be used to create holograms to facilitate teaching and learning. Imagine, for example, learning relativity from a hologram of Einstein, philosophy from Bertrand Russell, or using holograms to give guest lectures across the world. The use of holograms would certainly change the nature of video conferencing.

On the other hand, a teacher lecturing to a full lecture hall of holograms would obviously raise questions about the role of the teacher, about the use of lecturing, and about performance and presence in the classroom. Like the technology in the rest of this chapter, we are unsure if holograms will or should be adopted in HE. What is sure, though, is that if they are – as with any of the things we have mentioned – they should be seen as a tool rather than a thing with intrinsic value.

PAUSE FOR THOUGHT

If hologram technology was readily available and not limited, would you use it? How might you use it in your teaching?

CONCLUDING REMARKS

We have surveyed one some of the *possible* developments in technology. Some, such as 3D printing and AR, are here already, and within a short time will revolutionise the shape of teaching in HE.

Some of the other things we touched on, such as the 'internet of things' and 'reviewing and curatorship', are more about a reconceptualisation of HE through the development of technology. They will then form the lens through which we are asked – and we can always say no – to bring technology into HE.

We also noted that as technology develops it – ironically – becomes less recognisable as 'technology'. The future then is about ubiquitous multifunctional technology which we cease to identify as technology.

With this in mind, clearly it is our very ideas of education, university and humanity that will mould technology and form expectations in the market place. We then have the power to shape the future – we just need to be confident in what we want and how to ask for it. Perhaps then, the most important questions you can ask as educators are: '*why* do we give lectures, tutorials, essays, exams, grades, set our learning spaces out as we do?'; essentially, '*why do we do what we do in HE?*' Armed with answers to these questions, we can *then* ask: 'can any technology help me with that aim?' We are confident that as technologies develop, the answer to this question will be a resounding 'yes'. We are equally as confident that for us to remain in control in the future we need to have reflected on these big questions and have our eyes wide open.

NOTES

1 http://www.raspberrypi.org/
2 http://goo.gl/l4N6E
3 See for example: http://goo.gl/7eXJT
4 http://goo.gl/I6lmF
5 An interesting illustration of this is Udemy: http://goo.gl/y2A2e
6 Cited at: http://goo.gl/BlAeJ

7 Cited at: http://goo.gl/pdU4D
8 We acknowledge that this is yet another ethical debate which will become increasingly central.
9 http://www.elderscrolls.com/skyrim
10 http://goo.gl/6uUNV
11 http://goo.gl/C91wj
12 More ideas about practical applications of Kinect in education can be found in this YouTube video: http://goo.gl/gAipY
13 http://goo.gl/s38PX
14 http://horizon.wiki.nmc.org/3D+Printing
15 See, for example: http://www.thingiverse.com/
16 http://goo.gl/WaaWt
17 Cited at: http://goo.gl/Swb1X
18 http://goo.gl/zxCLp
19 http://goo.gl/wS3mV

USEFUL RESOURCES

A talk which uses Angry birds as a model for future technology reflection: http://goo.gl/qPHr2

Talk about the benefits of gaming: http://goo.gl/Z9alv

Slides about possible developments: http://goo.gl/bd5uf

Information on gesture-based learning: http://goo.gl/hYCdf

How to use Kinect in teaching: http://www.kinecteducation.com/

Horizon report on the possible developments of new technologies: http://www.nmc.org/horizon-project

Where does gamification fit in HE? http://goo.gl/x1oJv

Seven educational uses for 3D printing: http://goo.gl/Y0IlN

A general discussion of different future technologies http://www.explainingthefuture.com/index.html

References

Apampa, K. M., Wills, G., & Argles, D. (2009). Towards security goals in summative e-assessment security. Paper presented at the ICITST-2009: The 4th International Conference for Internet Technology and Secured Transactions, London, UK.

Anderson, L., & Krathwohl, D. (2001). *A Taxonomy for Learning, Teaching, and Assessing: A Revision of Bloom's Taxonomy of Educational Objectives*. Boston, MA: Allyn & Bacon.

Andrews, L., & Drennan, J. (2009). Students' perceptions, experiences and beliefs about Facebook in subjects at an Australian university. In *Proceedings of Australia and New Zealand Marketing Academy Conference 2009: Sustainable Management and Marketing* (pp. 1–6). Promaco Conventions PTY LTD.

Ashton, K. (2009). That 'internet of things' thing. *RFiD Journal*, 22: 97–114.

Atkinson, C. (2009). *The Backchannel: How Audiences are Using Twitter and Social Media and Changing Presentations Forever*. Berkeley, CA: New Riders.

Bailey, J. (2011). The birth of immersive learning and contemporaneous storytelling in a virtual maternity unit. (Strengthening midwives and midwifery practice). Theme paper/presentation 13th International Confederation of Midwives Conference. Durban, South Africa.

Barker, R., & Greeff, W. (2011). Vodcasting: An intelligent extension or pending derivative of traditional open distance learning tools? *World Conference on Educational Multimedia, Hypermedia and Telecommunications* 1: 58–66.

BBC News Wales (2012). Fabrice Muamba: Racist Twitter user jailed for 56 days. Retrieved July 2013 from: http://www.bbc.co.uk/news/uk-wales-17515992

Bell, T., Cockburn, A., McKenzie, B., & Vargo, J. (2001). Digital lectures: If you make them, will students use them? *International Multimedia Electronic*

Journal of Computer Enhanced Learning, 3 (2). Retrieved July 2013 from: http://www.imej.wfu.edu/articles/2001/2/06/index.asp

Biggs, J. (2002). Aligning the curriculum to promote good learning. Imaginative Curriculum Symposium. York, England: LTSN Generic Centre.

Bligh, D. (2004). *What's the Use of Lectures?* Exeter: Intellect.

Bloom, B., Hastings, J., & Madaus, G. (1971). *Handbook on Formative and Summative Evaluation of Student Learning*. New York: McGraw-Hill.

Boon, S., & Sinclair, C. (2009). A world I don't inhabit: Disquiet and identity in Second Life and Facebook. *Educational Media International*, 46 (2): 99–110.

Bosch, T. (2009). Using online social networking for teaching and learning: Facebook use at the University of Cape Town. *South African Journal for Communication Theory and Research*, 35 (2): 185–200.

Burgstahler, S. (1997). Peer support: What role can the internet play? *Information Technology and Disabilities*, 4. Retrieved July 2013 from: http://itd.athenpro.org/volume4/number4/article2.html

Buzan, T. (1976). *Use Both Sides of Your Brain*. New York: E.P. Dutton and Co.

Buzan, T. (1993). *The Mind Map Book*. London: BBC Books.

Cane, C., & Cashmore, A. (2008). Students' podcasts as learning tools. In Salmon, G., and Edirisingha, P. (eds) (2008). *Podcasting for Learning in Universities*. London: Open University Press and SRHE.

Chanock, K. (2007). How do we not communicate about dyslexia? *Journal of Academic Language and Learning*, 1 (1): A33–A43.

Ciobanu, D., Secar, A., & Morris, N. (2011). Can one tool change the culture of an institution? *ALT C 2011*. Leeds.

Clark, J., & Paivio, A. (1991). Dual coding theory and education. *Education Psychology Review*, 3 (3): 149–210.

Cohan, R., & Smith, R. (2007). *LearnHigher Oral Communication Literature Review*. Retrieved July 2013 from: http://www.learnhigher.ac.uk/resources/files/Oral per cent20communication/Oral_Communication.pdf

Crisp, G. (2007). *The e-Assessment Handbook*. London: Continuum.

Cross, J. (2006). *Informal Learning: Rediscovering the Natural Pathways that Inspire Innovation and Performance*. San Francisco, CA: John Wiley & Sons.

Danan, M. (2004). Captioning and subtitling: Undervalued language learning strategies. *META*, 49 (1): 67–77.

Dante, E. (2010). The shadow scholar. *The Chronicle Review*. Retrieved July 2013 from: http://chronicle.com/article/article-content/125329/

Deek, F., & McHugh, J. (2008). *Open Source: Technology and Policy*. New York: Cambridge University Press.

215

Dewey, J. (1933). *How We Think*. New York: Heath.

Dougherty et al. (1995). Cooperative learning and enhanced communication: Effects on student performance, retention, and attitudes in general chemistry. *Journal of Chemical Education*, 72 (9): 793–7.

Draffan, E. (2011). *LexDis*. Retrieved July 2013 from: www.lexdis.org.uk

Dron, J. (2006). The pleasures and perils of social software. *In Proceedings of the Higher Education Academy Information and Computer Sciences 7th Annual Conference*, (pp. 127–31). Dublin.

Duarte, N. (2008). *Slide:ology: The Art and Science of Creating Great Presentations*. California: O'Rielly Media.

Duarte, N. (2010). *Resonate: Present Visual Stories that Transform Audiences*. San Francisco, CA: John Wiley & Sons.

Dunlap, J., & Lowenthal, P. (2009). Tweeting the night away: Using Twitter to enhance social presence. *Journal of Information Systems Education*, 20 (2): 129–55.

Eaton, S. (2010). How to use Skype in the ESL/EFL classroom. *The Internet TESL Journal*, XVI (11). Retrieved July 2013 from: http://iteslj.org/Techniques/Eaton-UsingSkype.html

Exley, K., & Dennick, R. (2009). *Giving a Lecture: From Presenting to Teaching*. New York: Routledge.

France, D., & Wheeler, A. (2007). Reflections on using podcasting for student feedback. *Planet*, 18: 9–11.

Fuller, M., Healey, M., Bradley, A., & Hall, T. (2004). Barriers to learning: A systematic study of the experience of disabled students in one university. *Studies in Higher Education*, 29 (3): 303–18.

Gardner-Medwin, A., & Gahan, M. (2003). Formative and summative confidence-based assessment. *Proceedings of the 7th International Computer-Aided Assessment Conference*. Retrieved July 2013 from: http://caaconference.co.uk/pastConferences/2003/procedings/gardner-medwin.pdf

Garside, C. (1996). Look who's talking: A comparison of lecture and group discussion teaching strategies in developing critical thinking skills. *Communication Education*, 45: 212–27. Retrieved July 2013 from: http://www.infobarrel.com/Look_whos_talking_A_comparison_of_lecture_and_group_discussion_teaching_strategies_in_developing_critical_thinking_skills#dh1eIWB7BYk7KClB.99.

Garza, T. (1991). Evaluating the use of captioned video materials in advanced foreign language learning. *Foreign Language Annals*, 24 (3): 239–58.

Govender, I., & Mkhwanazi, P. (2012). Students' perceptions of podcasting as a learning tool. *Global TIME*, 1: 38–43.

Grace, S., & Gravestock, P. (2009). *Inclusion and Diversity: Meeting the Needs of All Our Students*. Oxford: Routledge.

Gray, D., Ryan, M., & Coulon, A. (2012). *The Training of Teachers and Trainers: Innovative Practices, Skills and Competencies in the Use of eLearning*. Retrieved July 2013 from: http://www.eurodl.org/index.php?tag=34&article=369&article=159

Grosseck, G., Bran, R., & Tiru, L. (2011). Dear teacher, what should I write on my wall? A case study on academic uses of Facebook. *Procedia-Social and Behavioral Sciences*, 15: 1425–30.

Haladyna, T., Downing, S., & Rodriguez, M. (2002). A review of multiple-choice item-writing guidelines for classroom assessment. *Applied Measurement in Education*, 15 (3): 309–34.

Halpern, D. F., and Hakel, M. D. (2002). Learning that lasts a lifetime: Teaching for long-term retention and transfer. *New Directions for Teaching and Learning*, 89: 3–7.

Harpp, D., Fenster, A., Schwarcz, J., Zorychta, E., Goodyer, N., Hsiao, W., et al. (2004). Lecture retrieval via the web: Better than being there? *Journal of Chemical Education*, 81 (5): 688–90.

Heath, D., & Heath, C. (2008). *Made to Stick: Why Some Ideas Take Hold and Others Come Unstuck*. London: Arrow.

Hinchliffe, L. (2000). Can the computer identify plagiarism? *The CATalyst*, 5–6 February. Centre for the Advancement of Teaching, Illinois State University.

Jenkins, M., & Brotherton, C. (1995). Implications of a theoretical framework for practice. *British Journal of Occupational Therapy*, 58 (9): 392–6.

Jenson, C., & Forsyth, D. M. (2012). Virtual reality simulation: Using three dimesional technology to teach nursing students. *CIN*, 30 (6): 312–18.

JISC. (2007). *Effective Practice with e-Assessment*. Retrieved July 2013 from: http://www.jisc.ac.uk/publications/programmerelated/2007/pub_eassesspracticeguide.aspx

Johnson, R. T., & Johnson D. W. (1986). Action research: Cooperative learning in the science classroom. *Science and Children*, 24 (2): 31–2.

Junco, R., Heiberger, G., & Loken, E. (2011). The effect of Twitter on college student engagement and grades. *Journal of Computer Assisted Learning*, 27 (2): 119–32.

Kandroudi, M., & Bratitsis, T. (2012). Exploring the educational perspectives of XBOX Kinect based video games. *Proceedings of the 6th European Conference on Games Based Learning* (pp. 219–27). Academic Conferences Limited.

Khuwaileh, A. (1999). The role of chunks, phrases and body language in understanding co-ordinated academic lectures. *System*, 27 (2): 249–60.

217

King, C., Guyette, R., & Piotrowski, C. (2009). Online exams and cheating: An empirical analysis of business students' views. *The Journal of Educators Online*, 6 (1): 1–11.

Koster, R. (2004). *A Theory of Fun for Game Design*. New York: Paraglyph Press.

Kruger, J.-L. (2012). Visual attention and comprehension: Same-language subtitling in the EAL (English as an Additional Language) classroom. *Subtitles and Language Learning Conference*. Pavia, Italy.

Lakhal, S., Khechine, H., & Pascot, D. (2007). Evaluation of the effectiveness of podcasting in teaching and learning. *World Conference on E-Learning in Corporate, Government, Healthcare, and Higher Education*, 1: 6181–8.

Leadbeater, W., Shuttleworth, T., Couperthwaite, J., & Nightingale, K. (2012). Evaluating the use and impact of lecture recording in undergraduates: Evidence for distinct approaches by different groups of students. *Computers & Education*, 61: 185 ut2.

Leblanc, G. (2004). Enhancing intrinsic motivation through the use of a token economy. *Essays in Education*, 11 (1). Retrieved July 2013 from: http://www.usca.edu/essays/vol112004/leblanc,pdf.pdf

Legg, A., & Wilson, J. (2012). RateMyProfessors.com offers biased evaluations. *Assessment and Evaluation in Higher Education*, 37 (1): 89–97.

Li, L. C., Grimshaw, J. M., Nielsen, C., Judd, M., Coyte, P. C., & Graham, I. D. (2009). Use of communities of practice in business and health care sectors: A systematic review. *Implement Sci*, 27 (4): 1–9.

Martin, A. (2012). Supervising doctorates at a distance: Three trans-Tasman stories. *Quality Assurance in Education*, 20 (1): 42–5.

Mayfield, A. (2008). *What is Social Media?* iCrossing. Retrieved July 2013 from: http://www. iCrossing.com/ebooks.

McGonigal, J. (2011). *Reality is Broken: Why Games Make Us Better and How They Can Change the World*. New York: Penguin Press.

McKenna, C., & Bull, J. (1999). *Designing Effective Objective Test Questions: An Introductory Workshop*. (L. University, Producer). Retrieved July 2013 from: http://caacentre.lboro.ac.uk/dldocs/otghdout.pdf

McKerlich, M., Rils, M., Anderson, T., & Eastman, B. (2011). Student perceptions of teaching presence, social presence and cognitive presence in a virtual world. *MERLOT Journal of Online Learning and Teaching*, 7 (3). Retrieved July 2013 from: http://jolt.merlot.org/vol7no3/mckerlich_0911.pdf

McKinney, J., & Iball, H. (2011). Researching Scenography. In Kershaw, B., & Nicholson, H. (eds), *Research Methods in Theatre and Performance*. Edinburgh: Edinburgh University Press.

McLoughlin, C., and Lee, M. J. W. (2010). Personalised and self regulated learning in the Web 2.0 era: International exemplars of innovative pedagogy using social software. *Australasian Journal of Educational Technology*, 26 (1): 28–43.

Medina, J. (2008). *Brain Rules: 12 Principles for Surviving and Thriving at Work, Home and School*. Seattle: Pear Press.

Michael, J. (2006). Where's the evidence that active learning works? *Advances in Physiology Education*, 30 (4): 159–67.

Michel, L. (2009). *On Teaching Fashion: Facebook and the Classroom. Worn Through*. Retrieved July 2013 from: http://www.wornthrough.com/2009/01/09/on-teaching-fashion-facebook-and-the-classroom/

Milgram, P., & Kishino, F. (1994). A taxonomy of mixed reality visual displays. *IEICE Transactions on Information Systems*, 77 (12). Retrieved July 2013 from: http://www.eecs.ucf.edu/~cwingrav/teaching/ids6713_sprg2010/assets/Milgram_IEICE_1994.pdf

Miners, Z. (2010). *Twitter Goes to College: Students and Profs Use 'Tweets' to Communicate In and Outside the Class*. US News, Education. Retrieved July 2013 : http://www.usnews.com/education/articles/2010/08/16/twitter-goes-to-college-

Mobrand, E. (2011). Facebook for teaching and learning. *Technology in Pedagogy*, 1. Retrieved July 2013 from: http://www.cdtl.nus.edu.sg/technology-in-pedagogy/articles/Technology-in-Pedagogy-1.pdf

Nicholson, G., Irvine, H., & Tooley, S. (2010). A test of podcasting effectiveness for lecture revision. *Proceedings of 24th Annual Australian and New Zealand Academy of Management Conference: Managing for Unknowable Futures*. ANZAM. Retrieved July 2013 from: http://eprints.qut.edu.au/39999/1/c39999.pdf

Nicol, D. (2007). E-assessment by design: Using multiple-choice tests to good effect. *Journal of Further and Higher Education*, 31 (1): 53–64.

Nicol, D. J., & Macfarlane-Dick, D. (2006). Formative assessment and self-regulated learning: A model and seven principles of good feedback practice. *Studies in Higher Education*, 31 (2): 199–218.

Novak, J. (1990). Concept-mapping: A useful tool for science education. *Journal of Research in Science Teaching*, 27: 937–49.

Oblinger, D. G., & Hawkins, B. L. (2006). The myth about student competency. *Educause Review*, 41 (2): 12–13.

Parson, V., Reddy, P., Wood, J., & Senior, C. (2009). Educating an iPod generation: Undergraduate attitudes, experiences and understanding of vodcast and podcast use. *Learning, Media and Technology*, 34 (3): 215–28.

Pearson, E., & Koppi, T. (2006). Supprting staff in developing inclusive online learning. In Adams, M. (ed.), *Towards Inclusive Learning in Higher Education: Developing Curricula for Disabled Students*. London: Routledge.

QAA (2011). Quality Assurance Agency's Quality Code, Chapter B6: Assessment of students and accreditation of prior learning. Retrieved July 2013 from: http://www.qaa.ac.uk/publications/informationand-guidance/pages/quality-code-b6.aspx

Rankin, M. (2009). *Some General Comments on the 'Twitter Experiment'.* Retrieved July 2013 from: http://www.utdallas.edu/~mar046000/usweb/Twitterconclusions.html

Rhem, J., & Glazer, F. (eds) (2012). *Blended Learning: Across the Disciplines, Across the Academy (New Pedagogies and Practices for Teaching in Higher Education).* Virginia: Stylus Pub Llc.

Rinaldo, S., Tapp, S., & Laverie, D. (2011). Learning by tweeting: Using Twitter as a pedagogical tool. *Journal of Marketing Education,* 33 (2): 193–203.

Roblyer, M., McDaniel, M., Webb, M., Herman, J., & Witty, J. (2010). Findings on Facebook in higher education: A comparison of college faculty and student uses and perceptions of social networking sites. *The Internet and Higher Education,* 13 (3): 134–40.

Rogan, F., & Miguel, C. S. (2013). Improving clinical communication of students with English as a second language (ESL) using online technology: A small scale evaluation study. *Nurse Education in Practice.* Retrieved July 2013 from: http://www.sciencedirect.com/science/article/pii/S1471595312002302

Rust, C., Price, M., & O'Donovan, B. (2003). Improving students' learning by developing their understanding of assessment criteria and processes. *Assessment and Evaluation in Higher Education,* 28 (2): 147–64.

Ryle, G. (1949). *The Concept of Mind.* London: Penguin.

Schechtman, M. (2012). The story of my (second) life: Virtual worlds and narrative identity. *Philosophy and Technology,* 25 (3): 329–43.

Schell, J., Lukoff, B., & Mazur, E. (2013). Catalyzing learner engagement using cutting-edge classroom response systems in higher education. In Wankel, C., & Blessinger, P. (eds), *Increasing Student Engagement and Retention Using Classroom Technologies: Classroom Response Systems and Mediated Discourse Technologies.* Bradford: Emerald Group Publishing Limited.

Schnackenberg, H., Vega, E., & Relation, D. (2009). Podcasting and vodcasting: Legal issues and ethical dilemmas. *Journal of Law, Ethics, and Intellectual Property,* 3 (1). Retrieved July 2013 from: http://www.scientificjour-nals.org/journals2009/articles/1461.pdf

Selwyn, N. (2011). *Social Media in Higher Education.* Retrieved July 2013 from: http://www.educationarena.com/pdf/sample/sample-essay-selwyn.pdf

Selwyn, N. (2012). Social media in higher education. *The Europa World of Learning 2012*. Retrieved July 3013 from: http://www.educationarena.com/pdf/sample/sample-essay-selwyn.pdf

Smith, P., & Smith, S. (1999). Differences between Chinese and Australian students: Some implications for distance educators. *Distance Education*, 20 (1): 64–80.

Sutherland, S., & Powell, A. (2007). Cetis SIG mailing list discussions. Retrieved July 2013 from: http://www.jiscmail.ac.uk/archives/cetis-portfolio.html

Tapscott, D., & Williams, A. (2007). *Wikinomics*. New York: Atlantic.

Taylor, D. (2012). Has LinkedIn taken over from the CV? *Guardian*. Retrieved July 2013 from: http://jobs.guardian.co.uk/article/4430480/has-linkedin-taken-over-from-the-cv-/

Traphagan, T., Kucsera, J. V., & Kishi, K. (2010). Impact of class lecture webcasting on attendance and learning. *Educational Technology Research and Development*, 58 (1). 19–37.

Ulbrich, F., Jahnke, I., & Mårtensson, P. (eds) (2010). Special issue on knowledge development and the net generation. *International Journal of Sociotechnology and Knowledge Development*.

UNESCO & Council of Europe. (2000). *Code of Good Practice in the Provision of Transnational Education*. Bucharest: UNESCO-CEPES.

Vajoczki, S., Watt, S., Marquis, N., Liao, R., & Vine, M. (2011). Students' approach to learning and their use of lecture capture. *Journal of Educational Multimedia and Hypermedia*, 20 (2): 195–214.

Valenti, S., Neri, F., & Cucchiarelli, A. (2003). An overview of current research on automated essay grading. *Journal of Information Technology Education*, 2: 319–30.

Vanderplank, R. (1988). The value of teletext sub titles in language learning. *English Language Teaching Journal*, 42 (4): 272–81.

Vanderplank, R. (1993). A very verbal medium: Language learning through closed captions. *TESOL Journal*, 3 (1): 10–14.

Vanderplank, R. (2012). 'Effects of' and 'effects with' subtitles: How exactly does watching a TV programme with same language subtitles make a difference to language learners and why does it matter to language learning researchers? *Subtitles and Language Learning Conference*. Pavia, Italy.

Volet, S., & Jones, C. (2012). Cultural transitions in higher education: Individual adaptation, transformation and engagement. *Advances in Motivation and Achievement*, 17: 241–84.

Volpe, E.P. (1984). The shame of science education. *American Zoologist*, 24(2): 433–441.

Walker, M., & Townley, C. (2012). Contract cheating: A new challenge for academic honesty? *Journal of Academic Ethics*, 10 (1): 27–44.

Warburton, S., & Perez-Garcia, M. (2009). 3D design and collaboration in massively multi-user virtual environments. In Russel, D. (ed.), *Cases on Collaboration in Virtual Learning Environments: Processes and Interactions*. Hershey, PA: IGI Global. As cited in Peachey, A., Withnail, G., & Braithwaite, N. (2012). *Experimentation Not Simulation: Learning About Physics in The Virtual World*. Retrieved July 2013 from: http://www.inter-disciplinary.net/wp-content/uploads/2012/02/peacheyepaper.pdf

Wenger, E. (1998). *Communities of Practice: Learning, Meaning and Identity* Cambridge: Cambridge University Press.

Wenger, E. (2006). Communities of practice: A brief introduction. Communities of Practice. Retrieved July 2013 from: http://www.ewenger.com/theory/

Wenger, E., MacDermott, R. A., & Snyder, W. M. (2002). *Cultivating Communities of Practice: A Guide to Managing Knowledge*. Boston, MA: Harvard Business Press.

Wray, J., Aspland, J., Taghzouit, J., & Pace, K. (2012). Making the nursing curriculum more inclusive for students with specific learning difficulties: Embedding specialist study skills into a core module. *Nurse Education Today*, (33): 603–7.

Yuen, S., Yaoyuneyong, G., & Johnson, E. (2011). Augmented reality: An overview and five directions for AR in education. *Journal of Educational Technology Development and Exchange*, 4 (1): 119–40.

Young, J. (2006). Wikipedia founder discourages academic use of his creation. *Chronicle of Higher Education*. Retrieved July 2013 from: http://chronicle.com/blogs/wiredcampus/wikipedia-founder-discourages-academic-use-of-his-creation/2305

Ziguras, C. (2001). Educational technology in transnational higher education in South East Asia: The cultural politics of flexible learning. *Educational Technology & Society*, 4 (4): 8–18.

Index